# BITING
# THE
# APPLE

# BITING THE APPLE

## ACCOUNTS OF FIRST YEAR TEACHERS

Kevin Ryan
Katherine K. Newman
Gerald Mager
Jane Applegate
Thomas Lasley
Randall Flora
John Johnston

**LONGMAN INC.**
New York and London

Biting the Apple
Accounts of First Year Teachers

Longman Inc., New York
Associated companies, branches, and representatives
throughout the world.

Developmental Editor: Nicole Benevento
Editorial and Design Supervisor: Judith Hirsch
Interior and Cover Design: Dan Serrano
Manufacturing and Production Supervisor: Louis Gaber
Composition: A & S Graphics, Inc.
Printing and Binding: Murray Printing, Inc.

Manufactured in the United States of America

9   8   7   6   5   4   3   2   1

Library of Congress Cataloging in Publication Data

Main entry under title:
Biting the apple.

  1. Teaching—Handbooks, manuals, etc.   2. First
year teachers—Handbooks, manuals, etc.   3. Lesson
planning—Handbooks, manuals, etc.   I. Ryan, Kevin.
LB1025.2.B573      1980      371.1'02      79-18008
ISBN 0-582-28107-5

# Dedication

*To our colleague and teacher*

James Kelly Duncan

# Contents

# Acknowledgments

Several special persons enabled each of us to survive, learn, and grow from our first experiences as teachers. These persons are special because they cared enough to try to understand what we were thinking and feeling. Their willingness to give time and patience bolstered our spirits during that first year, and the memories continue to nourish our personal and professional lives. We thank you—teachers and former teachers, friends, and family. You indirectly but significantly contributed to the First Year Teacher Study and *Biting the Apple: Accounts of First Year Teachers.*

We came together at The Ohio State University, six graduate students and an associate dean. We had something in common, a concern about the nature of the first year of teaching. The concern was first like a seed on a rock, filled with life potential, but in need of place and resources for growth. We found a place and planted the seed, hoping it would grow, hoping to investigate the first year of teaching as it unfolded for several people.

Eighteen new teachers in six school districts gave their consent to participate in our project, and thus allowed our seed to germinate. They agreed to let us observe, interview, and again get close to the first year experience. These new teachers courageously faced our intrusions into their life spaces, and indulged our interest by volunteering precious time and sharing personal concerns and joys. We wish we could express our thanks publicly, but we can reveal neither their names nor the names of the communities and school districts where they taught. We respect these persons' privacy, and we will not divulge any information that potentially could embarrass or hurt them or their colleagues, friends, and others who touched their first year experiences. Thus, though the accounts in this book are true insofar as reported to and observed by us, the names of persons, communities, and schools in the book are fictitious and any resemblance to other parties is purely coincidental.

Like a seed, a research project will not grow, become healthy and strong, blossom, and bear fruit without sunshine and sustained nourishment. Several colleagues at The Ohio State University provided these resources. Betty Myers was our sunshine. Her professional insight was valuable, and she freely extended her thoughtfulness and empathy. Betty was always there when we needed her, and she contributed far more to the First Year Teacher Study than she will ever admit. We thank you, Betty. The following persons responded to questions and concerns, and supported our efforts, ideas, and interest: Des Cook, Don Cruickshank, Kelly Duncan, and Chuck Galloway from the College of Education; Ojo Arewa from the Department of Anthropology; Ron Corwin from the Department of Sociology; and Randy Bobbitt from the College of Administrative Science. Ted Cyphert, Dean of the College of Education, provided access to support services and freedom to explore and work. Katie Barnes and Bruce Sampsel handled much of the correspondence, typing, and tape transcriptions. We are grateful for the time and energy Katie and Bruce put into the First Year Teacher Study.

Several persons were also kind enough to respond to our requests to read and comment on early drafts of the manuscript. Bruce Sampsel, Sylvia Marantz, Johanna Hartfield, James Cooper and the students in John Johnston's preservice teacher education class at The Ohio State University gave constructive criticism and compared their experiences to those of the teachers in the First Year Teacher Study. We thank them for their help.

Finally, we extend our appreciation to Carol Price for typing the manuscript.

# Biting the Apple: An Introduction

A few weeks before I began teaching some twenty years ago, I ran out and bought a large, green notebook. It was to be the diary of my first year of teaching. I didn't know what was going to happen to me but I sensed that something important was about to occur and I wanted to somehow capture it. For the first time in my life, I was to be truly tested. Finally, after years and years of schooling, the service, and odds-and-ends working, I was about to begin my chosen career.

At the end of my first day of teaching, I came home to my green notebook, but first I had to make lesson plans and do some beginning-of-the-year clerical activities. At 1:15 in the morning I opened the green notebook and wrote three or four sentences. I was exhausted, but promised myself that I would really get to it the next evening.

The next evening, I was up even later with lesson plans, but bravely put in two lines and made a second quiet promise to myself. Those two are the only entries in my diary of the first year of teaching. Something important happened to me during that year. However, I never captured it. It's there inside of me somewhere, but a victim of imperfect memory and the distortions of time.

As a classroom teacher, I witnessed the private drama of the first year unfold for numerous new teacher-colleagues. Sometimes there was a happy ending, and sometimes pain and failure. There was Cynthia White, a lovely, young English major from Smith College: well-trained, energetic, and very, very bright. She threw herself into teaching—at times, a little too hard. One afternoon, while I puttered around my room after school, I heard sobs from the room next door. I hesitantly walked in and there was Cynthia weeping over the desk.

"Well, what's the matter, Cynthia?"

Without looking up, she pointed toward one of the desks. "Look at that." I went to the desk and saw nothing. She said, "Look at the back." I did, and what I saw was a message scratched with a compass in the back of a chair: "Miss White is a bitch." Try as I might, I could not convince Cynthia that a bit of idle meanness from a single student was not some cosmic judgment by the great student body in the sky.

Cynthia felt she had been giving her all to her students and they, in her mind, had betrayed her. She got over it, of course, but her open, positive attitude toward her students was altered. She became more careful, and more guarded. She did a good job, though. It just wasn't the job of which she seemed capable. I left that school a year later and a few years after that I heard Cynthia had left teaching.

I have always harbored the suspicion that Cynthia would have had a richer career, and possibly, would still be teaching if she had had a better first year. I don't believe that Cynthia White is an isolated case. Many teachers have been affected, both positively and negatively, by their first year teaching experience. It seems to have a strong effect on them as professionals and as people. The purpose of this book is to call particular attention to this important induction phase into teaching.

It is difficult to speak about the first year of teaching. Although it is a single timebound period, it has happened to more than three million people currently living in this country. That means that there are three million different first year experiences. Out of these have come some views, or what I will refer to as belief systems, about the first year in the profession. There has also been some research done on it. In this introduction, I will explore my own belief system and summarize some of the major research findings concerned with the first year of teaching. Particular attention is given to the study out of which these accounts of first year teachers have grown.

# The First Year of Teaching: Some Beliefs

A belief system is a cluster of ideas about the way a certain portion of reality exists and works. People have belief systems about a variety of things, from religion to politics, from human relations to education. There is also a belief system about what happens during the first year of teaching.

Three million people have gone through the first year of teaching and have a belief system about it. So, too, do those planning to be teachers. They expect children, fellow teachers, parents, and administrators to behave in a certain set of ways. It is impossible for the prospective teacher not to have a belief system. However, not only does the new teacher have a belief system about the first year of teaching, but so do the other teachers, parents, students, and administrators with whom he or she will have contact. Since belief systems affect the way a person structures the world, it is particularly important for people considering careers in teaching to address some common beliefs about the first year and, also, to examine their own beliefs. What follows, then, is my view of some of the key aspects of the belief system that many people hold about the first year of teaching. My intention in this chapter and, indeed, a major intention of this book is to expose the reader to a number of factors and facets of the first year of teaching and have the reader come to a sharpened sense of his or her own system. This sharpened awareness of one's own belief system can then be tested against the experiences of the twelve teachers whose stories make up the heart of this book.

A number of years ago, Ashley Montagu, the distinguished British anthropologist remarked that "the largest personal sorrow suffered of human beings consists of the difference of what one was capable of becoming and what one has, in fact, become." This quote may apply to many of us in many different walks of life. It strikes me though, as having particular application to teachers. The difference between ideal education (the continuing development of the human potential of each individual) and what goes on in schools (assigning homework, prodding some to learn, giving others busy-work, testing and assigning grades) is great, and we teachers are painfully aware of the gap. Some aspects of schooling, such as the previous learning and personal history with which the child enters our classroom, are out of our control. But much is within our control. It is in this arena of personal control where we fail to live up to our human potential as teachers.

Many of us who have studied what happens to first year teachers believe that events during this initial year contribute to the gap between what they were capable of becoming and what they have, in fact, become.

We should first acknowledge, however, that for many beginning teachers the initial year in the classroom is an exciting and successful one. They planned and dreamed about becoming a teacher; student taught and learned how to apply their training in a real classroom; filled out placement papers and pursued job openings; and finally were accepted for a teaching position. And, then, the fun began. They were out of college, in the real world and doing what they always wanted to do. Their first year of teaching confirmed their judgment that teaching was for them. While their teaching situation may not have been perfect, life rarely is. Most of their energies went toward acquiring new skills and teaching approaches. They ended their year feeling that, by and large, it was a string of successes. These are the blessed few.

For most, the first year is complex and difficult. One of the major problems is that so many adjustments are forced on the lives of individuals beginning their first year of teaching, adjustments that have very little to do with teaching. Most have just left the security and regularity of the campus and, while they may be eager to take on the world, it comes on them rather fast. They need to find a place to live and settle themselves into it. For the first time in their lives they may need to purchase and maintain their own car. Some may be confronted with financial decisions for the first time: where to bank; how to handle checking accounts and credit cards; how to set up a budget and keep to it. Many begin learning how to cook. There are dozens of new things to learn and connections to be made: Where is the best grocery store? shoe repairman? auto mechanic? dentist? dry cleaner? What church should I go to? Then the little niggling items creep up. You need to get a phone number and have a phone connected, but the phone company only installs in your neighborhood on Wednesday mornings from 10:00 to 12:00. You tell the service representative that you are teaching at that time and find her as sympathetic as a clam. And, so on.

Another nonteaching adjustment that complicates the lives of many new teachers is the mating game. Graduation from college is the occasion for many young men and women to get married or, if not get married, to become serious about the search for a mate. In either case, there are straining adjustments to a new marriage and to learning to mesh one's life with another person, or to the loneliness and uncertainties of mate search.

But for most, these adjustments pale before the difficulties of adjusting to the role of teacher. Many difficulties emerge because new teachers are caught off guard. Actually *doing* teaching, moment by moment, is different than they had expected. Having been in school those many years and having seen so many different teachers in so many different situations, many beginners think they *know* what it is like to *do* teaching. But, alas, it fools them. The teacher's side of the desk is different. Behind it are hidden demands and subtleties which are quite unexpected.

One would think that student teaching might solve this problem. And, perhaps it does in part. But, student teaching, as many new teachers lament, is a long way from teacher training. Not long ago, a student gave me a cartoon showing the emergency room of a hospital. A nurse is helping an obviously dazed, battered, and disheveled young man down the hall. Another nurse explains to a doctor, "He's the fourth student teacher we've admitted today." It is not a particularly witty cartoon, but more to the point, it is not very accurate. First, the kinds of classes that would truly shake up a student teacher would rarely, and only mistakenly, be used for what is supposed to be a training experience. Colleges training teachers normally place student teachers with teachers in schools where they will receive good training, where they can learn skills and strategies and, ideally, where some of the professionalism and polish of a master teacher will rub off. Second, a student teacher's class is not the same thing as a teacher's class. The class *belongs* to the regular teacher. And while the student teacher may not be very mindful of that subtlety, the students are, especially those who are tempted to make his life miserable. They know that if they go too far, the real teacher, like an avenging angel, will deal with them. Third, the cartoon blurs the major distinction between student teaching and teaching which is the degree of legal, professional and ethical responsibility. The teacher carries a much greater burden of responsibility. But, while the cartoon lacks wit and accuracy, it may mirror a common belief of student teachers that "if I get through this experience, I will be a teacher." And, herein lies the problem. The new teacher all too often enters the classroom with a degree in one hand and a freshly issued teaching certificate in the other, with an unrealistic view of what teaching demands and of what he or she is capable. Much of the first year teacher's anguish comes from what is initially a too rosy view of how he or she will interact with and manage children, a view which may have roots in the student teacher experience. Many only learn they have to discipline children after making many awkward, painful and self-defeating mistakes.

Another difficulty involves the beginner's perceptions of what a school is. Gertrude Stein's famous line "a rose is a rose is a rose" has a parallel in the minds of many teachers-in-training. They believe a school is a school is a school. And why shouldn't they? Education textbooks and teachers tend to refer to schools as if they were not quite all alike, but that they exist on a rather narrow band of what is the actual spectrum of schools. However, as Russell Doll (1977) has pointed out, schools differ radically. For example, in schools serving the urban poor, both the families and the neighborhoods are in a state of deterioration. As Doll explains, few teachers are prepared to deal with the lower end of the school spectrum. However, these schools are often where the job openings are. They have openings because teachers have transferred out or have been driven out. So many new teachers walk into their first school with a head full of images of what will go on, images which are strikingly at odds with what confronts them.

Another difficulty is with the new teacher's actual assignment. Teachers-in-training usually prepare for specific job areas like high school biology or kindergarten. They spend a good deal of time preparing themselves for highly trained positions. It often turns out, however, that their assignments are in areas for which they have had little or no training. The newly trained biology teacher has one period of earth science, two of chemistry and two of general math. The kindergarten-prepared teacher is assigned to the third grade. Perhaps, later they will get an assignment for which they are trained, but initially, teachers may find themselves unprepared for what they actually are assigned to teach.

A similar problem occurs with extracurricular activities. A

school has a number of activities that students and their parents have come to expect. Administrators have learned the hard way that parents often get more exercised by some deficiency in the extracurricular program, particularly the sports program, than in the academic program. When a chemistry teacher who is also the track coach leaves, or when the fifth grade teacher who handles the music for the assembly programs transfers to another school, rather complicated gaps are left and need to be filled. Thus, when the new teacher arrives in September, he or she may be saddled with strange and unexpected assignments. The young man who hasn't worn sneakers since his last required physical education course is introduced at the preopening faculty meeting as the new track coach, while the young woman who quit piano lessons twelve years ago is shown the auditorium piano and told how creative Mrs. Schultz was with her assemblies. Frequently, then, the extracurricular duties, such as sports and clubs and study halls, are a most troubling part of the new teacher's work.

Another difficulty which surprises many beginning teachers is that teaching is a tough job. Oh yes, they had seen those posters which show some exhausted teacher, holding her head and they read the caption, "No one ever said teaching was an easy job." But somehow the message did not sink in. And, why should it? Teaching does not look physically exhausting. Indeed, it looks essentially like talking, carrying on conversations with groups and with individuals. Why, then, do they feel this bone-deep exhaustion? Why this near numb feeling? Why is it that all one wants to do is get home and crawl into bed? One reason is that new teachers are not in condition for the physical and mental demands of teaching. They are not prepared for the strain of being in command, of being responsible for so many people for so long each day. Ensuring that twenty-four first graders live through a school day, avoid pushing one another into the points of sharp tables, get to the bathroom before "an accident" happens, and cope with the trials and rebuffs of the playroom can be just as demanding as trying to keep the lid on a class of street-hardened teenagers. Both can wear one down.

There is always a strain to teaching, but it is particularly pronounced for beginners. They are like athletes who have trained for the season by reading, writing and discussing. They may know what to do, but their bodies cannot take the punishment of the game. This analogue has special meaning for the first year teachers for whom so much is new. After a while, however, the beginning teachers' bodies and minds become toughened to their routine of school so that they can be on their feet for six hours, responding to the many different messages and events of classroom life. They get conditioned, but it can be hell until then.

The surprising and intense fatigue of beginning teachers relates to another difficulty experienced by many first year teachers: depression. When exhaustion is added to a sense of failure, psychological depression is not far behind. It may be mild or it may be deep, but it is an unanticipated reality in the lives of many first year teachers. For some, the setbacks experienced in teaching are the first serious ones of their lives. They expected teaching to be satisfying, yet it does not seem to be. They had all sorts of expectations and plans but few of them are working out. They wonder how they will handle this child and that problem and the more they think, the more upset they become. When fatigue is added to depression, the depression is deepened.

These, then, are some of the issues which complicate and make difficult the lives of many first year teachers. Most of these issues come from the writer's reading and observation, and, possibly, imagination. However, there are more objective and less impressionistic sources of understanding of this special year and it is to those which we now turn.

## Some Relevant Research

If we define research as the process of thinking things through carefully, then we find a large body of literature devoted to the first year teacher. Indeed, I suspect that shortly after the first school was organized, thoughtful educators began to worry about the first year teacher. John Johnston, one of the coauthors of this book, did a recent study of the professional literature devoted to this topic between the years 1930 and 1977. Johnston's study, which I am drawing on very heavily for this section, began by identifying slightly over 300 articles and research reports dealing with this period in a teacher's career (Johnston, 1978). As a part of his study Johnston analyzed and then categorized all the published materials, that is,

books, journal articles, and microfiche, into five distinct classifica-
tions: (1) advice on the first year of teaching; (2) reports of first year
teachers' own experiences; (3) scholarly essays on the first year of
teaching; (4) reflective interpretations of first year teachers' experiences; and (5) empirical studies of the first year of teaching.

The first category, advice on the first year of teaching, is the
type of literature about the first year of teaching which appears most
frequently. These advice articles are written by first year teachers,
by experienced teachers, by principals, or school of education faculty members. They have titles such as "If I Were a Beginning
Teacher" (Jones, 1934), "New Teachers' First Days" (Hale, 1931),
or "I'd Like to Tell That Beginning Teacher" (Brown, 1942). Sometimes these advice articles deal with teaching in particular subject
fields, such as agricultural education, music education, or speech
education. Frequently they highlight a particular concern, like discipline or classroom control (Bell, 1971; Cambier, 1965; Elrod, 1976;
Peterson, 1960), or they deal with a generic teaching concern such as
planning (McClaren, 1972; Shadick, 1972).

The type of advice given in these articles varies a great deal. It
ranges from vague admonitions, such as "Be yourself," or "Set
classroom ground rules right away," to highly focused advice, such
as "Have a dozen sharpened pencils on the desk the first day of school
in order to prevent unnecessary trips to the pencil sharpener." It is
not uncommon to find the advice in one article contradicted by the
advice of another. There is also a portion of this advice literature that
concerns the care and feeding of first year teachers. It is written to
instruct college faculty or school administrators or supervisors about
how to assist first year teachers with their special problems
(Abraham, 1954; Brown, 1977; Lee, 1940; Smith, 1931; Wolford,
1931).

A second category is reports by first year teachers of their own
experiences. These first-person reports are descriptions of what their
first year of teaching was like (Ellis, 1939; Grinnell, 1940; Leiber-
man, 1975; Rost, 1939). It seems to be a regular occurrence in educational literature, that every few years some journal sponsors a sym-
posium of accounts of first year teachers' experiences. These are
usually told in direct narrative form, emphasizing highs and lows of
the year and unexpected events. These articles often end with a
stirring reaffirmation of commitment to a life-long teaching career.

Although one account was found to be negative in tone, they are usually extremely positive in tone, indeed, some border on being Pollyanna-like prattle. While these first-person accounts usually have real strengths, they tend to lack objectivity and interpretive commentary.

A third category of the literature is scholarly essays on the first year of teaching. The articles in this category normally combine the actual accounts of first year teachers with scholarly, and often discipline-based interpretations. Fuchs (1969) and Eddy (1968) bring an anthropological perspective to narratives or self-reports of first year teachers. Ryan (1970) includes accounts by three inner city and three suburban teachers followed by an interpretive essay. The literature in this category presents the raw data of teachers' experience and adds to that other perspectives which provide the reader with some interpretation of what the first year teachers were experiencing. (I see *Biting the Apple: Accounts of First Year Teachers* fitting into this fourth category.)

The fifth, and final, category is composed of studies of the first year of teaching which take a quantitative approach. Although there is a large number of studies in this category, they are of very uneven qualtiy. Most are limited in scope, poorly conceived and poorly executed. A large percentage of these are surveys of the problems of first year teachers. Often, these problem studies are based on principals' or supervisors' listings of problems that they believe the first year teachers under their supervision are experiencing. Among the common problems cited in these surveys are discipline, dealing with parents, and grading. There have also been descriptive surveys such as those dealing with first year teachers' reasons for failure (Barr and Rudisil, 1930) or surveys of classroom difficulties (Diamond, 1948; Johnston and Umstattd, 1932; Wey, 1951). Stout (1952) surveyed deficiencies of first year teachers, while Whitman (1966) examined the fears of first year teachers.

There are, however, surprisingly few experimental studies involving first year teachers. Muskowitz and Hayman (1974, 1976) have done creative and well-designed experimental studies that examine differences between experienced teachers' and beginning teachers' instructional and classroom management strategies.

There are other quantitative studies that describe special programs to induct new teachers into their role and to facilitate their transition from students to teachers (Collea, 1975; Hockstad, 1966; Noda, 1968).

Qualitative studies of the first year teachers using anthropological and ethnographical methodologies are relatively rare and more recent. The study out of which this book has grown and which will be described later, and a study of beginning teachers in California by Berliner and Tikunoff (1976) are among the few examples of this type.

Besides the studies that focus primarily on first year teachers, there is much research and writing that includes data on the first year of teaching. One line of research has to do with teachers' attitudes towards students. A favorite instrument used in this line of research is the Minnesota Teacher Attitude Inventory (MTAI), which is designed to measure "those attitudes of the teacher which predict how well he or she will get along with pupils in interpersonal relations, and indirectly how well satisfied he will be with teaching as a vocation" (Cook, Leeds, Kallis, 1951). This instrument has been used in over fifty studies of teacher attitudes and is fairly consistent. It shows a decline in positive attitudes toward students from student teaching to the first year of teaching. A recent study using the MTAI demonstrates what the researcher calls "the curve of disenchantment" (Ligana, 1970). The graph-line moves upward during preservice training as the prospective teachers' attitude toward children becomes more positive. However, during the first four months of the first year, the line takes a sharp dip, reflecting a strong change in attitudes toward students. So sharp, that the beginning teachers' scores are significantly lower than those of students just entering teacher training. After the first four months, however, the attitudes level out and a slight upturn begins.

Another researcher, Hoy (1969), measured changes in scores on an instrument called the Pupil Control Ideology Scale (PCI) for 162 graduates of a particular teacher education program. At the end of their first year of teaching, as a group the teachers had become significantly less "humanistic," more "custodial" in their orientation toward discipline and pupil control.

There is also the question of the new teachers' attitudes toward themselves. Wright and Tuska (1968) investigated the change in teachers' attitudes toward themselves and their behavior as teachers, using a Teacher Attitudes Questionnaire. At the end of their initial

year of teaching, the new teachers in the experiment rated themselves significantly higher on acting impulsively, controlling, and
blaming others for their problems. On the other hand, they rated
themselves significantly less happy, less obedient and less inspiring.
These studies and others present a rather persuasive case that the
first year teacher's attitudes toward self and students become, depending on one's point of view, more negative or more realistic.

Why this should be the case and for how long it endures we're
not really sure. There are, however, some suggestions that certain
aspects of the first year teachers' environment contribute to these
attitude shifts. The perspective of sociologists on the environment
and the work of the teacher (Lortie, 1975; Waller, 1932) has been
particularly illuminating. One of the issues these studies reveal is the
isolation of teachers from each other. Although schools are crowded
with people, individual teachers are separated from one another as
they ply their trade. Typically, in the American schools there is one
teacher per classroom. Teachers actually do not see one another
teach. Therefore, no great impetus for discussion of common successes and problems exists. As Lortie (1975) has pointed out, this
physical isolation of teachers one from the other leads to social isolation as well.

Physical and social isolation inhibits communication among
teachers, but there is something else that limits professional conversation. That is the absence of a shared language of teaching and a
shared body of knowledge about teaching. Again, Lortie (1975) writes
about education's "near absence of codified technology and the lack
of a developed technical vocabulary." They suggest that when
teachers finally do get a chance to talk to one another, squeezed in a
lunch line or on the way out of the building after school, they are
forced to talk about their work in very general language, which keeps
them from being exact about their professional concerns. Contrast
this condition with that of doctors who have a professional language
and a codified body of knowledge and who are trained to exchange
information and use colleagues to solve problems. The new teacher
still has much to learn about teaching and has a hard time learning it
from teaching colleagues. How the new teacher reacts to new colleagues and the new setting is another matter.

Sociologists have pointed out that when a new teacher enters a
school he or she is entering a multifaceted social situation. In re-

sponse, the new teacher, often unknowingly, adopts or creates a social strategy to deal with the complexities of the situation. Lacey (1977) recently has described some of these strategies. Among them is "internalized adjustment" in which the teacher simply accepts or conforms to the values and practices in the new setting. Skills, practices and values learned in preservice teaching are often put in cold storage and constitute what Lacey calls "latent culture" which may or may not be called upon later. Lacey also describes "strategic compliance" whereby the new teacher, not convinced by what seem to be the practices operating in his new situation, decides to go along with them for now. An alternative to this is "strategic redefinition" whereby the new teacher consciously tries to change or reform the school situation. As such, the new teacher sees himself or herself as a change agent in the setting.

These are just a few of the studies that speak to the experience of first year teachers. The picture this literature projects is perhaps best captured by Joseph Vaughn of the National Institute for Education. As he and other staff members studied the literature, they summarized it as follows.

> One result of this effort is a conclusion concurred in by thoughtful observers with a variety of backgrounds and concerns: the conditions under which a person carries out the first year of teaching have a strong influence on the level of effectiveness which that teacher is able to achieve and to sustain over the years; on the attitudes which govern teacher behavior over even a forty-year career; and, indeed, on the decision whether or not to continue in the teaching profession. [NIE, 1978]

## The First Year Teacher Study

The scientific tradition is very young in education. While research has told us something about this first year of teaching, there is still much more to know. Some of the most important questions are the ones about which we know the least. This book grew out of an effort to gain a better understanding of new teachers and their first year of teaching. Essentially, it is twelve accounts of twelve individuals making their way through the initial year in their chosen profession. These narrative accounts have emerged from a study of first year teachers, a study that is still going on. Seven of us are coinvestigators in this study and have written various of these accounts. To understand these accounts, the reader should know some of the background to our study.

We became involved in this study of first year teachers because we believe something strong, something very significant goes on in the life of the new teacher. All of us had been first year teachers and, at the time of the study, all were teacher educators. We shared a hunch that powerful forces and energies affect the lives of beginners. We had experienced the transition from college student and student of teaching to brand new teacher, and, later saw younger colleagues and our preservice students struggle during this transitional period. We wanted to understand what was happening in the lives of first year teachers. To go from this general concern to something more precise, we developed five questions which guided our research. They are:

1. What are the first year teacher's perceptions of himself or herself?

2. What are the first year teacher's perceptions of himself or herself as a teacher?

3. What happens in the classroom and elsewhere in the school that the new teacher perceives as successes and failures?

4. What are the new teacher's perceptions of students, administrators, fellow teachers, teacher educators, and parents?

5. How do these perceptions change over the year?

Our purpose in pursuing answers to these questions is not an idle one. As teacher educators whose work is involved with helping people become teachers and trying to equip them for the realities of life in classrooms, our questions are of fundamental importance to us. We have seen too many new teachers discouraged and sometimes defeated by their experiences. We have seen idealism too quickly reshaped into cynicism. We have seen the desire to reach out and inspire children to learn shunted aside quickly in a mad scramble to survive. We needed to get answers to our questions in order to forewarn our students about the special problems of the first year. We also needed to make ourselves as teacher educators, and teacher education as a whole, more responsive to these problems. A major inspiration was a curiosity about the process of learning to teach. As teacher educators we wanted to learn as much as possible about how people progress in their journey toward professional expertise.

To get answers to our questions we decided to study what happened to a group of first year teachers. Since we wanted to study teachers in a variety of settings, we contacted personnel directors in the urban, suburban and rural school districts around a large metropolitan center in the Midwest. Almost all of the school districts we approached agreed to cooperate as long as their new teachers were free to volunteer. However nice it may have been from a research design perspective to study all first year teachers rather than simply those who volunteered, we really had no choice but to confine our study to volunteers. Besides, we could have been quite uneasy sitting in the back of someone's class knowing that we were making that someone uncomfortable by our presence. During the weeks before school opened, we called people on the lists supplied to us, explained our study to them, and asked for their cooperation. We told them that one of us would be observing them on a regular basis, that we would want to have extensive tape-recorded interviews with them, and that we would not be able to be any help to them. We explained that in this situation we were "takers" essentially, and not "givers," because telling them what we observed, giving teaching materials to them or providing tips and advice would disturb the normal first year teaching situation.

We called thirty-six people to invite them to be part of our study. Half the teachers we contacted turned us down. Some were not too enthused about having a stranger in their class or spending hours in interviews. Most of the teachers who turned us down were really not first year teachers and so disqualified themselves. They had taught elsewhere but were new to a particular school district. The other half, eighteen individuals, agreed, with varying amounts of misgiving, to share their lives with us. And we are deeply in their debt.

We wanted our sample of eighteen teachers to be representative of the elementary and secondary teaching force. We took this into consideration as we went down our lists and made our calls. As it turned out, we were, in general, satisfied with the variety in our sample. Most of our teachers were in public schools, but we had some in parochial and private schools. We had teachers in rural, suburban and urban schools and, although the urban schools served many poor children, none were what are sometimes called hard-core, inner-city schools. We had teachers at all levels from kindergarten to twelfth grade. The high school teachers taught in traditional academic subjects, physical education and vocational subjects. The proportion of men and women in our sample mirrored the proportion in the teaching profession. While our sample contained a mixture of ethnic and religious backgrounds, we failed in our effort to include minority group members. Those we asked declined our invitation to participate. Finally, our eighteen teachers came from nine different teacher training institutions and they were teaching in sixteen different schools.

But having eighteen volunteers was not enough. We had to devise a way of capturing what was happening to them. First, we decided to limit ourselves to two primary data sources: classroom observations and the subject-teachers' own perceptions of what was going on in their lives. The latter data were gathered through five long interviews spaced throughout the year. Classroom observation, the other data collection procedure, created a number of questions: How often should we observe our subject-teachers? Should we use one of the available classroom observation instruments or should we develop our own? Should several of us look at the same subject-teacher or should we each observe a few? How are we going to find out what is going on inside their heads? If we ask them questions do we all ask them the same questions, or should each of us act alone? If we all observe different aspects of their teaching and ask them different questions, will we be able to make any sense of our data? If we completely standardize our observations and interview questions, will we be putting ourselves in a straight jacket, unable to capture the unique qualities of a particular teacher's classroom or psychological experience? We went back and forth over high level scientific issues, like Hisenberg's uncertainty principle, a principle which states that the very act of observing nature disturbs and alters it. Should we go into a classroom at all? Should the students be told what we are doing? Should we share our voluminous notes with our subject-teachers? What if they ask us "How am I doing?" or "What should I do to get that shy girl in the front row more involved?" These are just a few of the questions we wrangled and wrestled over.

Through what appears in retrospect, to be a Job-like degree of patience, the seven of us worked out a set of operational rules to guide our activities. We would observe our teachers semi-weekly in the beginning and gradually reduce the frequency as the year progressed. We would develop interview schedules with common questions for all teachers and we would all administer these at approximately the same time. Still, though, we were each free to ask questions and pursue issues of special interest. Most of these rules we followed faithfully.

One issue, whether or not we would help the teachers if asked, was particularly vexing. And although we agreed to play the role of "hands off" researcher rather than helper, we ended up breaking ranks in this one. In a few instances, when our teachers were frantic and depressed, some of our team had the good sense and compassion to respond to them as people in trouble and to give what help we could. The limited help we provided a few may have sullied the purity of our research, but we all slept better.

One other note about our study and its relationship to this book—we had eighteen individuals in the study but we have written up only twelve accounts. One reason for this is that we thought eighteen accounts would either make the book too long or force us to leave out too much to keep the book at a reasonable length. Second, we believe that the essence of what we found in our study is conveyed in these twelve accounts. We believe that they sufficiently represent the differences and similarities of the whole.

Our attempt in our study has been to capture and map out the lifespace of our teacher-subjects. By lifespace we mean the experience of living a particular life during a particular year. We hoped to understand the intellectual and emotional movements of our teachers. We wanted to find out what their successes and failures were; what their joys and private terrors were; what sparked their energies and what deflated them. We also wanted to see them as others saw them We wanted to see how they taught and how they interacted with their students, teaching colleagues and supervisors. In particular, we wanted to compare what they thought was going on in their classrooms with what other people perceived. Of course, we failed. Even though our primary methods of interviews and observation were often supplemented with countless informal contacts and telephone calls, we could not have captured all of what they were experiencing. While we felt that the majority of them were being extremely candid with us, we were not always there to capture their momentary insight or to hear about their latest success or frustration. Nor could we speak with all their students and thus provide a composite view of what all the students observed, thought, and felt about the events in their classroom. We had to stick with our method, however imperfect, of structured interviews and frequent observations. Out of mounds of audio tape cassettes, observation notes, and remembered phone calls, we have extracted the words we believe tell the story. It is an imperfect method and open to immense distortion. However, it was the best we had and we gave it our best.

## A Final Word

These twelve accounts of individual teachers making their way through their first year of teaching are not meant to be literature, but life. They are not stories, but data-based accounts of experience. This distinction is important since without it readers may be somewhat confused by what they encounter. Stories have conventions, patterns, and elements that contribute to our involvement, to the development of the characters, and to the unfolding of the plot. In a good story, there are few loose ends. Everything contributes to the final impact. Life is not so tidy. Things happen to us for which we never hear an explanation. Events begin, but never seem to develop. A large portion of the behavior we encounter and the events that whirl around us are never fully clear and are rather inconclusive. We could drive ourselves to distraction to find out why the man who passed us in the hall was chuckling to himself or what the students who had their hands raised would have said had we called on them. In life we must settle for loose ends. So, too with these accounts.

There are loose ends, unexplained happenings and unanswered problems which bob up, but then melt away. Some of this results from our not having all the facts, but a great deal is simply a part of life and a part of teaching. The student whose fidgeting has gone past the stage of getting-on-your-nerves and into hard-core irritation comes into class one day and somehow he is now calmed down. The student who is always on the border of insolence and seems to go out of her way to indicate that she can't stand you, one day comes into your class and works hard to get your respect and friendship. Life and teaching have their minor mysteries. So do our accounts.

And another consideration. Once upon a time, the orderly unfolding of the school year from September to June was given and could be counted on. We seem to be losing this inviolate quality of the school year in recent years. Now all sorts of factors intrude themselves onto the school calendar from labor problems to the weather. Schools fail to open on time because the teachers are on strike. Busing disputes close or disrupt schools for long periods. The particular year we chose to study our first year teachers had its interruptions, too. Two factors combined to close schools in the dead of winter: very cold and snowy weather and a severe shortage of fuel. The result was that almost all elementary and secondary schools were affected and went into some alternative way of educating their students. The closing was a clear break in the pattern of school and, predictably, it seemed to affect each of our teachers in different ways. In effect, though, it was an interruption in what is becoming the increasingly interrupted pattern of schooling.

While writing these accounts we made an effort to disguise events and persons, but at the same time to preserve the essential truthfulness of our accounts. Each one of these accounts has been checked with the teacher upon whom the account was based. For some teachers, it was an unsettling and difficult experience to relive their first year. All of them did it though, and all have agreed to our making their experiences available to a potentially wide audience. *Biting the Apple: Accounts of First Year Teachers* has no superstars or heroes, or, for that matter, villains. However, the young teachers in our study have been generous and brave in letting us share their lives with the hope that others may benefit from their experience. In this they have all acted in the highest tradition of the teacher.

KEVIN RYAN
THE OHIO STATE UNIVERSITY
SPRING, 1979

# References

Abraham, W. How are your new teachers doing now? *Educational Leadership*, 1954, *11*, 311-315.

Barr, A. S., and Rudisil, M. Inexperienced teachers who fail—and why. *The Nation's Schools*, 1930, *5*, 30-34.

Bell, W. W. Practical suggestions for the novice teacher concerning discipline. *National Association of Secondary School Principals Bulletin*, 1971, *55*, 50-54.

Berliner, David C., and Tikunoff, William J. The California Beginning Teacher Evaluation Study: Overview of the Ethnographic Study. *Journal of Teacher Education*, 1976, Vol XXVII, No 1, 24-30.

Brown, E. D. I'd like to tell that new teacher. *The Journal of Education*, 1942, *125*, 76-69.

Brown, R. E. Community involvement in staff orientation and in-service. *National Association of Secondary School Principals Bulletin*, 1973, *57*, 26-30.

Cambier, D. W. Good discipline and the beginning business education teacher. *Journal of Business Education*, 1965, *40*, 343-344.

Collea, F. P. A model for the preservice training of science teachers based on the intentions, perceptions, and verbal behaviors of first year science teachers. *Science Education*, 1974, *58*, 363-367.

Diamond, T. Difficulties encountered by beginning teachers. *Industrial Arts and Vocation Education*, 1948, *37*, 299-301.

Doll, Russell. Defining and limits of education innovation and change in (Barry L. Klein, Janet T. Collier, Olga S. Jerrett, and Donna K. Ulrici, eds.) *Innovative Practices in Teacher Education: Preservice Through Inservice*, Georgia State University, Atlanta, Georgia, 1977.

Eddy, E. M. *Becoming a teacher: The passage to professional status*. New York: Teachers College Press, 1969.

Ellis, H. A neophyte teacher speaks. *High School Journal*, 1939, *22*, 229-230.

Elrod, W. Don't get tangled in discipline problems. *Music Educators Journal*, 1976, *63*, 47-50.

Fuchs, E. *Teachers talk: View from inside city schools*. New York: Doubleday, 1969.

Grinnell, J. E. (Ed.). The teacher's first year. *Teachers College Journal*, 1940, *11*, 125.

Hale, F. M. New teacher's first days. *Grade Teacher*, 1931, *49*, 16+.

Hockstad, P. A program for helping new teachers. *Education*, 1966, *87*, 51-53.

Hoy, Wayne K. Pupil Control Ideology and Organizational Socialization: A Further Examination of the Influence of Experience on the Beginning Teacher, *School Review* LXVII (September-December, 1969), pp. 257-265.

Johnson, P. O., and Umstattd, J. G. Classroom difficulties of beginning teachers. *School Review*, 1932, *40*, 682-686.

Johnston, J. M. Conceptions of the first year of teaching: An analysis of periodical professional literature. (Doctoral dissertation, The Ohio State University, 1978).

Jones, F. C. If I were a beginning teacher. *Practical Home Economist*, 1934, *12*, 131.

Lacey, Colin. *The Socialization of Teachers*. London: Methuen, 1977.

Lee, J. M. Principal's responsibility to his beginning teachers. *Wisconsin Journal of Education*, 1940, *73*, 149.

Lieberman, A. May the best frog win. *Teacher*, 1975, *93*, 71+.

Ligana, J. *What Happens to the Attitudes of Beginning Teachers*. Danville, Illinois: Interstate Printers and Publishers, Inc., 1970.

Lortie, D. C. *School-teacher: A Sociological Study*. Chicago: University of Chicago Press, 1975, pp. 60-61.

McLaren, M. B. Instructional media and the first year teachers: A practical approach. *AV Guide*, 1972, *51*, 13-15.

Moskowitz, G., and Hayman, J. L., Jr. Interaction patterns of first-year typical and "best" teachers in inner city schools. *The Journal of Educational Research*, 1974, *67*, 224-226.

Moskowitz, G., and Hayman, J. L., Jr. Success strategies of inner city teachers: A year long study. *The Journal of Educational Research*, 1976, *69*, 283-289.

National Institute of Education. Request for Proposals (RP-NIE-R-78-0014) Washington, D.C.: Department of Health, Education and Welfare. 1978.

Noda, D. S. Beginning teacher development in Hawaii. *National Association of Secondary School Principals Bulletin*, 1968, *52*, 62-67.

Peterson, C. H. The beginning teacher and classroom control. *Clearinghouse*, 1960, *35*, 19-21.

Rost, B. A beginners beginning. *Peabody Journal of Education*, 1939, *16*, 365.

Ryan, K. (Ed.). *Don't smile until Christmas*. Chicago: University of Chicago Press, 1970.

Shadick, R. Facing the first day: Forget your fears. *Instructor*, 1972, *82*, 32-35.

Smith, E. E. The new teacher and the principal. *National Education Association Journal*, 1931, *19*, 227-228.

Stout, J. B. Deficiencies of beginning teachers. *Journal of Teacher Education*, 1952, *3*, 43-46.

Waller, Willard. *The Sociology of Teaching*. New York: John Wiley &
Sons, 1932.

Wey, H. H. Difficulties of beginning teachers. *School Review*, 1951,
*59*, 32-37.

Whitman, R. L. Fears of beginning teachers. *Ohio Schools*, 1966, *44*,
23+.

Wofford, K. V. The beginning teacher and the supervisor. *Educational Method*, 1931, *11*, 153-155.

Wright, Benjamin D., and Tuska, Shirley A. "From Deam to Life in
the Psychology of Becoming a Teacher," *School Review* LXXVI
(September, 1968), pp. 253-293.

# I've Done It on My Own

Clear Creek High School stretches its arms boldly across what used to be a large pasture. It seems to dig its fingers deep into the rich soil of the farmland searching for the nourishment which sustains rural life. Cows graze peacefully in nearby fields, oblivious to the orange and black buses parading past them six times a day. The school looks out of place in this pastoral setting. The long, low lines of brick, glass, and steel seem to be more a part of city style. Only the adjacent fields of corn and wheat serve as reminders of the school's heritage. Clear Creek became a school and a district from necessity. Small country schools were forced to merge for economic purposes and from this effort came Clear Creek Consolidated School District—three elementary schools, a junior high and a high school—all serving a student population of 3,100. The junior high and high school are housed in the same building, and students attend school on split sessions because the voters of the district failed to pass the last eight building proposals. While the number of students in the district has risen steadily as people from the city move out to become a part of rural life, the plea for more school facilities has not been acknowledged. Farm families like the split sessions: younger students can be home in the mornings to help with the chores, and older students can be home or out working in the afternoons. The community sees nothing wrong with starting the school day at 6:00 A.M. On the farm, days begin early.

Linda Fuller began her first year of teaching at Clear Creek feeling very much at home. She grew up in a neighboring community and felt that she and her students were kindred spirits—born of rural parents, brought up with traditional values. Linda left home for the first time when she went away to college, a small liberal arts school in the eastern part of the state.

Linda was a good student when she was in school, and college seemed to be a logical part of growing up. Because French had been easy for her in high school and because learning a foreign language might open many interesting doors, she became a French major. She wanted to be a translator or work for an airline. Although she was attractive and could have easily passed the qualifications for being a stewardess, there were no positions available when she was ready to be employed. While in college, Linda had taken enough education courses to get a teaching certificate. If nothing else, she thought she could always teach.

After college, Linda moved back to her parents' home and began looking for work. There were no jobs for a French major anywhere. The year following graduation was a frustrating one. Adjusting to living at home once again and not finding steady employment made Linda uncomfortable. She did some substitute teaching and waitressing to help pass the time. She really wanted a position where she could use her mastery of French but nothing appeared. Early in the summer she received a call from Clear Creek where she had substituted that year. The principal offered her a teaching position for the fall. Linda was relieved. She knew the school and she knew she could do a good job. She had been hoping for full-time employment and this was it. She accepted the contract and prepared herself to become a teacher.

Linda knew from her student teaching experience that teaching was a big responsibility. She knew the kind of teacher she had respected and she wanted to be able to gain the respect of her students. Teachers, she believed, were to set good examples as adults; they were to dress professionally, maintain appropriate distance from the students, be knowledgeable, be prepared, be in control. A teacher's job was to teach and not to be a pal to students though she believed teachers should be friendly and cooperative to all. She knew, also, that she was young, inexperienced, and not really far removed from the life of a student herself. She realized that most of her students would be bigger than she was. She wondered if her

5'4" frame would enable her to deal with problems should they arise. She knew she was making a commitment to a position that would require much from her but she was confident. She knew what she had to do and she knew she could do it.

Linda's first two days of school were spent in meetings—whole school teachers' meetings, new teachers' meetings, department meetings. She received her assignment for the year and the textbooks students would be expected to master. She discovered that she alone was the Foreign Language Department of the school. As such, she would have all college-bound students: three classes of first year French and two classes of second year—a total student load of less than one hundred students. In addition to her teaching responsibilities, she would be expected to manage a study hall in the auditorium and work with another teacher to coordinate the yearbook. She was also notified that this was the year for accreditation for the school and she would be responsible for describing the foreign language program of the school to the visiting evaluation team. Linda took all of this in stride. As she listened to the talk of other new teachers she heard them expressing feelings she hadn't experienced. She couldn't imagine why they were nervous and were having trouble sleeping. She wasn't. She was excited about finally having a job. She knew this would be a good year.

* * *

The second week of school came. The bell rang and students drifted into class. They talked quietly with one another. Filing into the neatly organized rows, they seated themselves facing the teacher's desk and the blackboard. Linda, seated at her desk busily sorting papers, only glanced quickly at the students filtering into their desks. The students talked about the upcoming football game, ticket prices, who's going. . . . "Shhh," Linda began. Standing up from her desk she moved to the blackboard. She erased the board, closed the classroom door and sat back down. The students whispered quietly. "Kathy, you missed the quiz yesterday. Will you come here? You too, Mark." Linda took two copies of the quiz and led the students from the classroom to the study hall to make up the tests. The students in the classroom remained seated and continued to talk about the evening game. There were 13 girls and 3 boys present in this French II class. Three minutes later Linda returned to the room, closed the door, and began distributing quiz papers to the now silent students. One boy seated in the back of the room began whistling. "Okay, it's time to be quiet now," she said firmly. Jon, the French exchange student, found an error on his paper that Linda had made when correcting it. They discussed the problem in French as the other students exchanged looks with one another as if to say, "What are they saying?"

"Okay, here are the answers. Watch your papers." Linda gave the correct answers to the quiz questions one by one. A question on the test: "Do you get very bored?" A student in the back of the class said aloud "Yeah." Others giggled. Linda ignored the behavior and asked particular students to give answers to questions. Some students responded correctly. Others made mistakes. She called on individuals methodically, up one row and back the next. "You guys are doing really good [*sic*] on your grammar. You just don't seem to know what you're saying." A student raised her hand. "Miss Fuller, how much does this quiz count? Did you count off for spelling?" Linda responded quickly, "You know how much quizzes count. I told you that the first week of school. I took one point off for each spelling error. If there are no more questions, pass your papers forward. Then open your books to page 4." The dialogue began. Linda grasped her textbook firmly in her hands, almost as if it were a part of her. The textbook, she thought, was what made her classes productive. Without it she would have been lost. The book was the same one she had learned French from in high school and the same one she has used in student teaching. Using it was comfortable, secure. "Who can answer the first question?" The class was silent. Linda called on Julie, a sleepy-eyed tenth-grader. "Come on, if you did the homework you ought to be able to answer it." Linda was somewhat irritated at the lack of response from the class.

There was a knock on the door. Linda got up and opened the door. The two students who had been taking the quiz in the auditorium returned to the room, put their papers on the desk and took their seats. Linda went to the board and wrote a word in French on the board. Jon, the exchange student started laughing aloud. Linda looked at him and at the board. She too began to laugh. They talked in French and she went back to the board and changed the word. The rest of the class sat in silence while Linda and Jon continued their conversation.

Linda turned to the class and asked a question in French. A student responded in French. The conversation was about the seasons of the year. "Who can tell me which season is their favorite?"

One by one each student in the class responded in French. "Now, who can tell me why they like the season they said in French?" Silence. Linda smiled: "I like summer when school is out." The class laughed. "Shhh. You guys are awful."

"Okay, look at number 8 on page 5." A student raised her hand. "Miss Fuller, does it snow in France?" Linda looked to the exchange student. Once again they talked together in French. "Jon says that it snows a great deal in France, especially in the mountains."

"Now, turn to page 7. You might want to take some notes here." A student on the side of the room muttered, "I doubt it." Linda gave him a scolding look. She read aloud to the students from the text about reflexive pronouns. They went through a set of questions. As she read the questions, the whole class responded in unison. They were all attentive and cooperative.

Someone knocked on the door. Linda answered. A cheerleader from another class wanted to speak to a student in the class. Disgustedly, Linda looked around but the student was not in class. She returned to the lesson. "Is everybody getting this?" Silence. "It's not really that important but you might want to know this some day." Again she explained reflexive usage. One of the boys started knocking on his desk. Linda ignored this. "Okay, let's do number 16." Then the bell rang and students broke into a stampede for the door and the conviviality of the halls. No one stopped to chat. Linda rearranged her papers for her next class. Things were going as planned.

Linda was pleased with the way the year had begun. The students, her classes, her duties—most were better than she had expected. Her students were brighter than she thought they'd be. To her, they seemed serious and mature, much like she had been when she was in high school. The students taking French had high aspirations for themselves. Some were sons and daughters of nearby townspeople, others' parents were farmers. Some parents worked thirty miles away in the city. Regardless, they all wanted to go to college and make something of themselves. She felt fortunate that she had the academic students to teach. She felt she did not share the behavior problems or the problems of apathy she heard other teachers discussing. Though it was early in the school year, her students were concerned about doing well. They always came to class prepared to learn. Though occasionally there were individuals who didn't do homework, the students always had books, notebooks, and pencils. The students believed that they had to have French to achieve in college, so they complied. Usually, whatever the teacher asked them to do they did.

Her study hall duty, on the other hand, was a source of constant frustration. Linda shared this duty with another teacher. Study hall was difficult for both students and teachers. According to Linda, most students viewed study hall as a break. Few of them ever came to the auditorium for the purpose of studying. Consequently, Linda felt she had to play prison warden, patrolling for quiet and control. She was always very businesslike in her behavior toward students. She took her job seriously. Parading around "the zoo" was not to her liking. When students made animal noises in the back of the hall or pitched pennies, Linda took action. She believed that if she were going to gain respect as a teacher she had to handle her own problems. She moved particular problem students to other parts of the auditorium. She talked to others. She sent others on errands. It was important for her to maintain control. Though study hall was a source of constant irritation to her, it was something that had to be handled and she did.

Linda had little contact with other teachers in the building. Because she was the only language teacher there was no one for her to turn to for ideas or help. She spent her planning period and her lunch period in her room working rather than in the teachers' lounge. The teachers in the building seemed cliquish. She viewed the school as a rumor mill—teachers always talking about kids or other teachers. Linda really wasn't interested in that. She wanted to keep her private life separate from her professional life. She did not want to be a teacher all the time. She wanted to feel that when she left the building she was not bringing the school home with her. While she thought most of the staff friendly, she did not want them to be friends; she just didn't feel they had much in common with her. Sometimes teachers would see her in the hallway and ask her where she'd been hiding. She just told them she'd been so busy with her classes that she hadn't had time to socialize. She thought they would believe her because they knew she was a new teacher.

By the middle of October her classes were going smoothly. The students were making progress through the text. Some French singers were to do a concert in a nearby city. Linda thought her second year classes would enjoy hearing them and she believed a field trip would be good for everyone. She called the auditorium, got performance schedules and ticket prices and began circulating the information to her students. As she was leaving school one afternoon she relayed her plans to an older staff member who suggested that she'd better clear this activity with the office before she did too much planning. Linda really didn't understand what the office would need to know, but the next day she went to see the principal. He wanted to know what night of the week the concert was being held. "Wednesday." He told her that he was sorry but that she would have to cancel her plans. No school-sponsored events could be held on Wednesday nights. That was community church night. The school and the church groups had agreed not to schedule events on the same night. The parents, school officials, and church leaders agreed that they all must work together for the good of the children. The community valued the moral and spiritual growth of their youth as much as they valued the academic. Therefore, the school had set aside Wednesday nights and no extra events could be scheduled. Linda was disappointed. She had counted on this field trip as a break in the normal textbook-bound classroom routine. But rules were rules and she believed they must be honored.

Early in December, a new exchange student came to Clear Creek from French-speaking Quebec. She had been enrolled in Linda's class. Two days after she began school the grandfather of her host family died. While the family was mourning, Annabel came to school anyway. She was very dependent upon Linda and came around every period for directions about where to go and what to do next. Early on a Friday afternoon Annabel came to Linda crying, saying that some students had pushed her against the lockers and hurt her arm. Linda consoled her, told her she'd be all right and told her to go on to class. About five minutes later another teacher came to the door saying she'd found Annabel crying in the hallway. Linda told the teacher to take Annabel to the office. About ten minutes later the principal and the football coach came to the door. They said they thought Annabel's arm was broken and would Linda come with the principal to take her to the hospital. She felt she had no choice, so the football coach stayed to watch over her class and she left. She felt very awkward. Annabel's arm was bruised, not broken and all was well in the end. Linda never expected teachers would have things to do like that.

Christmas was a lively time in Linda's French classes. As a break from the textbook routine the classes learned French carols and customs of French folks at Christmas. Linda and the students decorated the classroom with tinsel and red and green bulbs. She was glad for the holidays. She needed the break and she felt the students needed it, too. Little did they all know what a long break they would have.

During most of January the school was closed because of cold weather and snow. In the country, snow drifts had been 6–8 feet deep, making it impossible for buses to run. City schools were closed because of gas shortages, while Clear Creek had electric heat but too much snow. The closings came at a particularly bad time for Linda. The end-of-semester exams were to be given and grades had to be reported. Since Christmas the students had been very apathetic when in school and although she had not given any F's so far this year she was afraid she would have to give a couple to second year students who had not completed special projects.

By the second week in February school was back in session. Linda was really glad to be back. Staying at home for such a long time had been boring for her. Teachers in the district were being required to teach on Saturdays to make up some of the lost time and spring vacation was cancelled. The parents were very supportive of making up time and though Linda was personally not in favor of teaching six-day weeks, she felt that the administration and the school board wanted to see teachers earn their pay. "I can see their point, but it'll still be hard."

Valentine's Day brought Linda a surprise.

Dear Miss Fuller,

    I see a golden meadow around our feet with an early morning sun burning through the azure sky. I see happiness in your face as we stand side by side. The hills to our left make the carpet of gold stand out like a treasure. But with your tawny hair and noble dark eyes, I realize my treasure is you.

                                                    David

As a student, David was quiet and shy—a good student but a loner. Linda never expected this kind of attention from him. She'd noticed that since Christmas he asked regularly to come into her room during his study hall period to work. Sometimes she'd let him. He was no trouble. But she never dreamed he was a poet or that he had such a crush on her. She was far more aware of the "cat whistles" she'd gotten in study hall and of the boys in the hallways who would wink at her. More poems came.

> When I came across you my friend,
> In early morning rays
> We tried to go through eternity
> But went our separate ways.
>
> I'm in love with an older girl now
> But she doesn't love me
> I'm too young she said,
> But I wish that we were free.

What to do? Linda wondered. Should she ignore these papers as they came across her desk or should she confront David and tell him that she thought his poems were lovely but that she was his teacher? Undecided, she did nothing. David began discussing his problems with her—rumors were circulating among students in the school, students were making fun of him. Linda told him to just stay away from the students who were giving him trouble. Then David began writing her notes, "You're so wonderful. . . ." Linda really was confused and concerned. For nearly a week she puzzled about what to do. It was obvious that David needed attention, needed someone to talk with, but she didn't feel she was the one to provide it. She thought about talking the problem over with the school counselor but she didn't really want to get involved. She reacted by ignoring him. He was absent from school a couple of days and when he returned he came to her apologizing for going overboard with his attentions. She wasn't sure what had changed but whatever it was, she was relieved and glad the problem had disappeared.

As spring time grew near students around the school were becoming disruptive. Firecrackers and smoke bombs in the restrooms and lunchrooms were common. Teachers were asked to patrol restrooms between classes and to supervise hallways during the last ten minutes of their lunch periods. That was fine with Linda. If the principal needed her, she'd be willing to help.

One Friday Linda was in the teachers' lounge typing a test when the vice-principal came in and asked her to help search students' lockers for drugs and fireworks. Wanting to be helpful she complied. She said this seemed like an adventure so she went along with him. After the search she went back to the lounge to collect her belongings and the teachers there bombarded her with questions. "What were *you* doing checking lockers?" "Why were lockers being searched, anyway?" Don't you know that's a violation of students' civil rights?" "Why did they pick you to help?" Linda was really surprised at the teachers' questions. "I really didn't mean anything by it. I was just being helpful." The teachers there—all of them— were treating her like gestapo. She quickly hurried from the lounge to the privacy of her classroom. By the time she had arrived in class the students had heard all about the search and were upset. She tried to explain everything to them as best as she could. She tried to tell them about why the school was concerned about drugs and firecrackers. The students mostly seemed to understand, or they said they did, anyway. After school Linda went to the English room as usual to await the 1:15 dismissal bell for teachers. The teachers in there gave her a hard time, too. Again she was under fire with the same questions she had had earlier. She just turned around and walked out of the room and went home. She worried about this all weekend. She felt that she had been put into a no-win position. If she had said no to the administrators she might have destroyed the good relationship with them and contracts for the coming year were soon to be awarded. Yet other teachers seemed to think she shouldn't have helped. Why? Would this episode label her as an "outsider" forever? By Monday all seemed forgotten. No one said another word to her about the locker search. She was relieved.

Then April arrived. "Shhh. Get out your homework. Exercise 8, page 81." Linda arose from her desk, gradebook in hand, and began walking slowly up and down the rows glancing at students' papers. The students had their workbooks open to the appropriate page. "Did you have any trouble with this?" Silence. "We'll go over this today but we're not going to spend too much time on it. It's important, but . . ." her voice drifted as she saw a student who didn't do her work. She said nothing but noted the lack of work in her gradebook. She finished the walk and returned to the front of the room. "If you don't understand this, say something." Linda believed that it was the students' responsibility to speak up if they didn't know something or didn't understand.

The students on this morning were especially quiet. They were half awake as Linda continued with the lesson. "Today we're going to continue our study of the subjunctive. I know this isn't easy to understand." She went to the board and listed several examples of subjunctives. "Are you sure you understand this?" They all went over the homework. Linda asked a question. A student responded. When a student didn't have the right answer she went on to the next student until she got the answer she sought. She then referred students to the textbook for more drills. "Okay, open your books to page 223." She made a conscious effort to call on each student in the class at least once. Things were much the same as they were during the first weeks of school. Not much had changed.

"For tomorrow for your homework do page 225. This might take a little time. Go from the infinitive to the subjunctive. Does everybody know what you are to do for tomorrow?" Silence. "Okay, now look on page 229. I'm going to start a story about maids and servants. We'll take turns reading out loud. Marie, you read first." The student began reading aloud. "Good. Now Paul, you read." As the boy began reading Linda was called out of the room. The student looked up from the book puzzled and asked the others if he should quit or keep on reading. The students started talking to one another. A room once silent was now filled with conversation. The talk was about other classes, tests, students. Then Linda entered the room. "Okay, Paul, continue." The class immediately became silent.

As the lesson finished Linda sat down behind her desk. "You're going to have a writing assignment in your workbook. Write a paragraph about the story we read, like a book report. This will be graded. Try to make it long. That is all. Any questions?" The bell sounded. Class ended.

Toward the end of April, the school board made its annual review of Clear Creek. Each of the five board members roamed the building talking to students and teachers. The visit was unannounced to the staff. As Linda was teaching one morning she looked out her classroom windows into another classroom across the court-yard. There they were. All five of them lined up across the back of Mr. Kelley's math class. She stopped her lesson and stared. What would she do if they walked into *her* room? There had been a lot of talk among the teachers about who on the staff would not be rehired next year. Would these board members make that decision about her? She began checking herself out. Did she know exactly what she would be doing in class today? Yes. Should she change her plans and use the language laboratory that the board had reluctantly purchased for her predecessor? After all, they might be expecting her to use it. Hmmm. There is paper on the floor. The desk is messy. Only five minutes till classes change. Stop lesson. Clean up. Linda was ner-vous. Next period, in they walked. Her smallest class—only ten students and she had them all under the headphones. The board members all smiled and the principal gave her a wink. She had made the right decision. She was pleased.

The end of the school year found Linda bored and out of energy. She frequently wondered if she could make it until June. All of a sudden she had lost interest in her classes. She could care less about covering the textbook. She needed something different to help her survive spring fever. She never realized it could affect teachers. She knew students had had it for a month, but teachers? Hmm. Teaching had worn her out. What was she to do? Aha! Projects. Cultural projects. Independent student projects. The answers to a dull routine. Each student would have a custom or part of a country to research about the impact of France and French culture. A great idea.

"Okay, class, for the rest of the year we're going to do something different. You're going to do something different. You're going to do some research on France and other countries."

"Do you want us to make a report?"

"No. Make an outline. Or you can do it any way you want. Make it interesting." Linda read through a list of countries where French is spoken. "Tell about the language and the people. I'm not going to tell you exactly what to write about." Each student selected a country, custom, or region to explore. "Each of you will give a talk to the class about your country. We will start next Monday. Who wants to go first?" For the next three weeks students gave reports and Linda typed all reports for the students to use as study guides. The teachers had been warned by the office not to let up until the end of the year. Linda's students were certainly keeping busy.

As the school year ended Linda was given a two-year contract from the board. She said that two more years would probably finish her off—that by that time she would probably be ready to do something else. The end of the year was hard on her.

As she reflected on what she had done, she thought how good the year had been until the last month or so. She just couldn't wait for school to be over. She wondered why. The kids were driving her crazy and she felt bad. She wondered if she'd feel this way next fall. She thought she'd gotten soft as the year went by. She believed she was not as strict as she had been. Her attitude changed and she felt that since it was the end of the year she couldn't help it and neither could her students. The best she thought she could do was try not to be upset. She'd felt like this had been *her* year. She'd done it pretty much on her own. No one had helped her through. Now she needed a break.

# Mr. Hardy, Mr. Hardy!

A Coke and a lunch bag rest on a gravestone. On an adjacent tomb sits a tall, blue-eyed young man, polishing off his second sandwich with gusto. He talks to his friends with equal gusto, his arms fly as his rambling thoughts find expression. It has been a typically strenuous week at work—sandblasting tombstones in the machine at the shop and then transporting them to the cemetery to set them up. A morbid job? Not in the least. Dave Hardy is a lover of life.

Dave is one of those rare individuals who rushes eagerly and optimistically to greet life. He loves to eat, sleep, talk, and have a good time. He is active physically, emotionally, and intellectually. Dave is high on people; he thrives on knowing them and being with them. He radiates his eagerness to the world, drawing people to him. He thinks well of other people and himself. There is a dynamic quality about him, an impression of tentacles constantly out to the world, sensing, gathering, understanding.

\* \* \*

Dave Hardy was the youngest of seven children. He wanted to be a teacher all his life, except in grade school, when like other boys in Catholic schools, the priesthood was his goal. He took a Bachelor of Science degree in education at a Catholic college, majoring in German and minoring in history. His student teaching was a very positive experience.

Upon graduating from college, David decided not to look for a teaching position right away. He had worked so hard for so long that he needed a break. Through a friend, he found a job for a year sandblasting gravestones. Toward the end of the year Dave started seeking a position in the diocesan schools to teach high school German. He applied to his own high school, only to be turned down. Dave finally found a position at St. Mary's Elementary School. He had no training in elementary teaching. He was to teach fifth, sixth, seventh, and eighth grade social studies (his college minor) and sixth and seventh grade religion, for which his only training had been the required courses in his parochial schooling. Dave was not at all bothered by the discrepancy between his training and the teaching demands. He was looking forward to teaching with a confident, relaxed attitude.

While some first year teachers start out almost as strangers in their new schools, in many ways Dave was not. The parish schools he had attended as a child had much in common with St. Mary's. Furthermore, there was a network of ties which Dave discovered at St. Mary's. One of the teachers had known him when he was in sixth grade. Three of his students turned out to be his cousins. Another of the teachers had gone to college with him. "So," said Dave, laughing, "I'll really have to toe the line." With his performance visible to so many who already knew him or his family, he knew some people would be watching in a special way. But there was also security; these bonds gave him a sense of belonging.

Dave brought with him a deep intellectual and religious commitment to Catholic education. He perceived an atmosphere of discipline—in the sense of academic rigor—not found in public school. Further, he shared a central concern with a set of commonly held values which Catholic educators try to act out in the way they live their lives. From this milieu arose a sense of purpose for both teachers and children. The kind of teacher Dave hoped to be fit closely with his conception of Catholic education. He hoped to be demanding with respect to the subject matter, but fair; he would be an open person. He had had teachers like this and emulated them.

St. Mary's was a large complex—a church, convent, residence for the priest, and the school, with light pleasant classrooms, a gym, and lunchroom. There was one class each of grades one through eight; class size went as high as 33. The students who came to St. Mary's were third, fourth, and fifth generation German, Irish, and

British. They all knew their ancestors' nationalities, but were ethnically indistinguishable now. All were white.

Dave's only apprehensions about teaching at St. Mary's, and they were minor ones, revolved around what Dave perceived as the materialism of the parish. Although he fully expected to enjoy teaching there, he didn't know how comfortable he was going to feel with these people who would spend thousands of dollars replacing the stained glass windows when the old ones were perfectly good. He knew it might bother him sometimes to deal with how the students, in their naivety, took all their advantages for granted.

Furthermore, the St. Mary's parish was characterized by a certain religious conservatism. The priest would not use women as lay ministers, and had just recently held baptism within the Mass, a practice common in other parishes for several years. Dave expected that the parents would want their children's daily religion class to be taught fairly traditionally, with the teacher communicating the Church's teachings didactically and giving a strict interpretation of the Bible.

Considering himself a modern Catholic, Dave was not at all sure that his religious outlooks would jibe with those of the parish. He did not attend Mass weekly, disagreed with some of the Pope's stands, and found no personal meaning in such cherished traditions as the May Altar. However, Dave considered himself a practicing Catholic; he deeply believed in the basic message of the Church about how to live with one's fellow humans. He intended to teach his religion classes within the bounds of his own conscience, gliding over the "picky pedantic" points he disagreed with. Although he would be careful not to offend, he would not be at all surprised if parents and other teachers questioned, and perhaps even objected to his religion classes.

Dave saw his major goal as having the students learn their history. Although he realized that these ten to thirteen-year-olds would need more guidance than had the high schoolers of his student teaching, Dave did not see his job as reforming children or trying to make them perfect. He was there to teach the subjects. As for discipline, he didn't anticipate much of a problem; he hadn't had problems with discipline before. He saw himself as a patient person and felt confident that he could handle whatever would arise. He had no intention of being heavy-handed. "I'm not a ranter or raver; that defeats the purpose of the school." Rather he saw discipline as a matter of correcting the *behavior* of the child, letting the child know that the behavior is wrong, not that he himself is bad.

Dave anticipated a very positive school atmosphere. He liked the principal; he felt Tom would give him freedom in the classroom. He had met and liked the other teachers also. He felt good about the students; they came from a good background and from what he had heard, their parents were very helpful to the teachers. He really felt calm about teaching. Being so relaxed would work for him, he felt—it would give other people the impression he was competent. He looked forward to working with the children, and to giving of himself to help them.

The first few weeks were hectic. Dave found teaching harder than he'd ever thought it would be, but still enjoyable. He would arrive at school between 7:20 and 8:15, and, later toward the end of the week, stay until 4:30 or 5:00, cleaning off the piles of material which had accumulated on his desk, making bulletin boards, talking to the students and teachers. Home for dinner, and then back at school until 10:00 to prepare for the next day. He tried to get the sleep he needed. What was the use of preparing lessons if he was going to be too tired to carry them out well? Dave found that he was assigning many more papers than he had time to grade. He felt he was missing time for his personal life—time to do "dumb stuff" like re-pot his plants, or go out and just have a good time. "I'm so boring socially," he found himself thinking.

Dave felt his newness at St. Mary's in little ways. The textbooks were all new to him; he hadn't had time to read them, and consequently his first few days of classes weren't as well planned as he would have liked. Furthermore, he was not acquainted with all the materials available for his use. The library had many filmstrips, and his room's cabinets were full of supplementary texts, but there was no time to review them. He "felt dumb" not knowing the flow of the school. If he wanted to use certain audio-visual equipment for a lesson, how should he go about it? Where should he look for the adapter plug when it wasn't in its place? These were things which a new teacher wouldn't be expected to know, and would just have to learn as the occasion arose.

One thing Dave found nerve-wracking at first was performing all the administrative tasks in class, and finding out the procedure for

each. First you take attendance. What's the procedure for that? Then
a lunch count—how can the teacher handle that? Dave would have
appreciated someone to go over the details with him.

The first few weeks are difficult for a new teacher with respect
to discipline too. Dave didn't know the policies of the school. Does
the principal let the students go to the bathroom when they want,
and without a pass? What are the limits of acceptable behavior? The
teacher must make clear to the students a full set of expectations for
their behavior and the exact punishments for infractions. Dave
wasn't the type to sit down in advance and think these all out;
consequently he had to work them out gradually. In the meantime, it
was touch-and-go; he was in the process of discovering the limits of
his own tolerance, and the procedures that would work for him with
these children.

Dave found the atmosphere at St. Mary's all that he had hoped
for. It was warm and purposeful, an environment where people
treated each other well. Much of the atmosphere, Dave found, ema-
nated from the principal. He was open to teachers and students, and
believed deeply in the school's goal. To him the greatest offense in
the school was deliberate rudeness of one person to another, students
or staff. He felt confident that the teachers were making their best
efforts to teach well, and he set a tone of unmeddling support. He
asked teachers to submit their weekly plans, but admitted that he
didn't necessarily expect the teachers to teach specifically from those
plans.

If one place represented the heartbeat of the school, it was the
staff room. With an open door to the main corridor, it served as
teachers' workroom, lounge and lunchroom, meeting room and conference room. The teachers went there first in the morning for
orange juice or coffee, and bounced in and out all day, running off
dittos, talking to a student about makeup work, conversing. Amidst
much personal banter, in which the principal also took part, teachers
were constantly making plans for the next picnic or Mass or a team-
taught unit. There was no gossip, or deprecatory discussion about
the students. It was evident that the teachers were very much involved in their jobs.

Dave fit in well here; he thrived on being with people. The
other teachers found him talking constantly in a stream of enthusiasm for what was happening at the moment, what he was feel-

ing, what someone else was telling him. He moved rapidly over a range of topics, now the bulletin board he was preparing, now a bit of his personal philosophy, now how tired he was, now a joke. It was active, evolving talk, with significant thoughts embedded in rambling, and a delight in hearing his ideas as he expressed them. It was also talk that was sensitive to others.

Dave's goal for his teaching, beyond covering the subject matter, was to generate enthusiasm among the students. Dave knew from the beginning that he would feel successful if he sensed that the students were "with him," involved in what he was trying to teach. To this end, he knew that his greatest challenge would be to vary his teaching methods, to look constantly for ways of keeping their interest at high levels.

Dave decided to start his fifth graders with that basis of historical thinking, the hypothesis. He explained and illustrated the word "hypothesis" for them, and for homework told them to form some hypotheses about how people travelled in 1890.

\* \* \*

The next day.

Dave reviews the meaning of "hypothesis." He asks the children to take out their homework, and he walks up and down the rows checking it.

"Now, how do we check our hypotheses?" he asks. Ten hands wave in the air, and several more students call out. Dave writes their answers on the board.

"Do we have to write this down in our notebooks?" one asks.

"Yes," Dave replies. Thirty-three fifth graders open their notebooks and copy off the board diligently.

Now that they have a list of ways to check hypotheses, Dave asks them what hypotheses they have formed about how people travelled in 1890. Twenty hands wave in the air (twenty-five, maybe; some students have both hands up). Dave writes these answers on the board also.

"Write these down, and for homework go collect data on these. Don't look them all up. Ask people who would know." There is a minor roar of unbridled enthusiasm.

"Fifth grade!" Dave gently reproves them, and goes on to explain.

Joanie asks, "If we wanted, could we write an essay on it?"

"Yes," Dave responds, matter of factly.

\* \* \*

The next day.

Dave writes on the board, "How did people travel in 1890?" and lists the hypotheses from the day before. He calls them out one by one: "car," "train," "plane," "submarine," "unicycle," and the students respond "yes" or "no" in unison. Sometimes he asks where they got their information; they have asked parents and consulted the textbook and encyclopedia. When they get to "unicycle," there are few responses.

"Sandy, look up unicycle in the encyclopedia," Dave directs. Sandy goes to the shelf and takes down the U volume. In a couple of minutes she reports, "It's not in here."

"Okay," says Dave.

Meanwhile a dispute has arisen about the validity of Tony's data. "Your father might have made a mistake," Cathy tells Tony. Dave differentiates between conclusive evidence and hearsay. He compares hearsay to the game of "telephone." The children understand. Dave continues through the list. Most of the children have their hands raised constantly. At the end, unsolicited, they continue to call out other forms of transportation—"clipper ship," "subway," and the class weighs each hypothesis. Finally, Dave calls the discussion to a halt: "Okay, hand in your homework."

\* \* \*

The hypotheses lessons generated enthusiasm in several ways. They allowed for a great deal of student participation. Dave had an opportunity to show the students that he welcomed and valued their responses. The nature of the topic allowed that all answers, being hypotheses, were acceptable. Dave's assignment to go collect data on the hypotheses encouraged the children to do the homework the easy way, by asking their parents. The fact that Dave had given no indication of which hypotheses were correct lent an aura of detective work to the whole assignment. In class Dave demonstrated what he was later to call a strength of his—the ability to take advantage of "teachable moments." He took a disagreement between two students and used it as a chance to teach the difference between conclusive evidence and hearsay. Further, he showed the students that when someone, student or teacher, doesn't know an answer, it is natural to look it up right away.

In October, Dave jumped spontaneously into what he would later call a risky venture for a first year teacher in the second month of school. In his effort to stimulate involvement, he set up an experiment in prejudice with his sixth grade religion class. For four days all the blue-eyed students were to be considered superior to the brown-eyed students. They were spoken nicely to by Dave; they had exclusive use of a certain drinking fountain; they all sat on the same side of the room. The speed with which the blue-eyes adopted the role of oppressor was electrifying. The impact on the students was far greater than Dave would ever have expected.

On the evening of the first day a mother phoned Dave. She was upset; the school was supposed to teach the children love, not hate, she said. Dave could understand her point of view, but disagreed with her, and they talked for an hour and a half. Dave said he would be glad to remove her daughter from the experiment and do it in a way not obvious to the other children, but he would not stop the entire experiment. In the end, Mrs. Norris chose not to have her daughter removed from the experiment, although Dave had not changed her mind about its value. Dave wasn't upset by the criticism; he felt the discussion had been interesting. Whenever he and Mrs. Norris met for the rest of the year, it was with the sincerest cordiality on both sides. Dave was spoken to by various other mothers who came to the school for other reasons, and they were interested and supportive.

The impact of the experiment on the kids was so strong that Dave had to reverse the blue-eye and brown-eye roles after the second day. On the third day he used religion class to explore the experiment with the children.

*     *     *

The class comes in for religion. Blue-eyes and brown-eyes are seated on opposite sides of the room. Dave starts sternly: "It has come to my attention that some blue-eyed kids have been using the brown-eyed drinking fountain. If this continues, I'll have to do something about it." He continues with a frown, "blue-eyed kids take out your books." Then he turns to the others with a smile, "brown-eyed kids, would you please take out your books?"

Dave calls on a brown-eyed girl to read. A blue-eye leans over to her classmate and whispers with a dejected look on her face. Dave sees her, and chides the blue-eyes for talking. "I may have to have you write," he warns.

Dave has the student read one question from the religion book: "How have *you* experienced the struggle between good and evil?" He repeats the question in the book and calls on a blue-eye to answer. Patrick talks about how he is evil when he raids the cookie jar at home. Dave calls on another blue-eye. She talks about how she is mean to her sister sometimes. The discussion goes on, with almost no mention of the experiment. The students talk about how it feels, good and bad, to see others get in trouble. The teacher stays on the brown-eyed side, and periodically calls over to the blue-eyes to be quiet. Finally Dave brings the discussion pointedly to the experiment: "Brown-eyes, do you feel sorry for the blue-eyes?"

The brown-eyes chorus, "No. They aren't going through as much as we did."

Dave asks, "Brown-eyes, do you think you'll show more compassion?" He stops to explain compassion. Some say, yes; some, no. Dave talks to the students about the experiment. "After the experiment people can't hold grudges. Don't confuse it! This is our experiment."

The brown-eyes are not all reconciled yet. Tim says, "I'll be willing not to hold a grudge if we can keep the blue-eyes down for a while."

Dave begins to reply. The discussion is at a point of intense involvement for everyone.

\* \* \*

Unfortunately, the discussion fell victim to a common school interruption. The door opened, and in came Father Thompson, unannounced, to give religious instruction. Dave retired to the staff room, disappointed and a little irritated at having to cut off the discussion just when they were getting into a serious consideration of the experiment.

In the teachers' room he reflected on how the discussion had developed and the children's initial responses to the question on good and evil. One might have thought that their first response would be to talk about the experiment. But, Dave realized, the little evils such as white lies or raiding the cookie jar are what the kids tend to think of when the question of good and evil comes up. One thing had surprised him about the discussion; he had really expected all the brown-eyes to feel compassionate toward the blue-eyes after having been oppressed themselves. At this point, there was no such feeling. Dave looked forward to his next period with them: they would finish the discussion and he would show *Eye of the Storm*, a film about a grade school teacher who tried a similar experiment. On the whole, Dave felt the experiment had been a huge success.

The prejudice experiment, Dave's first potential rub with the parish, had gone by with no permanently upset feelings on either his part or the parents'. On the next issue he was not so lucky. He had been appointed lay minister, which meant that he served communion during the Mass. For this duty Father Thompson required that a white robe of fine material be worn. This bothered Dave; in his own parish ministers were deemed acceptable in the sight of God in their regular clothing. Dave asked the priest if he could get out of wearing the white robe, but Father insisted. "Enough," Dave said to himself, "I know when I'm beat," and he put on the white robe and braved the chuckles of his seventh grade boys.

Now Dave and a woman teacher alternated being lay ministers. One day as Dave sat with his class waiting for the school Mass to begin, Nancy came up to him and said, "Go up there and get the white robe on." In consternation Dave jumped up; he knew he was in the habit of forgetting things and immediately assumed that he had forgotten it was his turn to serve. He hurried to get the robe on. Along about the middle of the Mass, a series of realizations suddenly dawned on him: "It was Nancy's turn, not mine. This school Mass is open to the parish today because it is a Holy Day. Father never has women serve for parish Masses because he claims the parish isn't ready for it." Dave was immensely irritated. "If I had only realized this sooner," he thought to himself, "I would have gotten sick real quick. Or refused to do it on principle. That's one thing about the Catholic Church that bugs the hell out of me—their attitude toward women." Later on, Dave made his feeling known in the staff room, although he never did talk to Father Thompson about it.

Dave's classes were going well. The children would come in saying hello and crowding around him. He would start almost abruptly, initiating the discussion by telling them what page to turn to. If he were having them read from a book, never more than three sentences would be read before Dave would use the information as a starting point. A typical class found him holding a discussion, making a few important points himself and bringing out other points by questioning the students. Dave would move around the room, sitting on the radiator in the back, moving abruptly to sit at an empty desk, standing to one side of the room, or moving rapidly to the front board to write what he wished them to take down in their notes. Dave repeated or paraphrased much of what he said; he used advanced vocabulary, but always offered synonyms for the hard words, and expressed whole ideas in several ways. "Okay, today we have a filmstrip, to kind of reinforce, review, tell you about Abraham."

Dave would ask many kinds of questions. He might ask factual questions about the subject matter covered yesterday. Often he would engage students in historian's thinking, asking them for many possible explanations of an event. "How do you explain the story of Lot's wife?" He'd encourage them to think of many natural events which could have served as the basis of a biblical version. Or he would pose a hypothetical situation in which the students would be decision-makers, a situation analogous to the historical event being studied. The day the seventh graders studied the Diaspora, he asked, "What if someone sent everyone in this class away from here and away from each other? How would you follow the same customs you do now?" Often he would ask them for examples of a concept: "Give me some examples of how different cultures satisfy different needs." Or he would pose the moral dilemma faced by the people they were studying: "What if you were a Jew in the Spanish Inquisition? Would you convert or die?"

After posing questions, Dave would listen carefully to the students' answers. The first few days of school, he called on everyone whose hand was raised for each question. He often asked the children to repeat part of the answer so as to be sure of understanding it. He would give liberal praise to most answers, use them as the basis of his next comment, and would often refer back to them at a later time. By the second week, Dave had discovered that he simply wouldn't have time to call on each student who volunteered. He did try hard to call on everyone who raised a hand over the course of the period, though. There were usually hands raised all period in Dave's class.

"Mr. Hardy, I've got it. Would you *please* call on me?" would come the anguished plea.

"Fifth graders, you're not *listening*," Mr. Hardy would chide in reply. Sometimes Dave's questions took on a guess-what-I'm-thinking quality. Although on the surface the questions were open-ended, Dave would only call on students until someone gave the answer he had in mind.

With the middle of November came parent conferences. Dave loved them. He enjoyed meeting the parents and hearing what they had heard about him from their children. He laughed to hear that some kids perceived him as having a temper. One incident occurred during parent conferences which led Dave to have increased respect for his colleagues. One of the parents, curious to know an experienced teacher's opinion of Dave, asked the science teacher, "What do you think of the new social studies teacher?" Cindy wouldn't say anything about Dave behind his back. She told the parent that she didn't really know what Dave was doing with his classes and that it would be better for the parent to talk with Dave. Dave was very pleased to hear how professionally Cindy had handled it. He felt mildly irritated that the parent would not consult him directly.

As the fall wore on, Dave's admiration and liking for the staff increased tremendously. They were so friendly that he felt perfectly free to express his feelings. He could say, "Gee, I'm tired today; I'm really out of it," and he'd feel their support. He didn't look to them for specific teaching ideas, as none of them was in social studies, but he would consult them occasionally on a particular student who was being a problem for him. He would find out how that student acted for other teachers, and how they reacted. Then Dave would either try one of their suggestions, or integrate theirs with his. He borrowed from them in a continuous process of developing his own teaching techniques through synthesis.

The end of the first grading period was hard for Dave. He had a huge backlog of ungraded papers. Actually figuring the grades wasn't hard, but the hours of paper-correcting were wearing. He found himself getting involved, wanting so much to have each student do well on the test that he would pore over each one, trying his utmost to understand each student's position and find some credit-worthy statements.

Dave's relationship with students was for him one of the most rewarding aspects of teaching. His give-and-take relationship with the children wasn't long in starting. "How was it?" he asked a few eighth graders on their way out the door the third day of class, "Was it better today?" They answered yes.

"You seemed so out of it," he observed, but with concern in his voice.

Dave's early comments to his classes showed that he knew them quickly, had faith in them, and was comfortable with them. Upon introducing his fifth grade to a visitor on the third day, he said with a big smile, "This is my best class, or they think they are, and I hope they'll show you why." The ten-year-olds all turned around and grinned pleased grins at the visitor. In his eighth grade class someone had propped the window open with pencils. "You clowns," he said briefly, and closed the window. Between periods, at lunch, or before and after school, students sought Dave out to talk and laugh. He would participate in their jokes, learning the genre and making jokes on them, as well as being willing to be the butt of theirs. They might challenge him to a handslapping game, or engage him in a round of "knock-knock." As the students, especially the fifth graders, would come into class, they would gather around him, uncontrollably eager to tell him their latest news, or a joke, or ask one of a thousand questions.

"Mr. Hardy, look at my tooth!"

"Mr. Hardy, you know what my sister did?"

"Mr. Hardy, do you have a car? If so, you'd better look out!"

"Mr. Hardy, I couldn't finish my homework."

The lightheartedness often spilled over into the class periods. "Now don't throw popcorn on the floor," he'd tell them before a filmstrip, and they'd groan appreciatively. Another day he opened class with "Okay, seventh grade, let's start with state history, instead of religion." The class groaned. "I know you love state history," he told them.

Dave started asking review questions: "What slave state was added to compensate for free California?" One student after another got it wrong. A couple of students called out. Their answers were wrong. Other students talked out and Dave didn't stop them. The whole class was getting in the spirit, as more and more students called out wrong answers. The noise rose to a crescendo, everyone shouting out states at random. Once played out, the class watched Dave who looked at them with a twinkle in his eye and said, "No state, it was the Fugitive Slave Law."

"Oh, no!" they all moaned. Later in that period Dave asked, "What caused the Civil War, and if you tell me slavery, I'm going to knock you out of here." Several students chanted, "Slavery, slavery." Dave called on someone else.

Dave was willing to spend time outside of school as well. In the first few weeks of school, the fifth graders invited him to a birthday party, and the eighth grade cheerleaders persuaded Dave to take them TP-ing. Dave and a friend drove them around to the football players' homes and waited in the car while the girls draped the front yards with toilet paper. Dave loved it and discussed it with the football players the next day with great relish.

Did Dave like all of the students? As he put it, "Yeah, there are a couple of personality conflicts, but I like those kids even though I don't dig on their personalities."

Dave was able to discipline the students much as he had expected, correcting the behavior itself. In the beginning weeks he made many gentle reprovals, although harried at times, to the class and to individuals.

To the fifth grade: "Fifth grade," in rising and falling intonation.

To the eight graders, nicely: "What grade are you in? My fifth graders don't even do that."

To the sixth grade: "All right, sixth graders, this business of putting your mouth in gear and letting it run all period has got to stop."

To the seventh grade: "Don't make me do this; it's only the second week." These squirmy preadolescents would calm down for a while, and then the noise would mount again; stimulated by Dave's discussion in which he truly wanted students to participate. Then he would say, loudly and sometimes, sharply, "Quiet!" and "Be quiet!"

The principal behavior which Dave corrected was inattentiveness. Often he would call out the individual's name: "Bobby, you're not listening"; "Mary and Susie, are you going to be with us or be by yourselves? Come on, get with us." Often he would go over to the inattentive student, bend down, and tell him or her quietly to listen.

Sometimes Dave felt it necessary to administer a punishment. The second week he assigned his study hall a fifty-word essay (by Christmas such essays had increased to five hundred words) and soon had several students in for detention. Once during practice for a class Mass, he told the boys that if they didn't behave, he'd have them attend 8:00 Mass for a week. Fortunately they behaved—Dave certainly didn't want to get up early to go with them! In administering a punishment, Dave always warned the student in advance, then made certain the student understood what Dave thought he or she had done wrong, and gave the student a chance to answer the charges. As it turned out, he was not stubborn about carrying out the announced punishment. Often he settled for a lesser one, or dismissed the charge once the student understood what was wrong and admitted it.

Several weeks in the classroom brought Dave to the realization that he needed to be stricter with the children. He began keeping the students quieter and more attentive. As he came to know the age group, he found himself changing his view about the function of a teacher of these children. They are greatly influenced by their teachers whether the teachers know it or not. Dave realized that he was not only teaching subject matter; it was also his job to guide the children and help shape their characters.

As Christmas vacation approached, time dragged. Dave was tired and had a cold. His patience with the students was wearing thin. He was hassling the students a lot and raising his voice with them. One day he accused, "Frank, are you talking?" Frank shook his head.

"Don't tell me you're not talking when you're talking!" Dave's voice conveyed his anger. He seemed to have lost his motivation to correct the behavior rather than express anger with the child. He looked forward to a much-needed vacation of rest and relaxation, and catching up on school work.

Dave didn't get much of a vacation, though. The first week he was sick, and the second week friends came to visit. Dave returned to school tired, and again found himself hassling the students. Not only he, but some of the other teachers also noticed in themselves a "sit-on-'em" attitude toward the kids. They discussed this and realized that they did not like this attitude; it was contrary to the goals of the school and to their own personal aspirations as teachers. They began to make a conscious effort not to yell at the students, but to talk to them, correct them, be firm but patient. Things improved.

The month of January was one of inclement weather. Several days in the first two weeks were called off because of snow, ice, or cold. Dave was much relieved, and used these days to rest. With the gas crisis imminent, the diocesan board decided to close St. Mary's for the month of February and have the students meet two mornings a week in the convent. The teachers were to prepare learning packets for students to complete at home with daily work in each subject. Dave threw himself into creating packets enthusiastically. He had taken a computer-assisted instruction course in college and now used that knowledge in making worksheets. He sprinkled them with jokes, and wrote that the students should feel free to call him any time they had a question.

February was a month of frustration. In the mornings Dave would meet the students in the basement of the convent. It was 55°. There would be a flurry of activity as he collected their learning packets and passed out the next ones. He felt as if he and the children were just throwing papers to each other. Then in the afternoon it was back to the staff room in the school to prepare more packets. Those three weeks were busier than the beginning of the year.

In addition to the hectic rush of February, Dave suffered the disappointment of not being able to teach the Confirmation curriculum he had been developing. Before the gas crisis arose, he and Sister Rose, the English teacher, had been given responsibility to prepare the eighth graders for Confirmation. They had composed an excellent seven-part program dealing with themes such as courage, integrity, commitment, religious self-esteem. When the school closing prevented them from meeting regularly with the eighth graders, Dave and Sister Rose wanted to postpone Confirmation so as to be able to complete their course. Father Thompson absolutely refused, saying he couldn't change the date because he was obligated to the public school confirmees. Dave and Sister Rose disputed with him, but he wouldn't budge. They were both disappointed and discouraged. They would not finish the program before Confirmation, and there was no point in limping through it later. Dave was thoroughly riled at "The Good Father."

The last week in February was spring vacation. Dave loved it. He did nothing but sleep. After vacation he was glad to be back. The kids were glad, and Dave just "bopped around" and had a great time. His tendency to get angry with the students had disappeared.

About this time Dave deliberately began making major changes in his teaching methods. In several of his classes he assigned students to do group research on topics and to report to the class. During the report Dave would bring out the important points from what the students said. Several benefits accrued. For the students, there was the experience of taking responsibility for teaching the class. For Dave, preparation time was greatly decreased; he could go on his general knowledge, without having to familiarize himself with the students' textbook. Further, he was relieved of the pressure of coming up with six exciting lessons every day. He viewed these changes as definite progress; he had really been exhausting himself at the beginning of the year, even giving up his weekend evenings to prepare lessons. It was natural for a new teacher, he figured, but after a while it seemed ridiculous to sacrifice all his social life for his teaching job.

Further, Dave began to feel less pressure to cover all the material. He realized that he would never be able to get through the entire curriculum by June, so he just stopped worrying about it. If the students weren't getting one topic, they *were* getting something else in detail. Not getting through the curriculum was a mistake, but it was a mistake he would correct next September, and would not let upset him any more this year.

As the school year accelerated to a close, St. Mary's was a flurry of activity—special Masses, class picnics, the eighth grade trip, the patrol kids' trip to a baseball game. May was a blur. Dave loved being with the kids, but he was tired, and furthermore, eager to be off to Europe—he'd be leaving two days after school was out.

On the whole, Dave felt good about his first year of teaching. The students had done well; he was pleased with the way they could discuss the topics they had studied. Not only were they still constantly volunteering to answer his questions in class, but they were also making their own comments and asking him questions. Many class periods the students did most of the talking, with Dave just steering the discussion in the right direction. The students would refer to the subject matter that they had studied earlier, or what they had read in a book or seen on TV, or even played in a game.

"Mr. Hardy, Mr. Hardy! I have two questions for you. Do you know much about this time era?"

Dave answered seriously, "Oh, I know everything about this time." A few students groaned.

Billy continued, "Okay, you asked for it. *Who* were Alfred the Great and Aethelred?" He was reading from a paper in a challenging tone of voice.

Dave, answering quickly amidst the further groans of his students, replied, "Okay, Aethelred and Alfred were Anglo-Saxon kings in England."

Billy, impressed, told the class, "I got that from a game I got called *Feudal*." Even as he talked, four students were waiting with hands raised to ask other questions about the Middle Ages. Dave loved it. On days like this, it was the students who were getting *him* involved!

Teaching at St. Mary's had turned out to be more fun than he expected. Dave felt comfortable with the parents he'd met. They were just regular middle-class people, not the strange beings he had anticipated. No one had complained about the way he taught his religion classes. Dave felt good about himself. He anticipated spending time over the summer sprucing up the curriculum. Even though there was never enough time to do everything the way he wanted to do it, he had little doubt about being a good teacher.

# I Should Definitely Have It by Thanksgiving

## 4

When I was in high school, I knew I wanted to be a nurse or teacher. I decided on teaching. But when I went to college, I decided to go into a nursing program because I knew I could transfer if I didn't like it. After one year, I switched to education because it would have been selfish to stay in nurses training when I knew I really didn't want to be a nurse.

I plan to teach until I get married, then I want to start a family. I might come back to teaching after the kids are grown. With a college degree and a teaching certificate, I'll have something to fall back on if something happens to my husband. God forbid that should happen, but my cousin, Lynne, and her three kids have been on welfare since Bill, her husband, got killed in a car wreck. I don't want that to happen to me—you know—have to go on welfare because I'm not trained for a job.

\* \* \*

To the right of a bulky desk littered with papers and books stands Donna Hastings. Before her are sixth graders, a room full— twenty-nine in all. Miss Hastings appears the adult in the room, taller and heavier than the youngsters, rivaled only by tall, blond, Jo Ann. Miss Hastings is carefully and conservatively dressed in a tan skirt and white blouse. A navy blue blazer rests on the back of her chair. Miss Hasting's posture and expressions reflect a rural heritage. Her face is round, yet square-chinned, framed by a brushed-over bouffant of chestnut hair. Her hazel eyes gaze over seated eleven-year-olds and return to her planbook.

"Can someone tell me who provided ships and crew for Columbus to discover a way around the world? Sean, do you know?"

"Who? Me?" taunts Sean, then gives the correct answer before Miss Hastings can respond.

In the rear of the room Stan quietly closes a door cloistering John inside one of four plywood cabinets along the wall. Several boys snicker in anticipation. Lisa nudges Mary, points toward the cabinets and whispers. Both girls giggle. Stan snuffs a swelling laugh. Miss Hastings asks Jo Ann to read sentence number four.

*   *   *

This is the second day of Donna Hastings' second week as sixth grade core, and sixth through eighth grade social studies teacher at St. Ambrose School, a K–8 school in a mature, middle-class urban neighborhood.

As she stands before her students trying to appear confident, Donna has a nagging sense that teaching is considerably different than she anticipated two weeks ago. Neither her tasks, students, other teachers, nor her feelings are what she thought they would be. Frequent interruptions and procedural matters consume classroom time. Students talk and play and still run out of work in spite of her nightly planning vigils. She finds it embarrassing and difficult to attempt to get to know her new colleagues; in fact, Donna even has trouble involving herself in teachers' lounge talk. When she does, she often hears that she had done something wrong: "Kevin threw a football into my room. When I stopped him, he showed me your hall pass. Donna, I think you should talk to him, settle him down before he runs over you. Sister Celeste had Kevin in fifth grade last year and he behaved himself. You'll have to do like she did—keep him under your thumb."

Students inform Donna that she isn't like their former teacher. And the principal, Sister Theresa, who at first appeared to be a source of support, now seems a threat. Her office adjoins Donna's classroom, and the principal's voice can be heard responding to her ringing phone: "Good morning, St. Ambrose school, Sister Theresa speaking." Sister Theresa likewise can hear much of what happens in Donna's classroom. As a matter of fact, on the second day of school Sister Theresa came to Donna and asked if she could close the door for "We're so close, we don't want to disturb one another, do we?"

In addition to the adjustments necessary to her new job, Donna has had to make her new living arrangement feel like home. She and her roommates, a teacher and a department store clerk, moved their things into a two-bedroom apartment the weekend before school started, but have, as yet, to get settled. Clothes, towels, dishes, and other necessities remain in boxes, the kitchen is incomplete and the telephone has not been installed. The roommates have already undergone a major misunderstanding and are trying to find ways to become comfortable with one another. Also, Donna seems unable to garner the energy necessary to put her things in place because of the work she brings home every night, papers to grade, lessons to plan, and so on. Often she has tension headaches after school and doesn't feel like doing housework. Altogether, Donna wonders whether teaching and adult life are what she hoped they would be.

St. Ambrose sits in Avalon, a quiet residential community that clings to a major urban thoroughfare. Avalon's streets and homes reflect the community's history. A suburb begun in the late 1920's, Avalon's development was stunted by the Depression, but the community was able to breathe new life during the postwar economic boom, grow to maturity, and blossom in the 1950's. No longer a suburb, Avalon has been enfolded by the city but retains its suburban appearance.

Annual family income ranges from $16,000 to $30,000. The people are midstream Americans and Christians, mostly descendants of longtime area residents of English, Scot-Irish, and German background. Their occupations vary, but there is a fair sampling of middle management personnel, school teachers, university professors, pharmacists and other health care professionals, and a substantial number of persons involved in the construction and home maintenance trades. There are a few transient residents, most of these being upward-bound young professionals with growing families.

Avalon has two high schools, Bellevue and Carroll, public and Catholic. Both have had two decades of respect for their highly competitive academic and athletic programs. They send large percentages of their graduates to college. Most St. Ambrose graduates attend Carroll High, but a select few attend one of the city's exclusive prep schools.

*   *   *

Before she began teaching, Donna spoke proudly of her teacher education experience at a small Catholic college. She felt that her experience was the primary reason that she got the position at St. Ambrose, that her recommendations from student teaching cemented the contract. Donna felt good about her training because it assured her that she was able to teach. "The biggest thing that I learned in my education courses and student teaching was that I can teach. I really can teach. A good education program helps people find out if they are fit to teach. They can find out if they have the feel for teaching, if they can get rapport with students and at the same time get material across and control the class. Mine did that."

Donna believed that because of her home experience she would fare well. As the second of eight children, throughout her childhood she was responsible for helping her mother rear the boys. Donna assumed that she had enough practical experience to understand children and to manage them in a classroom. She felt that she would have few serious problems even though she would teach youngsters several years older than the lower primary levels she was trained for. Her family experience and student teaching contributed to her confidence that she would be successful. "Whatever concerns I had about controlling a classroom are pretty well gone. I know how to take care of them as they come. At first I was a little worried about the older students, but I'm not now."

As she began her year Donna expected that she would have a few problems. Some days might even present frustrations, but she looked forward to having "really nice days" frequently, days in which her plans would be "nearly perfect." Students would be prepared and willing to work, "everyone in a good mood, no one having a bad day, the class running so smoothly that everyone finishes their work and has time for themselves and time to do a lot of extra reading." Also, she imagined her ideal student would be one "I could teach and not have to give directions to."

The low salary paid teachers in diocesan schools was of some concern to Donna, but she was generally pleased to teach at St. Ambrose. In fact, she felt her assignment was nearly perfect. "Teaching in a parochial school has a lot of advantages, like there is a lot of cooperation and a good community feeling that you don't get in bigger schools. Parents and teachers can work together for a child's education and his own good. And teachers have better control."

Donna was concerned about being able to fully deliver on the principal's desire that she incorporate reading—specifically the teaching of reading comprehension—in the social studies program. She would try, though, and she anticipated that the students would be tolerant and helpful. "I'm prepared for healthy, intelligent go-get-'em kids, and they'll be interested in me because I'm new. We'll learn together, you know, help out each other."

The confidence that she felt Sister Theresa placed in her made Donna uneasy. This was a real concern. Donna believed that there might be a disadvantage in having her boss have high expectations for her at the outset: "If I don't do well in the beginning, Sister might lose confidence in me and think I'm not really a good teacher."

Donna was not aware of any special rules or policies at St. Ambrose. "They just make the rules as they need them. That's what I'll do, too. There's no reason to get bogged down in rules." Donna intended to be fair and even-handed in conducting class. "I think students expect teachers to yell sometimes and to give quizzes and homework and stuff like that. I won't. I won't give homework because students should have time to let down after school. They have enough work and pressure in their classes. So I'll only assign homework when it's important—like when they need to prepare for something I've planned for the next day. I'll never assign homework for punishment."

Teachers who humiliated students upset Donna when she was a student. She hoped she would never put down students. It was difficult for her to anticipate how she would handle a student who either failed to keep up with his work or "goofed off" in class. She thought she might ask if he understood the work. In some cases she would tell him directly to do his assignment. She might even apply peer pressure and reprimand him in front of his friends. But, as much as she could help it, Donna believed she would not form habits that would embarrass or humiliate her students.

Donna expected a good year. She felt prepared to teach. She believed her principal had confidence in her abilities, that the experienced staff would be supportive and helpful, and the youngsters would be ready, willing, and able to work hard and learn. Donna hoped that she would have her classes in order and on track within a few weeks. "By Thanksgiving I will know most of the students pretty well; I will have a pretty good idea what I can do the rest of the year. But, most important, I will have control. It takes at least a

month to get control and to get the kids to start learning. So I should
definitely have it by Thanksgiving."

* * *

It is Thursday morning, the second week of school. The tardy
bell pierces through the excited, playful sounds of twenty-nine
eleven-year-olds.

Miss Hastings calls out: "Didn't you hear the second bell? That
means be quiet!" She steps back, away from the stacked-high desk
that shields her from students, then quickly slides to the right to
escape shafts of early morning sun streaking to her eyes. She focuses
on the youthful mass, her class. She awaits silence. "Okay, everybody stand." Assured that all youngsters are giving her their attention, Miss Hastings turns and positions herself to view students and
crucifix simultaneously. "Our Father who art in heaven. . . ." begin
teacher and class.

Miss Hastings' posture is almost ambivalent as she leads students in the Lord's Prayer. She speaks each word correctly and
monitors student participation, but appears to place her thoughts
elsewhere.

Seven students pray intently, eyes tightly shut, bodies bespeak-
ing humility. Others stand casually, but speak clearly the prayer.
Three boys watch a jawbreaker roll slowly, then rapidly toward a
low spot on the tile floor. As it circles and comes to a rest, "amen" is
spoken—the only word said in unison. Thirty hands trace the Holy
Trinity.

"Are there any specials?"

Chris responds with a prayer for his aunt who goes to surgery
today. Karen lips a silent prayer.

Miss Hastings scans the room. No more prayers. She immediately pivots to face the American flag, hand over left breast. "I
pledge Allegiance to the flag. . . ." Students follow. No harmony, no
synchronization. ". . . one nation under God, indivisible, with lib-
erty and justice for all," is punctuated with a solitary "amen." Several youngsters laugh at forgetful Keith, now blushing and trying to
regain respect by feigning intentional error.

"Okay, how many people are buying lunch today?" Miss Hastings shifts her class into the final phase of their early morning ritual,
patterns cultivated in two weeks. "How many want milk?"

"Okay, get to work. You all know what you have to do. Get

your books and try to be more quiet." Most students approach shelves underlining the windows on the room's left. They talk while sorting through piles of workbooks. John gives Stan a piece of gum. Several youngsters leave the room to retrieve books from lockers. Sean distributes campaign paraphernalia. Pinned to Sean's football jersey are Carter-Mondale buttons. They match the green and white jersey. Miss Hastings sits at her desk helping Barb sort through books and papers in search of her worbook. Finally, they find it. Miss Hastings reminds Barb to turn to page 19.

Students work at their desks. Miss Hastings opens her plan-book, leafs through the pages, finds what she is searching for, reads, erases, and writes. Seven minutes pass as students and Miss Hastings manipulate thoughts, words, papers, and pencils.

A light rap at the door. A student calls out, "Hi, Miss Roan!" A teacher in her late thirties enters, quickly strides toward Miss Hastings shushing students with left forefinger lightly pressed to smiling lips. She and Miss Hastings speak in hushed tones for three minutes, throughout which Miss Hastings sits stiffly, holding a pen in left hand, left arm between her and the smiling Miss Roan. Then Miss Roan's voice rises, "Thanks for that." She surveys student faces and confidently steps toward the door. Behind her trail several youthful voices, "Goodbye, Miss Roan."

Students who several minutes ago went to their lockers now re-enter the room. Miss Hastings moves from her desk and positions herself near the door. "Everyone quiet in Group I over there by the window. And everybody in Group II should have this workbook, the blue map skills book."

Group I students focus on their worksheets. Some write. Billy hands a square of football bubble-gum to Joel. Group II students look toward Miss Hastings, anticipating her next announcement.

But, unexpectedly, "All right, we're going to the library now to get books for your social studies projects. Leave your books here. We're going down until ten minutes after nine, and you know the main rule of the library is *quiet*." Three boys snicker. Jo Ann and Paula continue a conversation they've had for the past five minutes.

"Line up." Students form a line along the window and across the front of the room to the door. "Quiet now! Okay, let's go."

The library is small and jam-packed with books, maps, globes, and audio-visual equipment, yet everything is comfortably, if not ingeniously, in its place. Miss Hastings already is seated at the librarian's desk, poised and ready to check out books. Mrs. Mowery, the librarian, leaves with an armload of books.

Mark asks Miss Hastings if she knows the title of a story he likes and describes for her. She has never heard of that particular story.

Keith and Charles play with a tan and brown bear that recently was comfortably seated on a shelf. Mrs. Mowery returns to the library. The bear returns to his lair.

Sean approaches Mrs. Mowery with campaign literature, but she is uninterested. As she quits his presence and makes her way among chairs and tables, Sean laughs, "This school is going to the Republicans."

Miss Hastings travels from the librarian's desk to a wall of books. She stands now, barely moving, gazing over the library, saying nothing, apparently unsure what to do.

Mrs. Mowery retrieves a projector that a fifth grader left in the hall moments ago. She sets it where it belongs, a space that is just right between a slide projector and a reel-to-reel tape recorder.

Nearly half the students are engaged in reading or seeking books. The remainder talk and share delights they find on illustrated pages. Some sit on tables. Kevin rests his head on forearms. Mrs. Mowery approaches the tables: "Tables are not for sitting. They're for doing work. Chairs are for sitting. Thank you."

David asks Mrs. Mowery where he can find information on the San Andreas Fault. She tells him three possible sources and appears pleased at the request.

Several youngsters stand near the librarian's desk. They have their books and now must wait for Miss Hastings to record their withdrawals.

Chris asks Mrs. Mowery: "Where are those books that come from other countries?"

"Do you mean about other lands and peoples?"

"Yeah . . . I mean, yes ma'am."

"Over here."

"Thank you, Mrs. Mowery."

From her vantage point, Miss Hastings monitors students. She sees that Jo Ann and Paula continue conversation as they leaf through *Glamour*. She says that they should find books to take back to class.

Mrs. Mowery: "Mark, this is library reading and research

period. You know what to do. Get to it." Mark stops talking and laughing aloud, but continues his delight with the *Sports Illustrated* football article.

The talking subsides now. Most students are reading or leafing through books and magazines. Miss Hastings walks with Keith to a set of books. Keith chooses one. Miss Hastings asks if she can see it, and he hands it to her. Miss Hastings leafs through the book, then returns it. But Keith has spotted another book which he retrieves with his left hand while taking the other in his right. Miss Hastings slips quietly toward Jo Ann and Paula.

Several minutes pass with everyone reading except Kevin and John. Kevin continues to rest his head. John wanders from shelf to shelf, apparently finding nothing that satisfies him.

Miss Hastings sits at the librarian's desk checking out books that students hand to her. "You people who don't have books yet, you have about three minutes to find one. Hurry up and get your books." The orderly line of a few minutes ago now becomes bulkier, bunches against the desk. Sean, Keith, and Mark converse in elementary "Donald Duck" as they await the registering of their books.

Five minutes have passed. Students have returned to the classroom, having come singly and unsupervised while Miss Hastings completed last-minute library details.

There are now low murmurs and intermittent chuckles in the classroom. A crude sphere composed of multiple sheets of notebook paper floats back and forth as Sean imagines he is a famous quarterback passing the pigskin to Mark, his favorite receiver.

Miss Hastings enters, her forehead pinched to a frown, lips tight. John, shoulders slumped, tentatively approaches her, speaks, and drops his head. Miss Hastings snaps: "Well, that's what you were down there for. Why didn't you get one?" John mumbles inaudibly.

Again, Miss Hastings: "It's too noisy in here. Be quiet. Next time I hear a sound, you'll have to get back in your regular seats." The level of sound diminishes. Lisa lightly strikes Mary's arm. "Shsh!" Paula looks directly at Mark who quickly gets the message and less noisily shuffles his papers.

There is stillness for a few moments. Then Donald Duck speaks from an unidentified location.

"Sean, is that you? You'd better not. . . ."

"Not me, Miss Hastings."

"Oh, okay. It better not be."

* * *

Tentativeness and lack of direction were not only there for students to see, but also were felt by Donna herself. She admitted feeling directionless in the classroom; in limbo at times. In spite of "well-planned" presentations, she found it troublesome to keep students quiet and on task. She seldom felt assured that they were working and that she was doing the right thing. As time passed, students began taking up the slack that Donna allowed by her not giving clear directions and not providing leadership. Students discovered other things to which they could direct their attention. Students generated their own activities and other means of occupying themselves in class.

* * *

It is the sixth week of school. A dozen collages are stuck on the walls of Miss Hastings' room accompanied by numerous notebook pages of student work. Also, Sean's campaign literature and bumper stickers are stuck on walls and piled in corners.

Smack! A milk dud slams against the rear wall. Smack! Another one. "Gotcha! Ha!" Milk duds fly, chairs collide, and chatter and laughter accompany the eighth graders' entry into the room. They dart and duck, trying to get to their desks without getting hit. As the milk dud battle wages, Tina and Mary Margaret calmly, almost routinely, compare lengths of their green and blue plaid uniform skirts. Scott and Terry zing milk duds and erasers at each other.

Miss Hastings enters, frowns, and wearily walks toward her desk. The air is filled with projectiles, squeals, and chuckles, but Miss Hastings shows no apparent sign of knowing. She shuffles through papers on her desk. Then, "Get to work! Terry, stay in your seat and pay attention! Turn around and be quiet, David!" Scott snickers, then zaps Terry with another milk dud.

Into the room come Melissa and Linda carrying tape recorders. They approach Miss Hastings' desk. Melissa clears a corner, turns, backs against the desk, hoists herself to the surface, and wiggles to a comfortable position. Linda asks, "Miss Hastings, do you want to hear the tape we did for our project?" Mary Margaret, Janet, and Tina talk quietly against the wall on the right side of the room. Billy and Mike, on the left, thumb through *Sports Illustrated* and discuss football. In the center from rear to front, the battle wages, fueled by

Terry's quick pivots and blasts at Scott who ducks and returns fire side-armed around Bob. Others enter the battle now, but they launch missiles less frequently and vigorously than Scott and Terry.

"All right class, we're going to listen to the tapes Melissa and Linda made as part of yesterday's assignment," announces Miss Hastings. Rick joins the two girls and Miss Hastings at the front. Linda depresses the "play" button, releasing another collage, this a collage of sounds, creaking doors, eerie voices, trucks shifting gears, spurts of rock music, juxtaposed cries of adolescents and babies, TV commercials, laughs and so on. Less than half the students listen. Some appear mildly interested while others feign listening. Even those who aren't battling vacillate between active spectatorship and feigned studentship. In kind and size the diversity of missiles increases—milk duds, paper wads, erasers, paper clips. More shots appear to find targets. Jack and Tanya have discovered that Bic pens, without inserts, can be used as peashooters if the objects used for shot are small enough.

The tape drones on. Miss Hastings takes a collage from her desk to an empty space on the wall. Moving a few pieces of student work to other locations, Miss Hastings presses tacks through the corners of the new collage. Zap! A milk dud slams into the wall, barely missing her elbow. She turns to face the battleground slowly, face first, then body. Left hand on hip, Miss Hastings glares at the center of the room. There is a hush, a ceasefire, but one can almost feel the pulse of those who await resumption of fire.

"You guys!" Miss Hastings accuses the boys in the center of the room, now looks toward Tanya, and turns again to her task. She sets the collage in place, pushing in the last tack. Her task completed, Miss Hastings returns to sit at her desk. The tape continues to unravel, but there are few, if any, listeners now.

Scott stealthily eases above Bob's shoulder, takes aim, and slams a chalk eraser against Terry's back. The battle is on again, first with spurts of activity, now rapid fire.

Miss Hastings sits at her desk leafing through papers, the battle raging before her, but apparently unaware—or is she? Rich and Linda stand to her left looking at the tape recorder, carrying on a conversation unrelated to the tape. Melissa leaves her perch on the desk. She walks to where she left her books before getting the tape recorder from her locker. The books are gone! Randy and David snicker. Melissa appears not to have been fooled. She knows the boys have hidden her books and demands that they return them now. Her demands turn to threats. The boys evade and taunt. Melissa scatters Randy's papers over the floor.

Miss Hastings: "Melissa, pick up those papers and sit down!"

"But Miss Hastings, they took my books!"

"All right, you guys, give Melissa her books." And Miss Hastings resumes paper-shuffling, eyes flitting back and forth from Melissa and the boys to the papers on her desk.

The tape plays and plays and plays. No one listens—not even Linda. More shots are fired. Tina and Mary Margaret sit closer to the door, hoping to lessen their chances of being hit. Melissa strides to Miss Hastings: "Tell Randy to give me my books."

"Randy, do you have Melissa's books?"

"No."

"Who has Melissa's books? Tim? David? Okay, you guys, quit playing. Give her the books."

Someone from the hall quietly closes the door to Donna's classroom. Hardly anyone notices.

\* \* \*

Donna sensed the slipperiness of classroom management and instruction during her first two weeks at St. Ambrose. But, after six weeks, she now knows she has serious problems. Authority and power have slid from her grasp. Her influence on students is negligible as far as she can tell. Although she believes that she plans good lessons, Donna also knows she has not involved students in appropriate activities. It seems to her that students refuse to respond to the lessons she plans, and presently they appear to be doing what they wish. "As far as preparing and presenting lessons, I feel completely sure of myself. I can plan and present good lessons. I spent the first three weeks getting acquainted and assessing what students need. I've also been talking with a lot of other social studies teachers to get ideas for the rest of the year. But control—I feel like I've completely lost control. I've lost my classes."

Donna finds her loss of control frustrating, but especially troublesome are the circumstances she confronts daily: continual talk, teasing and taunting, punning, and general playfulness including the freeing of insects, worms, and other critters in the room. "They think I'm scared of little insects and stuff. That just makes me mad! Playbaby stuff! I can't stand it. And there are those who think it's playtime all the time. They never bring their books. They constantly talk and sass back. Talk, talk, talk. That's all they do! Though they may not make really nasty remarks, there's always a smart aleck remark for everything I say. I've tried to separate groups, but that doesn't work. They still yell all the way across the room. So it's always something. I can't get a word in edgewise. All I want them to do is pay attention to me, act right and learn!"

Donna is angered by "the lack of respect that the students have for whoever's supposed to be in charge. They constantly talk while I'm talking. They don't even show Sister respect when she comes in. If there is one thing that we learned in school, it was that you respect the principal. When the principal walked in, we stood up and said, 'Good morning.' Now, I don't think these students should have to go to that extreme, but they should sit and look at her when she wants their attention. I just wonder what goes on in their homes, how they treat their mom and dad. I think these are students who'll run away from home when they are sixteen or seventeen."

In spite of her difficulties, Donna did have a day when she felt students were cooperative. "When they came to the door, I didn't give them a chance to start talking. I told them to sit down and open their books to a certain page, and I just bombarded them with my presentation. I started presenting and asking questions, calling specific names so people had to answer. I didn't give them a chance to start talking. Instead of saying, 'Does someone know the answer?' I said, 'Tom, please tell me who Magellan was? And I gave them three worksheets, one right after the other: presentation, worksheet, presentation, worksheet, presentation, worksheet. That seemed to calm them. But even at that, they still talked. They chattered while they worked—you know—like no one else was in the room. They did their worksheets, but their writing was sloppy, and only half of them thought out their answers. At least they did something. I have to say that my classes were better that day. It didn't last though. The next day was just like all the others."

There are days when Donna is frustrated enough to consider resignation, especially on days like the one with the milk dud battle. At the end of that day, she said, "I'm about ready to resign. Truthfully, I can't get any control over the students. All I get is headaches. I do a good job planning my lessons and I try to stay two to three days ahead of them. But they just play around and don't listen.

They give me all kinds of backtalk everytime I say something. I really don't know what to do. I'm about at my wit's end with them. The only thing I know to do is to send them to after-school detention or to Saturday classes. But I'm not about to spend any more time with them after school. And I can't assign them to Saturday classes all the time because Sister Theresa can't be there every Saturday—and they know that. Besides, if I keep sending them to her, she'll begin to think I'm not a good teacher. So I don't know what to do."

"I talked with some of their parents at PTA last week, and most of those students have settled down. But those are the really good ones. The bad students' parents don't ever come. That's why they're bad. Their parents don't care. I don't know, I suppose I should've called their parents a long time ago, but I couldn't because we didn't have our phone yet—you know—my roommates and I moved into our apartment the weekend before school started and we didn't get our phone until late. I feel it's just too late to call now."

Donna attributes some of the blame for her problems to the teacher who preceded her. She thinks the students became accustomed to informal classroom procedures and lax academic standards. The result, Donna feels, is that she cannot outlive the ghost of Miss Lucas. "I think the biggest problem I have with the students is their behavior. I think that's because of last year's social studies teacher. She let them get away with murder. And they always tell me 'Miss Lucas never did that' or 'Miss Lucas used to let us do that.' I'm sick and tired of hearing Miss Lucas this and that!"

Other factors that Donna considers troublesome are the attitudes of the staff members. The staff is not at all like she had anticipated in August. "I don't think they're a very good staff. Besides not giving me positive help, they don't cooperate very much. They don't do anything together or help each other out. And I can't talk to them. They seem so cold. I'm sick and tired of them sitting around the lunchroom complaining about how bad the students are. I couldn't believe the stuff I heard down there the first couple of weeks. I don't know, they're just cold."

By the sixth week, Donna still has not become well-acquainted with the rest of the staff. She fears approaching experienced teachers because she doesn't want them to know the severity of her problems, yet she knows they know she has problems. And Donna is feeling increasingly threatened by Sister Theresa. She fears that the principal hears nearly everything that happens in her classroom. Too, Donna feels it is unwise to discuss classroom management and instructional problems with her boss. She has assumed from the beginning that the principal will evaluate her on the basis of her disclosures. Donna is fairly sure that Sister Theresa will glean information from what she tells her, and that she will use this information against her. Furthermore, the few conversations between Donna and Sister Theresa have been limited and have provided little help. "I think that Sister Theresa is interested in each of the students, especially when she realizes that there are problems we can work together to solve. But she is one person who, when I've gone to her about my classes, has only said, 'sit on them,' or 'don't let so-and-so get away with anything.' I don't know what that means! Yet she has still come in here and yelled at the students several times. Of course, maybe it's my place to go to her and say, 'These students are really causing me to pull my hair out! What do I do?' But the talk over the lunch table hasn't given me sufficient satisfaction to pick myself up and go to her with my problems. I know she cares and wants her teachers and students to be happy here. And she's firm! I'm sure that if I were to send a child to her, she would handle the situation for me. I think she's a good principal and that she keeps the school in order. But I'm afraid to tell her my problems because she might evaluate me on what I say and think I'm not a good teacher if I can't handle my classes."

Beyond her problems at school, Donna is displeased with her living circumstances. She has two roommates. Tammy is a department store clerk who works from 2:00 to 10:00 P.M., and often dances until late at local discos. Mary Ann is in her third year of teaching at a local suburban middle school. Donna and Tammy share a bedroom but have not gotten along very well, although they seldom see one another. Their relationship is hampered by differences in values and preferred lifestyles especially with regard to sex. Donna is interested in men and wants very much to be married and have a family, but she firmly holds her ground on premarital sex. She will not engage in sexual activities until she is married or certain she is about to be married. Tammy, on the other hand, enjoys sex. She feels frequent sexual activity is important for her own well-being. This difference has been discussed and twice resulted in serious disagreements concerning sexual activity in the apartment. Donna said she could not condone Tammy having sex with anyone in the bedroom they shared. Tammy disagreed.

Donna, though she hardly knew Tammy before they moved into their apartment, had looked forward to living with Mary Ann. They had known each other since Donna was in the seventh grade. Donna and one of Mary Ann's sisters were the same age. Donna had anticipated that Mary Ann would be a good resource for her since she had two years of teaching experience. But Donna's anticipations did not materialize. Mary Ann was not a good listener. Rather than carefully listening and showing that she understood, Mary Ann freely gave advice. Donna found that the more she discussed her experiences and concerns, the more she received advice. The advice was not helpful. It caused Donna to build resentment. Donna did not detect a desire to help in Mary Ann's advice. Instead, she sensed judgments and criticism. As a result, Donna comes home in the evenings bursting but is unable to rid herself of frustrations. She has had to minimize her discussions of teaching in Mary Ann's presence.

This already tense apartment situation intensified one Sunday evening before the seventh week of school. Donna returned from her usual weekend visit at the parent's farm to find her bedroom door closed and Mary Ann watching television. Donna started to open the door when Mary Ann blurted, "Don't do that. Tammy and Steve are in there."

Donna immediately became angry. She was tired. It was already 8:30 and she had lesson plans to complete. But, most of all, Tammy and Steve were in her bedroom. Mary Ann told Donna not to be so "old-fashioned" and "country." "After all, you have to grow up sometime." Donna's anger heightened.

It was 9:30 before Donna finally had access to her bedroom. She argued with Tammy and Steve, but felt no satisfaction. She knew that this would happen again in spite of the clarity of her position. She felt she had lost control of her living space in addition to having lost her students.

Donna is aware that her problems often result from her own beliefs as well as from other peoples' behavior. She thinks that the students and staff at St. Ambrose cause her difficulty—as do her roommates. Yet she is also sensitive to the possibility that she might cause problems for herself. Donna vacillates between blaming others and blaming herself for her feelings. She hopes that once she learns the "tricks of the trade" she will become effective in dealing with both the external and internal sources of her difficulties at school. And in spite of all that has happened, Donna considers herself to be a potentially good teacher. "I think of myself as a very capable teacher as far as presenting lessons when I have time to prepare them. And I feel that I'm probably capable of controlling a classroom, although I can't control them now—but that's because I'm new. I don't know all the tricks of the trade—if there really are tricks. And if knowing the tricks doesn't help, then I don't know what I'm doing wrong or what I need to change. I really get down on myself a lot now. I just can't control the classes. There are times when I think I'd like a regular 9:00 to 5:00 job a lot better—like a secretary or clerk in a department store. But I can't quit now, not until I prove what I can do."

\* \* \*

It is the week before Halloween. The sixth, seventh, and eighth grade students are changing classes. Mark and Sean have just run from the room, ducking an eraser thrown by Stan. The eraser ricochets through the door missing its intended target, but strikes an eighth grade girl. She shrieks, then shouts, "I'll get you, Stanley, you creep!"

Sister Theresa comes into the hallway, surveys the situation, tells Stan, Mark and Sean to go to her office, and waits until decorum is restored. Then she turns toward Miss Hastings who now stands by the door to her room. "I just can't take much more of this, Donna. You're going to have to get this situation together. Straighten up this mess! Come see me during your planning period." Sister Theresa pivots and stalks into the office, harshly closing the door behind her.

The silence in Miss Hastings' room is heavy. Miss Hastings steps into the hall, closes her door, then rushes to the teachers' lounge.

\* \* \*

Donna was embarrassed, hurt, frustrated, and angry about her confrontation with Sister Theresa. But she now views it as inevitable. "Sister Theresa and I had not really talked about control and discipline. A couple of times, though, I asked her, 'Gee, what should I do with these students on such and such a thing?' and she would say in general, 'sit on them.' Well, I had no idea what that meant. So, to make a long story short, we had a blowout. She yelled at some of my students and then at me—in front of my students and all! So, anyway, she wanted to talk to me. The result was that she began observing my classes for a few days and made notes on things I needed to do and called me into her office again and sat me down and just gave me right down the line—one, two, three—the things I should do. They were suggestions, but I had to take them because in the end she'll be the judge of me. If I didn't start what she told me and if my students didn't improve, I would be in big trouble, and it would be my job. So I'm changing my methods. And I guess she's right. If there is no control, the natural outcome is going to be chaos."

Sister Theresa gave Miss Hastings definite instructions for changing her behavior and restructuring the environment—specifically, Miss Hastings should change seating arrangements, establish rules for classroom verbal and physical behavior, make her behavioral and instructional expectations known, sanction inappropriate behavior and reward appropriate behavior. She should plan lessons so that students know what to do at all times. Further, she should impress on students the importance of learning. One suggestion involved putting specific students on the spot to answer specific question at specific times. This would make it known that individuals must think for themselves and must fulfill their responsibilities as students.

For her part, Sister Theresa agreed to frequently observe Miss Hastings' teaching, and would use her observations to make further suggestions for improvement. She would handle recurrent and difficult problems so Miss Hastings could proceed with instruction unimpeded by inappropriate student behavior. But Miss Hastings must expect and require students to do good work, to learn, and to behave as Christians and good citizens. As long as Miss Hastings tries to fulfill her responsibilities, Sister Theresa will do what she can to support her.

Thus, Miss Hastings began to turn a leaf. She changed seating arrangements. She vigilantly monitored student behavior—or at least was more vigilant than before. She presented her lesson crisply, then assigned worksheet, workbook, and other written activities. She led students in oral reviews of written assignments, going through them item by item.

Sister Theresa frequently observed classes, took notes, and made suggestions. But Sister Theresa could not remain in the classroom for sustained periods because she frequently had to respond to her ringing phone. Her busy, part-time secretary was not always there to answer it herself. However, Sister Theresa was able to have conferences with students Miss Hastings found troublesome. The results of these conferences varied according to the nature and frequency of a student's misconduct. The principal verbally reprimanded many, assigned detentions to some, and, a few times, arranged parent conferences.

Donna's attitude and confidence, while not soaring, are improving. She feels better about her students, and finds herself less frequently angered and bothered with bitterness towards them. She seldom feels, as she did before, that she would like to "haul off and hit one. Sometimes when they would backtalk, I just wanted to hit them right across the mouth. I wouldn't do that, though, because that just isn't me. I'm not a violent person, but I would just get irritated and wouldn't know what to do, so I would let it pass. Now, if I'm not mad, I'll just look right at them and tell them not ever to do what they did again. You know, like 'Don't ever speak to me in that tone again. You wouldn't say that to your mom and dad or even to an older sister. So don't say it to me.' A lot of times I think these students need a good spanking. I wonder if their mom and dad ever hit them at home.

"It just took me too long to catch on to the fact that they will get away with as much as they can, especially since they know I'm a first year teacher.

"Now that I've gotten more control and things are getting better, I don't feel so bad. There are even times when I enjoy the students. I guess I really like each and every one of them—even the blabbermouths. I feel that it was probably my fault that things got so bad. Although they should know how to control themselves, I was at fault for not really controlling them."

Donna believes her students generally approve of the changes she made, that they previously were unhappy at being disturbed by walkers, talkers, and troublemakers. "Some of my students have come to me individually and commented, 'Oh, Miss Hastings, you should be meaner.' And I haven't gotten anything negative like, 'you're too mean,' 'you're too hard on us,' or 'you give too much work.'"

* * *

It is the morning of November 8. Miss Hastings stands in front and sternly governs six rows of young people. Students seated on the left have texts and worksheets. Students on the right have blue workbooks. Miss Hastings looks a final time over the left side for remaining questions, and succinctly answers John's. Then, "Okay, since you don't have any more questions, you can work quietly while I work with Group II."

Miss Hastings quarter turns, steps to her right, the book in one hand, the other on her hip, and positions herself before Group II. "Open your geography workbooks to page 48, please." The youngsters open their books with little commotion. Bill drops and retrieves his pencil. Tanya puts a large pink comb in her handbag.

Miss Hastings: "Joel, read question number 1 and tell us your answer." Joel reads and supplies the correct response. Miss Hastings rewards Joel with a "Good!" "Now, Tanya, do number 2." Her pattern set, Miss Hastings proceeds this way for the next twenty minutes, calling on students, awaiting their responses, rewarding correct answers with "okay" or "good," rephrasing questions or calling on other students when she gets incorrect ones. She reminds students in both groups to "pay attention" to prevent their eyes from straying, their voices from working out of turn. All the while, she extends forward a teacher's edition of the text when she calls on students, and clutches it to her breast when they respond.

Several Group I students busily try to complete assignments. A few doodle, tap pencils on desks, or fiddle with a variety of objects from paper clips to football bubble-gum cards to mirrors. Two rest their heads on forearms.

The door opens, and Sister Theresa enters. She finds a seat next to the window in front of Group I. Miss Hastings continues with Group II, carefully reminding John and Matt to raise their heads and "get to work like the others in Group I."

Five minutes pass much the same as before in spite of Sister Theresa's presence. Then the phone in the principal's office rings and Sister Theresa leaves, apparently without disturbing anyone—although everyone knows why she left. Class activities proceed in the same manner. A few youngsters become restless. Five Group I students have finished and placed their assignments on Miss Hastings' desk, and are leafing through magazines and talking with neighbors.

Mark asks Miss Hastings a question on his assignment, the fifth question from Group I and the third from Mark in recent minutes.

Miss Hastings appears frustrated at this distraction, but she answers, then elaborates on her answer. Group II students begin to talk. Carl snaps the back of Jo Ann's head with his pencil. Miss Hastings refocuses her attention to the text and Group II. She asks Tina to read on page 51. "Okay, the rest of you've gotta stop talking so we can hear Tina read." A murmur begins by the window and creeps to the back of the room. A number of students appear restless. Sean drops his pencil, looks toward Mark and smiles, then reaches under his desk to retrieve it.

* * *

Donna believes she is over the hump. She feels that she has completed a rough passage that all first year teachers experience. She believes, however, that it was especially rough for her. She feels she can and will complete the school year successfully. She still wants to teach younger children and wishes also to leave the city, so she intends to seek another teaching position for next year. All in all, Donna feels more comfortable at St. Ambrose, though she still has headaches. She no longer thinks of quitting and seeking a 9:00 to 5:00 job for the remainder of this school year.

Donna says that she has learned a number of things that she would like to communicate to other first year teachers, particularly with regard to classroom management and relationships with principals. "First year teachers should get in there and get an agreement with their principal on how they're gonna handle discipline. And they should go in strong with the students. Show them exactly what they want and make an example of the first student that steps out of line—squash him, give him that punishment or send him to the principal right away. But be sure to make an agreement with the principal beforehand. Even if it takes six weeks and you don't get any work done, you've gotta get control before you can teach."

Despite beginning to feel better about her teaching and her personal well-being, Donna entertains doubts and fears about Sister Theresa's thoughts. Donna wonders whether Sister Theresa will see the improvements she has made, whether she will respect her ability as a teacher after all that has happened. Perhaps more significantly, Donna has yet to blend her new self with the older self, the new Miss Hastings with what has been and is basically Donna. "I feel like I have two personalities now, like I'm two different persons, one who comes to school and teaches, and another who is just like the old me."

* * *

It is November 12. Miss Hastings enters Sister Theresa's office to respond to a note she found in her box when she arrived this morning. Sister Theresa asks her to have a seat, then begins a discussion of the grades Donna assigned for the first quarter. "You see, Donna I'm really uncomfortable about the grades you gave most of the students. They're too high. It's hard for me to believe that these youngsters could have earned A's and B's this quarter under the circumstances of September and October. I know they're working better now, but this has only been for a short time. I think you should reconsider your evaluations, and try to discover why you gave such high grades."

At first Donna was confused and upset. She didn't understand. She became angry, then cried. Sister Theresa said that she did not intend to embarrass Donna, but that she had serious professional questions about the grades assigned to many of the students. "You must rethink your criteria and how you've assigned the grades, and be sure that you've done the right thing. Besides, it isn't good practice to give such high grades when students have been disruptive and haven't completed many assignments."

Donna left Sister Theresa's office hurt and angry. Throughout the day, as students did their worksheets, Donna went through her grade book and considered whether she should change each student's grade. She lowered most of the grades.

* * *

It is early morning, November 15. Miss Donna Hastings knocks at Sister Theresa's door and asks if she can come in. Sister Theresa replies, "Of course, Donna. Come in. How are you this morning?"

Donna hands Sister Theresa an envelope. "Sister Theresa, I've thought a lot about what I'm going to say. I've had a lot of trouble here and you've been disappointed in me, and I've had these awful headaches since September. I went to my doctor on Saturday, and he thought they might be migraines. He suggested that I consider quitting my job for health reasons. So I'm resigning, Sister Theresa. I'm giving you my notice, and I will teach up until the last day of school before Thanksgiving."

# Math Teacher

5

Joyce Bond stood before the Basic Math class, feeling as if her mouth were full of cotton. Her consciousness was crowded with feelings—vulnerability, determination, and a strange aloneness. She didn't feel she really belonged there; she felt like the rookie she was. Her class seemed a mass of identical blurred faces. More faces drifted in. Part of her took control. "Sit at the front," she directed them firmly. It was the first day of school.

Little did Joyce know that a few months of teaching would earn her the nicknames Legskin and The Chopstick, fondly bestowed by some creative teacher-watchers. In a dress of brown, with a scarf of blue and white in a knot around her neck, with only a watch and wedding ring as adornment, she was stylish, yet with a "teacher look" to her as well. Her blond hair was cut long against her pale face. She was tall, but her slender stature made the classroom seem large.

Joyce's plan for the day was to administer to the ninth graders the first section of a three-day diagnostic test. It contained many of each type of problem to be covered during the year. Basic Math was essentially a review course; students who had previously failed math were registered for Basic Math in a final attempt to instill the fundamentals of the addition, subtraction, multiplication and division of whole numbers, fractions, and decimals. The pages of the test lay in separate piles on her desk.

The bell rang. A couple of students looked up expectantly and asked if she would assign them places. "Sit where you want," she answered nicely, and after a pause, remarked, "You'll only be moved if you're really mouthy." She gathered up the stack of page 1's, and began to pass them out.

"This is a test, to see how much you know," she called in a loud firm voice. As she spoke, the door opened, and a boy walked in, watching her as he found a seat.

"Why are you late?" she challenged.

"I just got back from my locker," he explained confidently.

Joyce looked down at her papers and replied, her voice slightly quavering, "Well, don't be late again." She finished handing out the tests, and the students quietly began to work.

Joyce sat down at her desk and called roll. Then she started to correct papers. Presently she called out softly, "When you're done bring up page 1. There's another sheet. And make sure your name's on it." Minutes passed, and a girl went up to Joyce with a question. She squatted down beside the teacher's desk, and Joyce bent over to answer the question. Lila plopped down crosslegged. Joyce was speaking with her easily and comfortably. Lila presently returned to her desk, and stood there, leafing through a book. Joyce got up and went to join her, squatting down beside the desk to continue the conversation. She was friendly and relaxed. As they talked, two groups of students on the other side of the room began to whisper, comparing answers. Presently, Joyce returned to her own desk, and commenced thumbing through some papers. She did not notice the whispering students.

Abruptly the Public Address system broke in as an adult male voice announced: "Would all freshmans [sic] who have not been photographed come to the cafeteria for ID pictures immediately."

The announcement was repeated and some students looked up.

Two boys who had not previously been talking now commented to each other about the announcement. Hearing them, Joyce addressed them in a no-nonsense tone: "You shouldn't be talking. You should be working."

The boys went back to their tests. Shortly the PA interrupted again, this time with names of specific students to report for pictures. Several students gathered up their books and left the room. The students who had exchanged answers earlier were at it again, but Joyce did not appear to notice.

"You should be finishing up now. I'll give you half a minute." Before the half minute was up, the bell rang. Students came by, dropping their papers on the desk, and left the room. Joyce gathered up the papers and breathed a sigh of relief. Class was over.

Joyce felt the class had gone well. Work had been accomplished, and the students had been quiet. She had really helped one student, and had dealt readily with the two boys who had talked. In her other four classes she also administered the first third of the diagnostic test. She went home that evening feeling that things had gone well. She had test papers from five classes to grade, and her weekly lesson plans to be submitted. All in all, she was exhausted.

Joyce Bond's father was in the service, and Joyce had lived in nine places by the time she entered high school. Her family remained in one town throughout her high school years, however, and Joyce attended school with a cross-section of suburban and rural young people. She was in the accelerated classes. Her family valued good grades, and so did Joyce. Math classes turned out to be the most exciting courses in high school. Her math teacher truly inspired the students, and led Joyce and three others through two semesters of college calculus. Joyce worked hard and loved the subject.

Joyce chose to attend a small rural, liberal arts college. She majored in math, almost completed a history major, and took the secondary teacher education sequence necessary to become certified. She enjoyed her college days, developing her vocal ability and becoming a member of the gymnastics team.

One summer she took courses at a university near her home. There she met Terry Bond, a pre-law student much like herself in that he was a serious student, an athlete, and a friendly, wholesome person. He was accepted at law school, and Joyce landed a position teaching high school math and coaching girls' gymnastics in a nearby suburban-rural school. They were married the summer following college graduation, and Joyce approached her new job with the knowledge that her income would keep the roof over their heads for the next several years.

Toward the end of the summer, Joyce and Terry moved into a tiny two-room apartment near the law school. Joyce spent the last weeks before school arranging their wedding presents, scanty furniture and many books into homey spaces. She joined the choir of the church down the block, and continued to run two miles every day.

What did she think about her upcoming teaching job? A complex of thoughts crossed her mind. Prominent was the image of herself as an inspirer of young people who might come to her classes hating math. She felt strong in her knowledge of mathematics, and saw herself as a patient teacher who was willing to take as much time and effort as would be necessary to communicate the information to her students. She knew she was willing to make the subject matter relevant to them; in student teaching s.ie had made up word problems for her slow learners dealing with subjects of great interest to them—cars and driving.

Other images were dark. She had forebodings that the students would be giving her an especially rough time, this being her first year. Others told her often that she didn't look her age. She expected to have minor discipline problems; these had occurred during student teaching. Discipline—the picture was cloudy here. She believed that students should be relatively quiet and attentive. But "relatively?" She wasn't sure exactly what would cause her to take disciplinary action. Lack of respect for other people, for one thing, but she didn't really know how to describe what she meant by that. Yet she had worked with young people before, and had been successful. They would expect her just to be herself, not put up a front. Possibly there would be personality conflicts which would make it hard for some students to learn from her, but in general she hoped to be known among the students as being warm, and easy to talk to. She liked the idea of herself in the role of counselor to some of the students, although she wasn't too clear on just what problems they might have.

Her main goal would be to communicate the subject, and she intended to evaluate herself on how well the students progressed. She foresaw adjusting her teaching over the year so the students could learn better. She knew her greatest satisfaction would come from seeing the students learn, especially one who might have been struggling for a long time to grasp a certain point.

Out of this swirl of thoughts, one was crystal clear—this would be a year of proving herself, proving that she was capable of handling the job. She had her doubts. "I'm just worried," she thought sometimes.

Harington School District held three days of preschool orientation. Teachers were greeted, informed about the system, and initiated into the ways of writing lesson plans. They were given a test on behavioral objectives and each new teacher who did not pass the test attended a workshop to learn about them. Harington had recently embarked on an effort to identify goals and objectives for all high school courses. The two courses which Joyce was to teach, one section of Algebra and four sections of Basic Math, had complete lists of objectives developed for the year's work. Teachers were expected to cover all and only the objectives in the given order. Every week, it was explained to the new teachers, they were to file a plan for the next week. The plans, nicknamed "green sheets," were to include a goal, a rationale, objectives, and methods for the week. After the orientation Joyce was confident that she could plan her lessons and fill out "green sheets" satisfactorily.

By the end of the first week, Joyce felt her classes were not going well. Seventh and third periods were the worst. Friday when she walked into third period several boys were already talking loudly and making jokes. Without speaking to the class, she passed out the tests they had been working on for the past two days. The boys continued talking. "They *know* they should be quiet," she thought. Most of the class settled down, but the boys still talked. Joyce could feel her irritation mounting. Finally she spoke to them in a high-pitched, cross voice: "You should be quiet and working!"

"What's work?" Jim sassed back.

"Be quiet!" she ordered. There was a slight pause. Then another of the boys asked, "Do we get a grade on this paper?"

"No."

"Then I'm not doing it." Mike threw his pencil on the desk. Joyce did not reply. The boys' comments continued, and Joyce's tension increased. She felt that her yelling at them had no effect. "Maybe they'll take me more seriously if they know it will affect their grade," she thought.

"Just as a warning," she told them, "if you talk you'll get five points deducted from your grade in this class. Also for gum chewing." She placed a blank piece of paper in front of her, and the room became a little quieter.

Now began the coughing, paper rustling and pencil tapping. Joyce called roll. Some students continued to talk. Presently Joyce commented in a low voice, "I don't want to hear it. Keep your mouth shut." The comments continued.

"Keep *quiet*." Now her voice was full of disgust. Most of the students were working, but the boys kept laughing. She tried again: "If you don't want any more points deducted, I suggest you keep your mouth shut."

"How many did I lose?" Jim called out.

"Fifteen."

Jim to Mike, "I don't even have any yet!" and to Joyce, "How do you get points in this class?"

From the desk, she answered him, explaining.

Still the boys wouldn't stop talking. Joyce thought of another approach; she sent John to the corner to sit. Now the boys called out questions from their seats.

"What will we learn in this class?"

"When do we get books?"

"Can I throw this paper away?"

"What do you do while we work?" Joyce answered each one seriously and politely, looking directly at the students. They continued to question her. Finally the period came to a close. On their way out, Jim, John and Mike detoured by the teacher's desk, looking to see how many points they had lost during the period. "Wow, man!" they hooted. One of the girls paused at the door and said in all sincerity and sympathy, "Have a nice day, Mrs. Bond."

Joyce was upset. It was just a few kids, but she knew they could ruin her class. How could she handle this? She tried to think of the alternatives: keep them in class, but they would just ruin it; send them to Enforced Study; have them suspended. But how could she take those measures? It was only the first week of school. In quiet desperation she asked some of the other teachers in the math office what to do. Most of their suggestions she felt wouldn't work, knowing her students as she did. One teacher advised her just to tell them to be quiet and give them problems. Joyce went ahead and gave them lots of problems, but they wouldn't be quiet. She became so harried that she didn't take time to explain the work before giving the assignment; she just hoped they'd read the section on their own.

The second and third weeks were more of the same. At first Joyce acted as if she were deliberately ignoring the noise; it was the students who were the losers if they wouldn't listen. Then she decided to use her voice. She prided herself on her strong voice when her temper was aroused, and decided she would not let the students talk above her. She would be heard. So she started shouting— directions, answers, discipline. But the students still wouldn't be quiet, and she was exhausting herself. She began to feel resentful of the few who wouldn't settle down. It was just three or four in her bad classes; the rest were fairly cooperative. But those three of four "morons" (as she thought of them sometimes) just didn't want to learn. All they wanted to do was play; math was just a place to be instead of study hall. By the end of the third week, Joyce knew she was in a deep tunnel, with a long way to go before the light at the other end appeared.

Despite the many terrible moments, Joyce felt she was handling the job. She spent all evening every evening correcting papers, and working out all the homework problems for algebra. She didn't want to fumble in class if a student asked her to explain a problem, and she tried to antcipate every possible question. She was having no trouble filling out the "green sheets." Best of all, she felt most of the kids were learning. The grades were distributed on a normal curve, even though her curve was lower than she would have expected. Her main concern as a teacher was trying to get the material across, and she felt she was doing that. Although she felt really tired every day and had had two colds, and in spite of the discipline problems, Joyce had a generally positive outlook about her work.

There was finally a ray of hope for seventh period. Joyce conquered one behavior problem. The students were accustomed to clustering restlessly around the door for several minutes preceding the last bell, and then, as Joyce put it, "whooshing into the hall like a vacuum was pulling them." Every day she had told them or yelled at them to stay in their seats until the bell. Finally, by the fourth week, they no longer congregated by the door. "An improvement," Joyce thought, pleased.

October and November were months of attempts and accomplishments in achieving discipline. There was no drastic change, no marked taking of control. Rather Joyce made a series of sporadic attempts, many of them ineffective, to gain control. Once or twice she tried sarcasm as a means of shaming students into taking the class more seriously: "The answer is 41, for those of you who did it." But it didn't feel right; Joyce was not naturally inclined to treat people disdainfully; hers was a more cheerful and friendly personality which reacted to individuals positively.

Early in October, Joyce reached the point of drastic action. Seventh period came, and students wouldn't settle down. Two of her worst troublemakers started chasing each other around the room. Joyce had had it! She marched them down to the office. The next day, she had just started to explain the work to the same class when two students talked. Action again! She marched the next two offenders to the assistant principal. They were given the choice of three days suspension or a swat. One took the swat and came back to class. The students were "gems" for the rest of the period. Joyce really felt good about having taken that action.

Joyce began to feel as if she were winning the battle between seventh period and herself. She saw her tolerance for bad conduct getting lower and lower. Upon reflection it occured to her that maybe one reason she had been so tolerant was because of her younger brother—he had always been a smart-aleck, and she had learned to live with it. Other teachers would probably have gotten fed up much sooner. She was generally a calm person, although she knew she had it in her to blow up under the right circumstances.

Seventh period was only a small victory; she certainly couldn't take students to the office every time something went wrong. She tried threatening students with tearing up their papers if they talked, and actually did it a couple of times, but she couldn't do it for everyone who talked, so it didn't really solve any problems. One day she said to Walter, angrily: "Do your own work, or I'll tear your paper up." Jim, whose paper Walter had been copying from, sat back with an indulgent smile intoning, "Tough! Tough!"

Joyce did find something fairly effective; instead of staying at her desk until a student asked a question, she began circulating around the room while the class worked on the assignment. This enabled her to identify and help students who were having trouble, and let the students know her attention was on them. Sometimes she would have an offender take another seat. This worked to an extent. In seventh period she tried using the overhead projector so she could keep her eyes on the class at all times. This had been suggested by the department chairman, and helped.

There was also a change in the way Joyce handled herself during the homework review. At the beginning of the year she would loudly read the number of each problem, and then she might or might not read the problem itself. Sometimes she would call on students to read the answer, but other time she accepted answers just called out by students. Sometimes she would affirm the answer by saying "correct"; other times not. If students missed answers, they either asked their neighbor, or they called out and Joyce would tell them the answer even if it had been three or four problems earlier. Now, instead of being determined to be heard above the noise, she decided to speak in a normal voice, soft compared to the noise the students usually were making, and to give the answers only once. She would not repeat whenever the students asked her. This way the students would learn that they had to pay attention. If they didn't get the answers it was their fault. Still, this new approach didn't seem to get any more students paying attention than had been before.

As only a few people were causing the problems, Joyce readily saw the need to contact parents. For weeks she carried intentions of making phone calls. But the mere thought of it made her heart pound and her palms grow sweaty. She hoped that if she called the parents they would talk to their children and straighten them out a little bit, but truthfully, she didn't know how they would react to being called. While one part of Joyce said, "I'm definitely not going to put up with this any more," another side was reacting, "I'm scared." Finally she called one student's home but could only reach his sister; she didn't pursue the matter by calling the mother at her office. Parent Night came in October, and parent conferences in November; Joyce was very nervous about these, but only the parents came whose children were doing well. They and Joyce reinforced each other.

It was about the middle of November that Joyce's disciplining finally began to take effect. At the suggestion of the department chairman, she made seating charts and required students to be in their seats. If students continued to talk after she had told them to stop, she told them again. If a student out of his seat did not return the first time she directed, she would repeat her direction. Two of the most unruly students were permanently removed from seventh period.

Joyce began to see herself in a new light; she saw herself as more dominant than she would have thought. For the first time she realized that she had to have absolute control in the classroom. She never would have dreamed that she would want to command such a disciplined classroom. Coupled with this determination was her realization that she still had a long way to go, that she had a lot to learn about handling students. She still felt baffled about what to do to maintain discipline. Where she had originally seen her patience as a strength, she realized that in some respects it had acted as a weakness in causing her to put up with bad behavior for so long. At least things were getting better. And she, being a perfectionist, had every intention of continuing to improve.

A marked contrast to Joyce's discipline measures in the classroom were her means of handling her non-teaching duty. She was assigned to spend half of lunch period sitting outside the girls' room closest to the cafeteria. "Oh, so you have Potty Patrol," the other teachers told her. From the beginning, Joyce was determined to be on top of the situation. She sat inside the lavatory. This way she could tell if the girls tried to smoke. The first time she saw smoke drifting from under doors she marched the girls down to the office. But the assistant principal refused to suspend them because Joyce had not actually seen the cigarettes in their hands. Joyce gained a reputation fast. Girls would look in, say, "Oh, she's here," and go back out. In some ways it was a pleasant period for her; she became acquainted with several girls and would willingly let herself be included in their chatting and banter.

While Joyce's relationships with her classes continued to be trying, her relationships with individuals began and continued to be a source of satisfaction to her. Joyce always felt more comfortable conversing with one student than with the class as a whole. She welcomed students' questions and often went to their desks to help. She didn't mind if groups of students clustered at her desk waiting for her attention. The young people would often converse with her before class began, complimenting her on her clothes, discussing the latest performance of her gymnastics team, or discussing whatever topic happened to be on their minds. In these conversations, Joyce was always friendly and attentive. As the year wore on, she saw most of them develop a personal loyalty to her; they would be quieter when the department chairman came to observe, as if eager to show her in a good light. "Strange," she thought, but felt glad. Occasionally she would make a joke or pun to the class; when they groaned, she loved it.

November through February was gymnastics season. Joyce coached the school's first girls' gymnastics team, and found many problems to iron out. Her gymnasts, on the whole, did not have much of a background. Next there was a problem of where to practice. Several times they had to drive to another school. When they stayed at the high school, they had to clear the cafeteria, moving tables, and sweeping the floor. They had to haul the mats down from the gym balcony and wash them. Students were constantly wandering through their area of practice. To make matters worse, the male coaching staff was not always cooperative. One day she asked the basketball coach if she could borrow a few boys for five minutes to carry down mats, and he yelled at her. Then as she mopped the mats with the mop that was for everyone's use, the coach told her to be sure to put back "his mop." Joyce was so furious she "felt like hitting him in the face with the mop." Instead she continued to mop the mats vigorously, almost violently. Her gymnasts knew she was mad.

Furthermore, the parent's Booster Club had voted money for a new set of parallel bars, ones suitable for more difficult stunts. The bars would need to be fastened down to the gym floor in sockets. The basketball coach refused to have the sockets put in the basketball floor although, Joyce maintained, the floor would not be hurt. By the end of the year he had not yielded, and Joyce knew she would have to take the battle to the parents for support.

Gymnastics was a high point in Joyce's day. It was a more free and open situation than her classes. She and the girls could joke, but if the fooling continued, Joyce's yell would bring the girls back to practice. She worked them hard, including almost every day of Christmas vacation, and although they lost every meet, she felt pleased with their progress. Several individuals were doing well, even if the team wasn't. At the end of the season, two girls won prizes at the district meets. Still, it was somewhat of a relief to have the season over. Joyce wondered how teachers who coached three seasons could do it—"They'd never see their spouses," she thought.

Harlington School District had a tax levy before the public. Levy and school bond issues were up in many districts, and in November most had been rejected. Harington's was to be voted on in February, and the district was acutely aware of public relations. Each teacher was required to write ten letters and make four visits to parents, urging them to vote for the levy. Joyce planned to write the letters, but had no intention of making the visits. She lived too far away, she told herself, and was already putting in extra time. Besides, she knew what it felt like to get the door shut in her face. When the faculty meeting came in which teachers were to submit records of their contacts, Joyce stated what she had done: she had phoned the parents of four of her gymnasts; she had not written the letters or made the visits. She was very concerned about the levy, however; if it did not pass, her position could well be cut and she would not be rehired the next year.

The month of January was cold and stormy; school was cancelled several times. Joyce really enjoyed the free time. She had not been ready to come back after Christmas vacation. Then word came that the schools would be closed for the month of February due to the gas shortage; teachers would meet their classes once a week, formally, and as much of the time as possible on the other four days informally. Teachers were to prepare the month's assignments for each student to work on at home. Furthermore, each teacher was to call ten parents of first period students, and explain the closing procedures to them. Joyce didn't phone the parents. Two weeks into the closing was the levy vote. It passed, and Joyce was very happy. It wasn't until April that Joyce came to feel comfortable calling parents. Contacts with them had been a real source of anxiety.

At the beginning of March, school resumed the regular schedule, to continue in session without a vacation until June. For Joyce these were months of feeling more relaxed, reflecting on the year's experiences, and just hanging on until the end. Gymnastics was over, and she had more free time. Her classes and she had become used to each other. Although there were ups and downs, things went fairly smoothly. Her contact was renewed.

At the beginning of a typical class toward the year's end, students would be talking and some walking around. Presently Joyce would yell at them to be quiet and within a few minutes they would settle down. She would write five preliminary problems on the board, and the class would do them and go over them. Then she would pass out a worksheet or write the assignment problems on the board.

As students got to work, one after another would call out procedural questions.

"Do we have to show our work?"

"How many points is this worth?"

From the front she would answer each individual's question. Occasionally she would tell someone to turn around, or sit down, or get to work. The student she was speaking to would comply either sooner or later, or give some smart answer back, such as "I *am* doing my work." Joyce did not reply to this back talk. She would sit at her desk grading papers, or go around the room glancing at students' papers to see whether they needed help. When the students finished the assignment, they would converse among themselves until the bell rang.

Joyce received her final recommendation and felt it was fair. The department chairman commended her preparedness with respect to content, her eagerness to do a good job, and her cheerfulness. He saw lack of class control as the greatest problem, one that had influenced other aspects of her performance.

Looking back, Joyce felt good about her first year of teaching. She had wanted to do the best she possibly could; in some ways she had, and in other ways she hadn't. She had tried to treat the students as adults, tried to reason with them, but that was impossible. By June her attitude toward the students had changed. Next year she would buckle down and "sit on them" the first two or three months and really make them behave. She knew she was capable of doing it; it was "just a matter of *doing* it." She had made the normal first year mistakes, and now she felt much less worried than she had been at the beginning of the year.

Throughout the year she had been striving to do better. Even though she could see improvement, she thought of herself as a perfectionist. The advice people had given her had been only minimally helpful; she mainly had to find out for herself. Other math teachers had encouraged her by keeping her spirits up. She didn't think the school could have done any more to help her adjust. She was the type who had to learn for herself, making her own mistakes, learning the hard way.

# Just So They Have Fun

Bill Moore began the school year with confidence. Although he was new to teaching, he felt he understood children. He knew he would be accepted by his fifth grade students. He knew he would be successful.

To Bill, teaching was an art. It could not be learned; it had to be felt. He believed a teacher needed to know certain educational concepts and possess certain technical skills, but the essential prerequisite for teaching success was to like kids. The teacher who liked children would be able to provide meaningful classroom experiences and enable students to enjoy the learning process.

Broad-shouldered and muscular, Bill had the stature of a basketball player. His blond hair, blue eyes and tanned skin accentuated his athletic appearance. When he walked around the room his size was particularly noticeable; he appeared Herculean compared to the small eleven-year-olds seated at their desks.

Bill discovered how enjoyable teaching and children could be during an outdoor education trip in college. He spent four days working with underprivileged boys at a YMCA camp. The experience made him feel needed and gave him a sense of self-worth. Originally a marketing major, Bill became bored with computing figures and understanding theories of consumerism. He felt that teaching was an opportunity to work with real people, not abstract symbols.

Bill began teaching at Flowing Brook Elementary School. It had an enrollment of 500 students and served children in a lower middle-class, suburban community. Most of the students' parents worked in factories; a few held white-collar positions. The homes surrounding the school were small and architecturally simple; all manifested a certain sameness.

The students wore nice but unpretentious clothing. Occasionally a girl would flaunt a new dress; a boy, new tennis shoes; but these occasions were rare.

There were thirty-two students in his classroom, a room intended to hold only twenty-five. The room had a few seasonal decorations attached to the dull blue walls, walls which had not been painted for three years. A melange of colorful leaves dotted the bulletin board and a couple of commercial posters hung above the blackboard.

The textbooks and curriculum guides outlined specifically what each teacher should teach and Bill had them carefully stacked next to his desk. Faculty members at Flowing Brook were not encouraged to deviate from the adopted subject matter sequence. The teacher provided a subject matter-centered curriculum and offered a strong emphasis on the basics.

Bill found it difficult to adjust to a traditional school. He did his student teaching in an open space school and believed that the open concept was the ideal. It enabled the students to enjoy school, their peers, and the teacher. He wanted students to be able to talk when they wished and excuse themselves for a drink or to go to the restroom without asking for the teacher's permission. With few problems anticipated, the year began.

*   *   *

Alphabetizing was the first major English unit of the year and Bill wanted to make sure that students knew the alphabet well enough to locate words in their dictionaries. "Okay, let's work on those dictionaries for a few minutes." Bill waited impatiently while the students found their dictionaries. His frustration with the students showed on his face; his look was serious and intense. He finally said, "Let's go, hurry up." The students moved slowly around the room until a student in the back of the room reinforced Bill's request and yelled, "Hurry up." The student demand, along with some individualized disciplining by Bill, produced results. The students were reseated, dictionaries in hands.

"Okay, Let's see who can look up the words the fastest." There was a pause and then Bill called out the first word, "Crime!" The students furiously scanned their dictionaries for the correct page.

"I got it," responded one student. Another student repeated the statement, only to be followed by a chorus of "I got it" as other students simultaneously located the correct page.

"Hey!" Bill demanded quiet. "Hey!" His second attempt was louder and more adamant.

The quiet was broken by a frustrated student, "I don't want to play the dictionary game!"

"I don't want to play either," remarked another student.

Bill ignored the comments and gave the next word, "Jigsaw!" Jigsaw was followed by a long list of words: border, smash, motion. . . . Bill moved away from his desk and walked around the room as the students continued to look up words. The room was split almost evenly between those involved and interested, and those bored and indifferent. Bill stopped at one girl's desk to respond to a question. His inattentiveness to the class as a whole seemed to cause the other students to get louder. Bill looked up at the students seated near a corner table, "Hey, hold it down." The noise level decreased as the students at the corner table buried their heads again in their books.

* * *

Bill spent a great deal of time during class at his desk. He gave directions, answered questions, and covered lesson material while sitting at the large wooden desk located at the front of the room. Students lined up and waited for his assistance. Class control was difficult because Bill had to help the students standing at his desk, and, at the same time, keep the students at their desks quiet. The difficulty of working with one or two students and keeping the other thirty quiet was particularly noticeable whenever the students worked on independent projects or reports.

One day early in November, for instance, the students were working on sports reports. Bill was helping students at his desk when a loud crash jarred the room. Bill looked up and observed two students, Frank and Dave, standing next to an overturned chair. "Dave, Frank, get back up here. Who told you to go back there?" The students meekly picked up the chair and returned to their seats. Bill looked at the class and said, "All right get out your English books." The students walked around putting some materials away,

getting others out. Bill gave them about five minutes for the transition in activities. "Okay, Joan, please read the directions for the
assignment on prefixes." The class quieted down. The students discussed the definition of a prefix and gave examples. "For tomorrow I
want you to do page 103." The class got louder when Bill stopped
talking about the assignment and returned to his desk.

"Don! Amy!" Bill called out the names of two students who
were not working on the English assignment. The students started
back to work but the rest of the class got louder. Bill stared at the
restless students and said, "Mark, you owe me fifty sentences."
Mark was leaning back in his chair and staring out the window.
There was a pause, the class became a little quieter. "Mike, you owe
me fifty sentences." Mike was talking to a neighbor. The class got
very quiet. Bill commented, "I guess you folks like to write sentences."

*   *   *

During the first part of the year the lessons in Bill's classes were
not dramatic and the planning for instruction minimal. By Christmas the curriculum guides and textbooks were followed almost reli-
giously. The teaching was straightforward. Classes started with a
short discussion of a concept and after the discussion Bill gave an
assignment. All students did the same work on the same assignments. Bill developed very few individualized lessons; he relied on
the packaged materials developed by publishing companies or other
teachers.

Bill taught the lowest reading group for the fifth grade, a group
he was assigned by his supervisor. There were about twenty students in the group and all read below grade level. The students spent
most of their time working on self-instructional materials and
memorizing word lists. Students were encouraged to work on the
self-instructional packages but they were seldom given time to look
at books in the library.

The reading program Bill used was new and experimental. It
emphasized the basic skills and reflected the unwritten philosophy of
the district: a teacher should not develop materials for students when
packaged materials from a publisher are available. Teachers were
expected to use various science and reading programs purchased and
adopted by the school district and to implement the programs in the
form recommended by the publishers.

The principal told Bill during the first evaluation in October to develop better lesson plans. Initially Bill wrote down only the concept he planned to teach (e.g., alphabetizing or prefixes); he thought up the method and sometimes the assignment when class began. This approach was, in part, a carryover from his student teaching. After talking to the curriculum coordinator, however, Bill developed his plans in more detail. He began including both the concept and methods of instruction. The sequence for teaching concepts and objectives was determined by the various district guides. Bill did not have to determine the "what to teach" just the "how."

Bill wanted to have a reputation as fair and likeable but he felt the school expected him to be tough. Rules were created, therefore, for the students to follow: a raise-your-hand rule, a sit-up-straight rule, a work-hard rule. As long as the students were quiet, the rules were not implemented. When the class was calm, students could respond without raising their hands or carry on conversations with peers. Once it started to get noisy, Bill got tough. The toughness usually manifested itself in a verbal reprimand with Bill calling out a student's name and then delivering a punishment. "Joan, you have fifty sentences to write. Susan, you have the same." Bill's disciplining, particularly at the beginning of the year, was seldom nonverbal and private, it was overt and public.

During late winter the students were working on an assignment when Bill attempted to call the class to order. "Hey! Hey! Hey! What's all the noise? Everyone should be done with their worksheets so turn them in." The class got quieter. "Okay, let's get our books out." Bill walked to the side of the room, waited, and then called on a student to begin reading.

"Nancy, get your own book." Nancy and a friend were sharing a book. Nancy responded, "I want to share with Susie." The class got quieter, Bill looked sternly at Nancy. "Get your own book!" This time it was a command, not a request. Nancy responded pleadingly, "I want to share with Susie." Bill glared at Nancy but did not repeat his command. Nancy moved toward her desk but did not get her book. Bill turned away and called on another student, "Okay, John, would you read next?"

A few minutes later, Bill yelled across the room at John, the student who just finished reading. "John, you know the rule for sitting back in chairs." John looked sheepishly at Bill and bent his head down. "Stand up and pick up your chair." The class was absolutely quiet. John stood up and picked up his chair. He held his chair for the next seven minutes. John held the chair in a variety of positions to keep it from dropping. Bill finally walked over to John, took the chair, unfolded it, and told John to sit down.

* * *

The final evaluation by the principal was conducted in March. Bill thought that he was doing a good job. The students were enjoying school; they were learning. The principal disagreed. She felt Bill did not have sufficient control; there was too much freedom in his classroom. According to the principal the students needed to be controlled. They must ask for permission to get a drink of water, raise their hands to answer a question, and sit in straight rows while working on assignments. The principal felt Bill was not tough enough. The evaluation was negative. Bill suddenly felt defeated and uncertain.

Other than managerial problems, the principal described very little Bill needed to do to improve. She simply told him to be tougher and plan better. Bill found himself asking questions to which there seemed to be no clear-cut answers: How do I plan better? What is good planning? How do I get tougher? Do I have to make students line up for the restroom? A drink? Do they have to be quiet before leaving the room? Bill began to question his ability to teach. Teaching suddenly seemed difficult.

In accordance with the principal's "get tough" policy, Bill cracked down on misbehaving students. His action created an immediate parental reaction. One parent became angry and protested Bill's inconsistency and questioned his fairness. The parent, Bill, and the principal discussed the problem. Although Bill felt threatened, he stood his ground. More importantly, the principal supported him. The principal's support gave Bill renewed confidence. He knew what the principal wanted and he knew he could do it. He could be tough.

* * *

The weather was warm; the room was almost hot. The students were observing a filmstrip. "Hawaii consists of many islands. The islands were created by volcanic action." The students looked at the picture of the islands as one student read the captions. Bill repeated word for word what the student read. The pattern continued until the filmstrip was completed. The students stood up to stretch. "Sit down! Sit down! We have another filmstrip." Bill was firm, the students sat down. Bill started the projector and called on another student to read. "The active volcanoes of Hawaii are Mauna Kea and Mauna Loa." Students struggled with the words, Bill assisted with the pronunciations. He repeated what had been read and discussed it with the class for a few minutes. "John, read next." John tried to read but found the words difficult. Bill took over but like the student he struggled. "The major cities of Hawaii are Honolulu, Kalaupapa, Kahului, Kaitua, and Niulii." The warmth of the room made it difficult for the students to concentrate. Only about one-third of the students looked at the filmstrip; many students played with pencils or fidgeted with books; some had their heads down on their desks.

The filmstrip ended. Bill told the class that there would be a short break. They stood up, started talking and moving around. Bill reacted, "Sit down!" The students looked at Bill but did not settle down. "Before we go to the restroom we all have to sit down." A few students returned to their seats, many remained standing. "4 . . . 3 . . . 2 . . . 1 . . ." When Bill started counting backwards the students ran to their desks. When seated, they put their heads down.

The class was excused for the restroom by tables. "Table 1, you may go . . . Table 4 . . . Table 2 . . ." He excused only those students who were quiet. "Table 6 you are all excused except Mary." The students at Table 6 left, Mary put her head back down. Bill waited, "Okay, Mary, you can go."

Mary looked up somewhat angrily. "What did I do wrong?"

Bill responded immediately, "You were talking. No talking is permitted."

The students returned from the restroom. They straggled in and wandered around while Bill worked at his desk. The principal started talking on the intercom. "Once again, today, someone has set off a firecracker in the restroom. This will not happen again! *All* teachers will accompany *all* students to the restroom and drinking fountains! No students are to be allowed in the hall by themselves! Teachers, this is partly your fault! You have become lax in watching students outside your rooms. Now, let's all do our jobs, and let's put an end to this."

The announcement ended, Bill looked at the class. "Are there any questions concerning what Mrs. Johnson said?"

One student raised his hand, "What would happen if they

caught someone with firecrackers?" The students all focused their attention on Bill. A "Yeah, what happens" look appeared on everyone's face.

"Well, if someone is caught he could go to jail, if the judge finds the person guilty."

The students looked frightened. A girl desperately waved her hand and called, "Mr. Moore, Mr. Moore!" Bill gave her permission to talk. "Mr. Moore, what if someone sticks a firecracker in your pocket and you don't know you have it, would still go to jail?" The students were both frightened and excited as they waited for an answer.

"Well, if you had them and you didn't know it, you probably wouldn't go to jail. The judge would probably set you free."

Bill asked if there were other questions. The class sat quietly. One girl raised her hand, "Mr. Moore, if someone goes to jail is it all right if we visit them?" The students were excited at the possibility. Again the class's attention focused on Bill. He nodded affirmatively. The students responded with excitement; there was clapping and smiling.

"All right, quiet!"

One boy was very excited and called out, "Can we really visit?"

Bill responded quickly, "John, you have talked out of turn. You have one mark." The class got totally quiet. Bill leaned back and put a mark next to John's name.

*   *   *

Bill started the year hoping his students would enjoy school and learn. To a certain extent this was accomplished. Bill viewed enjoyment in interpersonal terms—joking around, solving riddles, and playing games. He often had relaxed conversations with students about sports and current events. The students enjoyed Bill's warmth and often responded physically by touching him affectionately and putting their arms around him, almost like children with a parent. Bill wanted to be liked by the students but he had difficulty knowing how close to be with them. How much joking around should a teacher do? How warm could a teacher be before students would take advantage of the closeness?

One day late in the school year, for example, the students were working on an English assignment. One girl called Bill over to her desk and said she had a riddle: "What has eyes but cannot see?"

Bill stood quietly for a second, a number of students gathered around, smiling and staring at Bill's puzzled face. "I don't know," replied Bill. "What does have eyes and cannot see?"

The girl's smiled broadened as she answered, "A potato!" The students who were staring at Bill exploded in laughter and the students around the room looked up to see what had happened.

The class became very loud, Bill's facial expression immediately turned serious, "All right, get out your math books." The commandlike statement caused the class to get quiet. Bill walked to the front of the room, picked up his math book, his face still set in seriousness, and the lesson began.

Knowing how far to go with jokes, how much to plan, how to discipline and how to develop interesting lessons were problems which plagued Bill throughout the year. At the end of the year he had developed some solutions based on what he thought the principal wanted. He was, nevertheless, still struggling to find a teaching style which would permit his open approach to exist in a traditional school. He was still struggling to see himself as a teacher.

# When There Is No Way

"Pearl . . . Pearl, come on. Let's finish this section before the class ends."

"You finish it. I'm done. I done all the work today I'm going to do. So you better finish it."

"There are only three more problems. Come on, what's the answer to this first one? Are you supposed to add here or subtract?"

Therese Gorman points to the problems but studies the face of this young woman, sixteen years of age and still in ninth grade, still studying simple word problems in math, and still seemingly unable to master them. Pearl returns the gaze. She is obstinate.

The other four students in the class continue their work at other stations. One station is on the multiplication tables; Dianne works alone there. Robby and Bonita play a game which requires them to add and multiply scores; they punctuate the class period with outbursts of bickering. Timmy works on the problems from a text; if he finishes this and does well, he may be placed in a regular math class like Joe. Trace and Willie are absent. They rarely come.

Pearl fiddles with her rings. She glances from them to the teacher and back. Timmy approaches and asks Therese to review his papers. Therese agrees to do so, and Pearl, too, examines his work. Momentarily, Pearl resumes her own.

The bell rings to end the period. The eighth graders come bursting into the room. Therese tells Pearl she'll have to finish the problems for homework. Pearl retorts, "You do it! You finish it!"

Timmy waits expectantly. Billy and James chase each other knocking over chairs in their path. "Billy! Billy!" and the boy hesitates. "You sit right where you are. James, you sit over there. Now!" Lynette is laughing uncontrollably in her seat. Fox threatens her with his fist. "Timmy, how about stopping back after school? Then we'll review your paper. Okay?" His disappointment shows, but he doesn't object. Therese quickly gathers the materials from each math station and moves them to the cabinet.

Nine youngsters make up the eight grade group. All are classified as Educable Mentally Retarded (EMR), but the classification does not seem quite right for all the youngsters. Fox is a tall, slim fellow; his real name is Fredericks, but by some twist of syllables he has always been Fox. Rubin and James are like twins: short, childlike frames, but aggressive and cocksure spirits. Rubin probably doesn't belong in the EMR class. Dan is too heavy; he's very quiet and seldom looks directly at anyone. Dan and Billy and Perry are the only white youngsters in the class. Like their black classmates and the general school population, they come from poor homes. Lynette is the only girl, an unpredictable mixture of tomboy and young woman. She will not be intimidated, but she's easily hurt.

The sun has warmed the room measurably. This, the last class of the day, will find heat added to the mounting exhaustion Therese already feels. By contrast the youngsters are energetic, even volatile. It is an eighth grade class in health; the topic is nutrition. Therese distributes magazines to each student. "After we have a short review on the basic food groups, then we're going to plan our menu for the picnic. Does everyone have a magazine?" The youngsters page through the issues, satisfying curiosity, and not particularly attending to the question. Dan sits quietly. Lynette approaches Therese and whispers in her ear. Therese nods, the girl takes a note and leaves the room. Fox asks, "When do we get started? And when did you say was the picnic?" Therese does not respond but gestures to Fox that he should raise his hand to speak. Fox settles for no response.

"Who can name the four basic food groups? Raise your hand." The lesson begins. Rubin and James are laughing at something Rubin has found in his magazine. Therese sees, but ignores their momentary distraction. "Billy, do you know one group?" The boy mumbles a response. "That's right. Good! Now say it so everyone can understand." The boy responds again and the lesson goes on. Some students participate, some are less willing. The questions and answers take much more time than planned.

Having identified each of the food groups, the youngsters are given the task of finding examples of each in the magazines. "Cut the pictures neatly and paste them on the paper so it looks like a meal, if that can be done. Then label each of the food groups. Does everyone have scissors? Paste? Rubin. James. Get to work." The youngsters move into the task. Dan is the first; gradually, others also begin. Lynette returns to the class and sits. Therese stoops to explain to her what she is to do.

Fox calls from across the room, "I'm tired of this." Therese ignores the comment but moves generally in his direction. She stops at another desk and works momentarily with the student. "I'm tired of this. I have to go to the bathroom. Give me a hall pass." Therese moves directly to the youngster. "Fox, how is your work coming? I see that you've got two of the groups selected. Which ones do you yet need to find?"

"This magazine stinks. Give me a hall pass."

"I can't do that. Besides the period is almost over."

"You said we would plan the picnic menu. When are we going to do that? Why do we have to do this?" Fox has grown impatient and his voice is loud.

The other youngsters listen; some stop working. "Now, Fox, we'll get the menu planned. We would have done it today except it took so long to get started. But there's plenty of time. We'll do it the first thing tomorrow."

"I want a hall pass. If you don't give me it, you're going to have a big problem to clean up." He snickers at the image he has created, and others laugh too. Therese chuckles, "Gee, I hope not. That would be a first time problem for me. I expect you can wait until the bell."

Fox persists, his voice now very loud, "I'm telling you! You gave Lynette a hall pass. Why does she get one? She must be teacher's pet." Fox looks at the girl who has settled to work. James now joins in, "Yeah, Lynette is the teacher's pet. You don't mess with Lynette or the teacher'll get you." Lynette now retorts, "Shut up or I'll bust your head. You just wait!" Therese moves away from Fox and encourages the class to return to work.

Fox and James continue their barrage: "Mrs. Gorman likes

Lynette. She thinks she's a sweet girl. What she don't know. . . ."
The boys laugh and are joined by others. Lynette bristles and stands
up. "I'm going to bust you. You're dead!"

Therese intervenes, "Lynette, just ignore what they say." She
moves and rests a hand on Lynette's arm. "Come on, let's finish this
work." The confrontation is avoided, and the girl resumes the task,
distracted, but steady with Therese's attention. In moments, the
boys also resume work, except Fox who rests his head on the desk
and covers it with the magazine.

Therese circulates about the room. She works her way to Fox.
At his desk, she stoops and speaks softly, peeking under the
magazine. "Fox, I know you're in there. What's wrong? You were
working so well this morning." The youngster is silent. "Fox, don't
you want to talk to me?" Therese's voice is nearly a whisper; the
conversation is private. "Fox?" Still, there is no response. Therese
stands and touches his shoulder. He reacts: "Get your hands off me,
bitch!" He jerks but does not come out from under the magazine.
Therese moves away to her desk.

The bell rings. Students begin to scatter. "Put your papers on
my desk. Make sure your name is on it." The door opens to the
adjoining room and seventh graders and ninth graders come charging in. "Tomorrow we'll work on the picnic menus." The comment
is lost. Two youngsters resume a game of tag and zip out of the
room. A seventh grader is fumbling with the pencil sharpener. Pearl
comes in and warns she will not do any homework in math. And Fox
languishes to his feet. "Fox, let's talk after school. Okay?" The boy
ignores the comment and exits. "All of you are supposed to be some
place. Ninth graders, you have gym." A seventh grader approaches
Therese, holding onto her forearm: "I don't remember my schedule.
What's today? Do I go to art or study hall?" Therese looks into his
eyes and touches his hand. "Today, Joey, is Tuesday. Today you go
to art." Then Timmy is there, asking if she could review his math
paper during ninth period. "Well, Timmy, Mr. Simon and Mrs.
D'Angelo and I are supposed to meet. But if we don't, I'll review the
paper. Where will you be if I need you?" The lad is pleased. He
hurries to the gym.

Five minutes into ninth period, the room is quiet. Therese
gathers the handful of papers that have been turned in and the few
which were left on desks. Through the door which joins this room to

the next she hears Ann, Mrs. D, as the youngsters call her, humming a snappy tune, belying the exhaustion which they share. She too is recovering from the day. Jeff emerges from another room, actually a large storage room which they use as the third classroom in the EMR suite. He whistles a sigh to Therese on his way out the door. Therese calls to him, "Mr. Simon, are we going to meet today? I wanted to . . ." But he interrupts that he has to meet with a trio of former students who need help completing job applications. "We can get together tomorrow. There are some things we all need to speak about."

Therese turns back to her work. Her thoughts turn to Fox and his behavior. She reviews the incident in her mind. ". . . he didn't really mean it . . . he was just having a bad day. I know I should be careful of touching them but I touch them to show I care. If they know I care for them, that I really love them, it will be all right . . . but they must see that I care. I wish I could talk to Mr. Simon about it. Why do I call him Mr. Simon? He's Jeff to me. He'd know how to handle the situation; he'd know what to do." The door opens and Timmy peeks in. "Mrs. Gorman, can we go over the paper?"

"I thought you went to gym. You're not supposed to leave the gym once class has started."

"I know, but Mr. Vance doesn't care. I told him I wanted to speak with you and he said I could go. He doesn't care. He says that us special kids are his overload, so he doesn't care if none of us show up."

"Well, come on in and we'll go over your paper, but you know if you're going to get into regular classes, you're going to have to work extra hard to show the teachers that you can do the work and that *you* care. Leaving a class doesn't seem to show that you care." The admonition is only half heard. The youngster settles to a table and waits expectantly. Therese sits opposite him and they begin the review. In the background, the humming continues, punctuated with lyrics. And the sun continues to tempt a drowsiness from the new teacher.

After 4:30 she begins to think of home. She has graded all the papers she needs to for tomorrow. She has yet to produce the master for a new math station. She'll have to do it at home. She packs her supplies. Her husband will not like her getting home so late; that means a late dinner for him. She selects two math books to use as references in her planning. He'll ask why she can't come home right after school, and why she brings work home with her. She straightens the desks into irregular rows. He'll not want to hear what went on today. She closes the windows. He'll say the house is unkempt; that she's not doing her job as a wife. She takes her purse from the desk drawer, lifts her books and exits, locking the door as she leaves.

The school seems empty, as is the parking lot but for two cars. She stops momentarily and looks at the building in which she has begun her career. The dock area is right next to the main doors, separated by a cracking brick wall. Trash and papers litter the entrance. "How can the kids even be proud of their school. It always looks so messy." She pictures the spot as it is during the lunch hour with youngsters lounging on the few remaining benches while others cavort around them. She wonders if they ever notice that it could be different, better. A slight breeze brings afresh the odors of the nearby landfill and factories, and Therese shakes off her reverie. She drives from the school, "her school," on the industrial edge of the city. She drives past the crumbling wood-frame houses, past the corner grocery where students hang out, past the factory entrance, and onto the freeway which will take her crosstown. It's going on 5:00 and dinner will be later yet.

*   *   *

Dinner was late, and for the fourth time in as many weeks Therese and her husband Jack had words about the changes her teaching position had brought to their lives. He objected to the time she spent at school and the hours of paperwork she carried home. "Teaching is nothing but talking and giving assignments. Why does it take you so long!" She argued back that teaching was important to her, and that it was important to her students. They reached no peace. After dinner when Jack settled in front of the television, Therese settled with math papers and books and planned a new learning station to replace one that would soon be no longer of use.

Planning was particularly difficult for Therese—math was the only subject she had dreaded teaching; she would have opted for language arts or reading, given that choice. When she arrived at the school for the first time in late August, she was told she would be the math teacher on the team. Jeff and Ann had divided responsibilities before they met Therese, and she felt there was no chance to rethink the decisions. Planning for math was also difficult for Therese because Jeff had taught the subject last year. She felt she might not be able to meet his standards. The help he offered her in preparing was supportive yet intimidating; it left her feeling obligated and dependent. As she set about the task of organizing another learning station, she couldn't help but wonder if Jeff approved of her use of learning stations to teach math, and of her teaching in general.

The team of three EMR teachers was assigned the responsibility of schooling just over thirty youngsters. The three were part of the large junior high school, but they functioned rather autonomously. They made their own schedule and planned their own curricula. The youngsters, too, were isolated. Although they participated in the inevitable youth subculture, they were schooled separately. Only a few efforts to mainstream youngsters and a handful of special subjects like home economics, shop, and physical education, brought them into formal contact with other teachers in the school.

The three teachers presented quite a contrast. Ann was older than either Jeff or Therese, but it was only her second year of teaching. She had spent the first year in another school, and coming to Wilson Junior High meant learning new procedures. She worked hard at teaching, but in the early weeks of the year it became evident that she would have problems. She was unable to manage the class. Even the docile youngsters ignored her directives. She persisted in her efforts and was rewarded with occasional order; for the most part, however, she was frustrated and preoccupied by her own limitations. Therese and Ann became confidants. They could speak to one another of things that other teachers did not care to understand. Although Therese was the newer of the two, she often found herself listening, giving advice, and consoling. She liked Ann, and they grew close.

Jeff was the experienced member of the team. He had been at Wilson for five years and had sustained many changes in team personnel. Jeff had established himself as an informal leader in the school, a position of some influence. He protected the EMR program from encroachment and neglect, and worked with other teachers on the larger school problems—discipline and the relations between principal and faculty. He was a committed teacher, and his commitment was readily evident. Therese respected Jeff: she respected his experience, his position in the school, and his belief in the work. She bowed to his organizational abilities. She sought his advice on matters and respected his judgment. At the same time, however, Therese felt encumbered by Jeff's authority. She felt left out of some decisions about the EMR program which he made alone. She was not secure in her own decisions until he concurred. But the encumbrance was not great, and it was gradually supplanted by mutual respect. Together Therese and Jeff were the strength of the team.

By the beginning of the second month, the team had developed a comfortable working relationship. Therese managed the math program. She took on the responsibility of accompanying the EMR students to shop and home economics, and occasionally to typing and gym, so they could participate and succeed as a part of regular classes. She managed to find spots in the regular academic classes for a few students like Timmy who could keep up, with help. Ann taught language arts and with help from Jeff and the vice-principal, she managed a semblance of order. Jeff taught the modified social studies and managed relations with the larger school. Though the three seldom met formally, their work was complementary.

Therese's daily schedule became familiar. Homeroom with twenty-five assorted youngsters began the day; in half the auditorium her group talked and rustled, while in the other half Mr. Chesney, the shop teacher, held his group silent and restrained. The difference was obvious to Therese, but it did not bother her. She proclaimed no strong commitment to the homeroom group; she would not see most of the youngsters all day long.

Seventh grade math was her first class of the day; it was often the best. The students were new to the school and just discovering their place in it. They were easily managed. Working with the seventh graders Therese was able to feel that something was being accomplished.

A planning period followed. Early in the year she would spend it in the teachers' lounge. She wanted to make friends but found the teachers generally unfriendly. None of the black teachers lounged there, and Therese heard they spent their free time in another part of the building. This disturbed her. In the lounge the teachers complained about the ineffectiveness of the principal: "There's no sense in taking a kid to him. He'll just pat the bastard on the head and send him back. You're better off to paddle the kid yourself. Solve your own problems. But do it with a witness." And the teachers spoke no

better of the students. Therese found the lounge stifling, and as the
year went on, she used her planning period to accompany the EMR
students to regular classes; she spent less and less time in the
teachers' lounge.

After planning period, Therese had study hall duty, shared
with Ann. Therese could not understand why two inexperienced
teachers were given this difficult duty. After several weeks, however, it became apparent that only about half of the forty-nine students who were supposed to report ever would, and repeated notes
to the office regarding the absences generated no concern. Therese
grew content to police who ever came, keeping them quiet and in
their seats. Ann helped.

After the study hall, Therese had a forty-minute lunch and a
slate of afternoon classes: eighth and ninth grade math, and eighth
grade health. The last period of the day was set aside for team
planning, but it was seldom used as such. Tutoring, paper-grading,
individual planning, and meeting with other teachers were most
often the tasks at hand. It all made for a full day and a busy evening.

By the beginning of the second month, Therese had grown
competent and comfortable in the environment of Wilson Junior
High. She learned from incidents. One time a girl who she did not
know bumped and pushed her down the hall at class change time.
Therese was befuddled by the girl's behavior, but not angered. She
asked another student who the girl was, so she could later contact the
girl about it. After school that day, the girl came on her own to
Therese's room weeping. She pleaded with Therese not to call her
home. "I'll get beat. My dad will beat me if I'm in trouble." When
asked why she behaved as she did, the girl replied, "Because you're
new here, and me and my friend thought we'd give you a hard time."

And there was the day Therese received a sharp note from the
school attendance secretary, reprimanding her for not submitting the
homeroom tally. The note was penned on the principal's stationery,
and demanded some explanation. Therese spoke with the attendance
secretary: "I really think I turned it in. I spent half the morning
looking through my papers, and I can't find it. What might have
happened is that I gave it to Sheila to bring to the office—Sheila is
that new girl who has had trouble in school. I don't know her very
well but I thought I could give her this responsibility to help us
develop a sense of trust. Well, maybe she forgot to get it to you. I can

make a new list." Shortly thereafter, the secretary found the original mixed in with other lists. Therese felt relieved. A week later, when the secretary misplaced the tally again, Therese learned that she need not have responded with such concern.

She also learned about herself. "I'm not as patient as I thought I was, or as I should be. I spend most of my time disciplining and handling problems. I don't really think I'm teaching. During student teaching it wasn't this way. Mrs. Brockman could help me out, and she had so many good ways of doing things. Of course, she has younger children to teach, and some of the things that work there could never work in junior high. But she was such a dynamic person; she was always ready to tackle a problem. I don't think I'm like her. I can't be her; I have to be myself. But I do miss talking with her and getting the advice and pats on the back she used to give me. She was patient, and I thought I was patient too. I've started to give detentions as punishments. I know I once said I wouldn't do that, but it works. It works well. The kids listen better when they know they may be headed for a detention, even if it's just a short one. They also listen when I tell them I'll send them to the office, to the vice-principal, that is. So if it works, I'll use it. Mr. Chesney said he'd make a paddle for me in shop; he's making one for Ann. I don't think I want one though. I suppose if he makes it, it won't hurt to have it in the room. Every teacher has one."

It was in the second week of October when Therese first heard of Davey Williams. In the lounge where she had gone to grade papers, a trio of teachers talked of the boy: "The kid is a real problem. He shouldn't be in school; this isn't the place for him. He really belongs in that special school downtown."

"Did you hear he threatened Bonnie Dohrn? She has him for math. Yeah, she tried to get too close to him. She took him to some basketball games and gave him special attention in school. She was trying to help him. He loved it, but when she gave others some attention, he got angry."

"Do you mean he was jealous?"

"Well, I don't know if that's the word, but it was like that."

"I saw them once, coming down the hall. He was holding her arms from behind, just sort of rough-housing. But it looked too rough to me. He's a big kid, and strong. He's a rough kid. I guess I wasn't really surprised to hear that he had punched her. The kid is barely in control of himself, and he can't be controlled by others."

"The kid's got no conscience. He doesn't belong in school. What's going to happen to him? Anything?"

Therese listened to the conversation with limited interest. She did not know Davey, and she did not know Bonnie Dohrn well either. It was interesting to know that other teachers had such problems, but it was a problem she did not have to address.

She had her own. At home, things were not going well. She and Jack continued to fight. He had begun to drink heavily and sometimes he didn't come home till after seven. "He spends hours, and I get worried about how he'll drive home. Then when he comes home we argue. He doesn't want me to teach. He doesn't want me to work at all, I think. Last night when he came home he started complaining, and I pretended to cry. I pretended to cry so he would stop yelling. I've never done that before; I don't know why I did it, but I knew what I was doing." Therese's parents were the source of some consolation. They too were teachers, in a small town in the southern part of the state. On the phone they talked long and frequently about both school and home problems. Therese gained comfort from the conversations, but she knew that the problems were hers alone to face.

In the first week of November, Davey was added to the list. The principal transferred him from the regular program into the eighth grade EMR class. Jeff suspected that the youngster's IQ scores were altered so that he could qualify, but that the actual purpose was to defuse the explosive situation that had developed in the regular classes. Davey began with Therese just where he'd left off with Bonnie Dohrn. He pushed her and shoved her in class. He would place his arm around her and call her his girl. "I don't know how to take it! I don't know if he's trying to be friendly or if he's really being abusive. He has a temper and gets very angry at times. It worries me: he's so strong I could never really defend myself if he starting hitting me. And you know he's really capable of hitting a teacher, like he did Mrs. Dohrn. The other kids in the class are standing up for me. They tell him to sit down and leave me alone. That's nice to see, but they don't control him either. A couple days ago after school Davey was waiting in the hall for me. It was getting late and most of the kids were gone. He wouldn't let me go by. Then a couple students came whom I don't even know. They said, 'Let that lady alone. Don't pick on her.' So he did leave. But I don't know what would have happened if they hadn't come by."

Therese wanted the boy to have a new start, and she did not want to react coldly toward him. "I don't know if it's because I expect him to be so bad that he is, or if he's just that way." She moderated her behavior toward him: his misbehavior she ignored; if he grabbed her arm or hugged her, she calmly told him to stop; his good behavior she praised. To this pattern of response, Davey grew hostile. He became more angry in his frustration: he could not get her attention as he wanted it. Therese felt that she was making progress in the relationship. Then Davey discovered that as he worked his anger on other students, he once again could command the situation. "I can't just let him hurt other students. They're not able to defend themselves against him. I have to step in. I can't ignore it. But then I'm back to where I started with him!" Of all the students, Davey strained her patience the most, and of all the students he was the first whom she thought seriously of paddling.

The week following Thanksgiving was quiet. More students than usual were absent, including Lynette, out with a cold, and Rubin, who had been suspended on Monday for something he did during the lunch period. When some students were absent, things seemed to go much better. On Monday afternoon, Therese found an old file of math papers used in previous years. She was surprised to find that teachers other than Jeff had taught math. "I thought he had always been the math teacher. Now, I find that he only started last year. It makes all the concern I've felt seem rather unnecessary. When I asked him why he didn't want to teach the math again this year, he said he thought it would be the easiest subject for me to break in on. I didn't understand it that way before."

On Tuesday of that week Therese's study hall duty was changed to lunchroom duty. The numbers of students had gradually diminished enough to make two supervisors unnecessary. Ann continued at the post. Therese liked the change. In the cafeteria she could be more herself: she could talk with youngsters and not worry about the noise; she could take time to get to know other students; she could spend time with Jeff and the vice-principal who already held duty there. She was happy with the switch.

Therese continued a practice she had begun just before Thanksgiving: she kept a notebook with her and wrote down things that students did. She originally had no purpose other than anecdotal record keeping. But she discovered that the students responded strongly to the practice. "They are very concerned about what I write, even if I'm just writing a note to myself. It's amazing! If they think I'm writing about them, they shape up quickly. Mostly, I let them see what I've written. If it's bad, they sometimes get angry. Sometimes they are surprised what I've written. It's just another way of fostering good behavior."

For the first time Therese paddled two youngsters for misbehavior. Jeff acted as witness. "It just had to be done. Fox and Perry simply wouldn't take me seriously. They wouldn't settle down. I think they were surprised, more than hurt, that I would do it. They didn't think I would. Well, now they all know that I will if I have to. And I won't make idle threats."

On Friday she received at school a bouquet of roses from Jack. They had spent Thanksgiving separately, after continual arguments. Therese had decided to ask for a divorce. "I don't see any other way to work this out. He really doesn't want me to teach, or do anything for that matter. He expects me to sit home, take care of the house, and have his dinner ready when he wants it. That's what his mother did and that's what he expects of me. Well, I can't do that. I wasn't brought up that way. We've talked about it, but he just can't change, or won't change. I can't expect him to. I guess I've seen it coming for some time now. Last year we almost parted ways. I took a long vacation at my sister's home and thought about it a lot. I came back hopeful. Things didn't change much though. Now that I'm teaching I don't have time to put up with all the aggravation. I may love him, but I can't be his wife. I've moved out of the house; I'll be staying with friends until I can find an apartment. A lawyer is drawing up the papers, and it should all be settled shortly. I guess I'm determined to go through with it this time." She was content in her decision.

In ninth grade math period that day only Pearl and Bonita were present, and the three of them talked, spurred on by the roses, of life, of marriage, and of divorce. Therese was impressed with the sensitivity they displayed toward her concern. Several teachers, too, offered her solace: she could call on them for whatever they could do to help or if she ever wanted to talk. She was invited to the Friday after school "T.G.I.F." party that day, and each Friday following.

Therese headed into the holidays mildly content with what had been her first semester as a teacher. She had not only survived, she had made a place for herself. Her commitment to teaching and to the youngsters had strengthened. She had proved to herself that she could teach. She was determined that the progress made would not be lost come January. She was determined to move forward.

*  *  *

Therese is among the earliest arrivers on Tuesday of the second week after the holidays. She rushes in out of the winds and flurrying snow to the warmth of the building. Timmy is there early, also. He greets her and accompanies her to the room where she sorts papers that need to be graded from those which already have been. Timmy talks to her throughout this time. "What's that smell you're wearing?"

"It's perfume, Timmy. Don't you like it?"

"Oh yeah, it's all right. I like it, I guess. You always wear perfume, don't you? And you like to wear earrings. I like those earrings. My sister has earrings like that too. She wears them all the time."

"Sometimes I don't wear earrings. Sometimes I do. It's like you. Sometimes you wear your watch, and sometimes you don't. I like to dress up to come to school. So I fix my hair, and I put on nice clothes, and sometimes I put on earrings."

"I was going to get a new watch for Christmas, but it didn't work out. My Mom says I may get one when I get to high school."

"Say, by the way, how's your work coming in Mr. DeLema's math class?"

"It's okay. He gives us a lot of work. He said that I am doing pretty good, but I don't do well on his quizzes. I may get a D in his class."

"We should work together more so you can do better. How about coming after school a couple days a week?"

"Well, I don't know if I can. Say, when do we go bowling?"

"What makes you think you're going to be one of the people going? Do you think you've earned enough points to go?"

"I've been good. You know, I don't know how many points I have. I don't know how that works. When do we find out who's going?"

"Well, Mr. Simon and Mrs. D and I will sit down on Friday to add up points and decide a cutoff number. Then, if we can make the arrangements, we'll go next Friday."

Robby, another ninth grader, now rushes into the room. "Hey,

Timmy, the gym is open. Let's go shoot some baskets. Mr. Vance will let us until homeroom." Robby darts out. Timmy pulls together his books and papers and heads for the door.

"Timmy, what about that extra help in math?"

"Well, I don't know if I can come after school." The boy is gone.

Therese returns to paper sorting, and checks the supply of materials in each of the learning stations. She reviews in her mind the things she wants to do today. "I've got to see Lynette right off the bat to remind her of our agreement. I've got to think to say something nice to Bonita. I've got to be sure Davey is here for detention after school. I've got to ask at the office if Trace has moved as the kids say he has. I want to check for new home phone numbers for James and Rubin."

Her catalogue is interrupted as Lynette bursts into the room, chased by a boy whom Therese does not recognize. They are laughing and out of breath. "Hi, Lynette. Say do you remember our agreement?" The girl attends more to the boy who now begins to exit, "You're dead, girl! When I get you after school, you'll see." He laughs, and she does too. Then he's gone.

"Lynette, do you remember our agreement? If you are good for two weeks—that means no detentions, no going to the office, no fights—then you and I can spend a Saturday afternoon together. Do you remember?"

"Yeah."

"Well, do you think you're going to make it? You have until Friday. I thought maybe we could go to a movie, if you make it."

"What movie?"

"Well, I don't know. But running down the hall is going to get you in trouble. And who was that fellow? I don't know him. If he doesn't go to school here, you better tell him to stay out of the building."

"He went here last year. What movie can we see?"

"You'd better think first about being good for four more days. Come on, you better go to your homeroom."

"I got time. Let me carry your books. I got time."

Together they head off down the long hall, toward their respective homerooms. Therese wonders if the girl will make the two-week goal, and if it will be of any value in the long run. Halfway down the hall, Bonita and Pearl stand at an open locker. Therese stops. "Bonita, hello. Gee, that's a nice purse you have there. Did you get it for Christmas?"

"No, It's old." Bonita glares back. Pearl shoves something in the locker and shuts the door.

"Well, it does look very nice. It matches your sweater too." The girl remains unresponsive. Therese continues down the hall, and Pearl and Bonita return their attention to the locker. At the doors to the auditorium, Therese insists that Lynette give up the books and head toward her own homeroom. The girl does so with a sprint that could easily win her an office referral. Therese turns and enters the shared homeroom.

Homeroom goes by much as it always has. Attendance is first, followed by a handful of announcements. Momentarily, Mr. Roberts, the principal, looks in through the doors but says nothing and leaves. Small talk with the youngsters and a few moments shared with Mr. Chesney fill the time. "Have you found any use for that paddle I made for you?"

"Well, yes. I've used it a couple times now. But not much, really."

The bell rings and the youngsters bolt through the doors. Therese hurries too, through the crowded halls and down to the EMR suite of rooms. The seventh graders are there, nearly all, ready for class to begin.

Davey is in the room as well. When Therese enters he goes with her to her desk. He clasps her forearm. "Hey, Miss Stevens, are you going to marry me? Now that you're not married, are you going to marry me?"

"Davey, let go of my arm. You know what I'll do if you don't behave well."

"Man, you're always sending me down to the office. It's not fair. You never send anyone else down there."

"Let go of my arm. Now." The boy releases her. "Aren't you supposed to be with Mrs. D this period? You'd better go to class."

"That old hag. I hate her. She don't teach me nothing."

"Maybe you don't give her a chance. Go ahead, go to class, before you're late." The boy lingers, and begins to bully one of the seventh graders. "Davey, I'm going to write a referral right now if you don't go." Therese readies the pad of blank referrals and a pen.

The boys looks at her across the room, frowns, and mutters some-thing as he goes to the adjoining room. "Man, you. . . ."

Therese begins the math lesson. "Do all of you have a ruler now?" She surveys the room for exceptions. "Okay, I'm going to give each of you a different size piece of colored paper. I want you to trace it on to your paper and then measure it on each side."

"Mrs. Gorman, why aren't we doing stations today?"

"Dummy! Why, don't you know that her name is Miss Stevens, now that she is divorced?" Lester chides his classmate, and Joey is embarrased by his mistake.

"That's all right, Lester, I sometimes forget myself that my name has changed. Joey will try to remember from now on. Joey, I explained yesterday that we would work on stations three days a week, and on a unit on measurement the other two. That way we're not always doing the same thing. Okay?"

The boy nods, and the class sets to work. Therese moves among them keeping them on task, correcting their errors, answering their questions. After twenty minutes or so most of the youngsters have completed the simple task of tracing and measuring. Therese suggests that they exchange papers and do it again. Two boys com-plain that they don't want to, but with a bit of coaxing are soon engaged in the task. The second time it goes more quickly; there are fewer questions and fewer mistakes. "Okay. Now choose something in the room to measure. Don't choose something too big. Choose something straight or flat." The youngsters move about the room deciding upon and noting the size of various objects. "No, Lester, I don't think you should measure Laurie's head. It's not straight or flat enough." Everyone chuckles at the joke, including the girl. Just before the bell rings, Therese collects the materials and papers. "Now that was a good class. You all get points toward bowling. How many of you learned something?" Half the youngsters raise their hands. "Tomorrow we'll do stations. Do you all remember which station you were working on? Check your folders." The bell rings and again the room is the center of traffic.

Davey comes in, but stands at some distance. He glares for a moment at Therese and then exits. Bonita and Pearl come in and sit down. "Bonita, I really do like that purse."

Pearl now retorts, "You like it so much you can have it. Bonita don't like it half as much as you. Bonita will give it to you." Pearl snickers at her offer, and coaxes Bonita to agree. Bonita remains silent. "Maybe Bonita will sell it to you for five dollars. Bonita needs the money." Pearl now begins to take the idea half seriously.

But Therese quickly puts an end to it. "No, I don't need another purse. I was just saying how nice it looked." Therese gathers her books and heads out of the room as Jeff enters. "They're all yours Mr. Simon. Enjoy your class."

Therese heads for the home economics room where Lynette will be this period. The girl is not there, unexplainedly. "I haven't seen her, Miss Stevens. Do you want me to send for you if she shows up?" Therese decides to use the time instead to make phone calls. In a workroom off the main office she finds a telephone and the quiet she needs to converse. Seven parents are on her list: three she has never met or spoken with before; with three she has tried to keep regular contact; one is the parent of a new ninth grade boy.

"Hello, Mrs. Thomson? This is Miss Stevens, Perry's teacher at school. I just wanted to let you know that Perry has been doing pretty well this week, and I was hoping you'd take a moment to encourage him to keep up the effort. . . . No, I didn't know about that. But I'll ask him about it when I see him at study hall." The conversation continues for several minutes, and ends on a good note as Perry's mother thanks Therese for calling.

Five more phone calls are tried. Two numbers have been disconnected or changed. For two there was no answer. Robby's father answers the last attempt; the conversation is brief and dry. Therese is just able to convince him that Robby is not in trouble. He too appreciates her interest. The planning period is consumed.

Therese gathers her materials and heads to the study hall. After a month or so of lunchroom duty, she has once again been assigned to supervise study hall. Ann had asked that Therese return to the former duty, and though Therese preferred the other she did not complain of the switch. She reaches the auditorium just before classes begin to change, and as the students enter she prepares to check the seating chart against the youngsters present.

"Judy, you're not supposed to sit there. Move over three seats."

"But we have to work on this together, Linda and me."

"You can't talk in study hall. Now move over."

"Mrs. D always let us work together."

"I want you to move." Reluctantly the girl changes seats, and

Therese completes taking attendance. Ann, who has stood by answering several students' questions, now folds her arms and tells the youngsters to get busy studying.

"But Mrs. D'Angelo, I need help on this."

"Mrs. D'Angelo, can I go to the bathroom?"

The woman moves to the front corner of the room, and there remains silent and staring. Therese sits at a desk on the stage. She watches the youngsters and occasionally reprimands those who are on the verge of mischief. Toward the end of the period Ann leaves; Therese notices, but thinks little of it. The period ends, and again Therese gathers her books and papers.

The youngsters have gone and just as Therese is about to exit, Ann comes in. "I'm sorry about leaving you alone this period."

"Oh, that's all right. Everything went fine." Therese notices that Ann has been crying. "Are you okay?"

"Yes, I guess so." She begins to cry again. "I just can't understand it. When I'm in here alone, the kids just don't listen. They're so bad. But you came back and in one day you had them in order. Why can't I do that?"

"Ann, you shouldn't let that bother you so much." They take a pair of seats in the auditorium and sit to talk. Therese pats Ann on the forearm. "You see, together we handle the study hall. You do one thing and I do another. The only way I can keep order is by not attending to what the students ask about, and complain about, and want to do. If I listened to all of that, it would be chaos. So I remain strict and hard. You could do the same thing if you just didn't listen so well. And when you say you'll send them to the office, do it. Or they soon learn you don't mean it. But don't feel so bad about it. We can do this together." Therese speaks sincerely. Ann has become a close friend.

*   *   *

The first bowling expedition went well. Very well, actually. The youngsters who had gone—three-fourths of the EMR classes—enjoyed the trip and were very well behaved. The manager of the lanes invited them back whenever they could come. Jeff and Ann and Therese revelled in the success it represented, and in the hope it held for rewarding future good behavior. "The next time, we should be more particular in giving out points; we don't want this to become too easy." Plans were set for another visit in three weeks.

Lynette never made the two-week good behavior goal. Always something would happen. Therese began to grow weary of sustaining her support for the girl, especially when it seemed that Lynette put forth so little effort herself. Therese was puzzled, but still continued the offer, hopeful.

January showed Therese that the progress she had made in the first half of the year was not lost. She had, in many ways, strengthened the base she had earlier established. The bowling trips were a sign that the team could work well together; they were supportive of one another. She was an important part of the team. On her own, she initiated steps to address particular problems. The agreement with Lynette, the attention to Bonita, the handling of Davey—all were signs of increasing competence. Therese had begun to contact parents regularly, speaking for herself and for the team. Though it was time consuming, and not always immediately productive, Therese felt it was important and useful in the long run. She had also begun to plan and teach as she believed she should. The unit on measurement promised to be successful; for the ninth graders, a unit on how to set up an apartment was both practical and involving. She saw herself really teaching for the first time.

The end of January and all of February brought the full force of winter storms to the city. Paralyzed by snow and bitter cold, urban life slowed; emergency procedures had to be put to use to supply many vital services. The schools closed as fuels grew scarce, and special arrangements for continuing with education had to be made.

For the EMR youngsters the closing of school essentially brought a halt to their work. The youngsters could not function well on independent study, and the weekly meetings at a new location provided little more than time away from home for the few who attended. Two field trips during this time—one to the City Science Museum, and one to the County Court—were well attended and were worthwile. Therese spent part of the time visiting homes herself and preparing materials for the eventual return to normalcy.

In March, winter subsided and school did resume. The youngsters seemed anxious to return. The closing of school had taken a large part of their lives away. They seemed glad to return to their friends and their teachers. Once again, points began to accumulate toward a trip to the bowling lanes. Learning stations and newly planned units got underway too. Also returning were some of the individual problems and heartaches of working with these youngsters.

In the teacher's lounge a new topic dominated discussion. The impending court ruling on desegregation had generated many rumors throughout the city district. Teacher reassignment on a massive scale apparently had many teachers worried. "But not here at Wilson. I found out—I guess I was sort of surprised—that no one expects Wilson to be much hurt by this. The teachers say we can only get better as a result. Teachers leave Wilson as soon as they can, anyway. So, some are even looking forward to it. But most of the teachers here feel that, if anything, Wilson will be better off. Of course that doesn't account for the teachers who will be coming here against their wishes."

Talk of desegregation was complicated with talk of teacher cutbacks. "They say we'll lose four or five next year. I'm one of the newest people here. But I was told that Mr. Roberts likes the way the EMR program is going, and he won't split up the team. Well, it's also true that they need three of us here, and maybe more. So I think I'm pretty secure in my job, even if there are cutbacks made. I've thought about it some, and I don't know if I'd like to leave here. I like working with Jeff and Ann. We get along well. I'm not sure I'd find that elsewhere."

In the second week back, Mr. Roberts sent Therese a note that she had to be observed twice before the end of the year, and the observations had to be two months apart. There was a need to do one quickly. Therese was surprised by the sudden urgency, but not particularly concerned about the observations and consequent evaluation. Mr. Roberts had instructed her to pick a time and date and notify him of her choice. Therese talked with her mother about the process. "She's been teaching many years, and even so, she's having a hard time with the evaluation this year. It's got her pretty upset. I don't know if it's that she wants things to be perfect or if it just gets harder after so many years."

Therese chose a seventh grade math period; it was the least difficult of her classes. She had planned to do something special, but was absent the day before the observation. "I just came in and did what I normally would have done. I sent Mr. Roberts a note to remind him to come in. It's a good thing I did, because he's one to forget it. Well, he observed for about thirty minutes, then got up and left. He made no comment, no note. That bothered me more than anything, I suppose. At least he could have said something. I tried to catch him after school but I couldn't find him in his office. Oh well, I think it went well."

Sometimes things did not go well. Early in April, Therese had a particularly exhausting and trying day. "It was really bad today. I think all the teachers felt that way. I was pushed and shoved all day long. First, I was separating Rubin from Denise—she usually gets herself into situations she cannot get out of—I had to pull him off her. Well, he turned and grabbed my arm and pulled so hard, I thought it would come out. Then Lester was choking Lynette. I mean really choking her. I don't know why. She was crying and he came charging through the doorway and nearly knocked me over. I couldn't stop him.

"Davey is going to court. His mother wants help with him. I've spoken to her but I don't fully understand what's happened. She has her hands full at home with Davey and his brothers. I hate to call her anymore to complain. I feel sorry for her. Well, today, Davey did it again. He was messing with the dirt in the flower pots, spilling it all over my desk. I started to clean it up and he started spilling it on my hands. I pushed his hand away and he slapped my hand. I said, 'Davey, please don't!' But he didn't stop. I spend so much time talking to him, giving him so much attention. It's like he needs all this attention just to get by. Later I found my purse full of dirt. I don't know who did that.

"Finally, after class I noticed that Billy had a cigarette behind his ear, I told him to put it away but he wouldn't. So I took it. Well, he grabbed my purse and wouldn't give it back. I felt tears come into my eyes. I just walked out of the room and thought, 'Let him have it.' Even Davey tried to get it back for me but he couldn't; he saw how upset I was. Later Jeff got it for me. I don't know how. It was just a lousy day. Ann and even Jeff agreed. After school the lounge was full of teachers who felt that way."

Jeff and Therese talked about her feelings and the way teaching sometimes is. "You know, Therese, I read an article about people who get divorced. They go through stages afterward. I'd say you're at the stage when you need nurturance and you need to achieve." Therese wasn't sure. "I don't know if I am or not, but I don't feel that simple." Therese's personal life had stabilized. She had found a nice apartment and she was beginning to make new friends. "Sometimes it gets pretty lonely being alone. But now friends call sometimes or stop by. The woman who lives next door teaches; we get together and talk.

"Sometimes I think I'm not as dedicated as I should be. I don't take work home as much as I did. Oh, I get it all done, but I try to do it at school. When I go home I'm tired, and I want to do something for myself. If it's been a bad day, I don't want to think of school. Sometimes I find myself saying, 'Those damn brats, they don't deserve me!' But I really don't feel that way."

It was the end of April before Therese had heard anything about the observation Mr. Roberts had made. Then it was only that she should schedule a second appointment for sometime early in May. She did so, and once again things seemed to go well. Mr. Roberts first observed Ann's class, and then came into Therese's. After ten minutes he asked if he was supposed to be watching her or Jeff. Minutes later he left. At the day's end, he stopped Therese in the hall and told her how well he thought her class was going. He was not noted for his compliments, and Therese felt good about his praise. It helped to confirm her confidence.

Shortly after the day of the visit, Therese again had cause to examine her dedication. With but a few minutes to go in the last period, Lester slammed the window on her fingers. It was accidental, but Lester had been fooling around. Therese's hand bled, and she was in great pain. She told the class to dismiss themselves at the bell, and she headed off down the hall, bleeding and crying. "I never felt so vulnerable as I do as a teacher. You can get hurt so many ways. I'm not used to being hurt. At times like this I want to transfer right out of here. I feel like forgetting these kids. In many ways they need me. Jeff has talked about transferring. He could do it anytime he wants. But he doesn't. He always stays on. Besides, transferring would mean starting all over again—new people, new procedures, new kids. There would be no guarantee that it would be any better. Most junior highs are pretty much alike, I guess. I'll probably just stay here." The wound required some stitches, and a visit to the hospital. Therese took the next day off, calling Mr. Roberts to explain. He raised no objection.

*   *   *

The bell rings and the seventh graders begin to exit. Robby

comes in from Mrs. D's class and approaches Therese. "Can I stay here this period?"

"Where are you supposed to be, Robby?"

"Well, I finished my thing in shop and Mr. Chesney says it's too late to start a new one now."

"So what will you do if you go to shop this period?"

"I don't know. Nothing."

"Then take this note to Mr. Chesney to tell him you'll be with me. Then we can work on math."

"I ain't going to work, but I'll be right back." Robby rushes out of the room. Other youngsters mill about. Rubin and Perry chase one another, and Lynette somehow becomes involved. The three topple a chair and desk and then hurry to the adjoining room before they can be reprimanded.

Davey swings open the door and announces himself. "Hello, Miss Stevens, it's me." He comes over to her and grabs her arm. "Did you miss me?" This is his first day back from a week's suspension.

"Davey, let go, now. Or you'll end up in the office."

"Let me see your hand. How is it? Does it hurt still?"

"It's okay, now." She shows him the scar as he releases her arm. "It will be completely healed in a while." She returns to her paperwork. "You'd better go to class. You'll be late." Just then the bell rings; Rubin walks in; both are late. Davey puts his arms around her: "Are you my girl?"

"Davey, let me go! I've told you, you should not behave that way. Now, let go." He releases her, and he and Rubin chuckle as they head into Ann's class. "You don't know what you got in me, honey." And he slams the door behind him.

Momentarily, Robby comes back in. "What did Mr. Chesney say, Robby?" She continues sorting papers.

"He said it's all right."

"Come on, let's do some math. Get your folder out."

"I'm not working. I told you I wasn't working. I got better things to do than math."

"What? Like what? Go ahead, get your folder."

The boy delays. "What are you doing?"

"Just putting these stations in order. Someone mixed up the sheets of paper. While you're sitting at my desk, why don't you straighten out the things under the plate of glass. Fox and Lynette messed them up. But be careful to not break the glass and get cut."

Robby eagerly sets about the task as Therese continues with her own. The two work for minutes in silence. Robby arranges the pictures, lists, and cards in a design. "Where do you want this, Miss Stevens?"

"What is it?"

"It's a poem. I don't like poems." The boy reads it, half to himself.

> I believe I am always
> divinely guided.
>
> I believe I will always
> take the right turn of the road.
>
> I believe God will make a way
> when there is no way.

"What does this mean, Miss Stevens? Why do you keep it on your desk?"

"Well, sometimes I think about it, Robby. It's sort of there to remind me."

"I don't like poems. Where do you want it on the desk?"

"You choose a place. You're doing that very nicely." The boy places the poem where it best fits into his design, and carefully replaces the glass plate. He momentarily admires his work.

"What else can I do?"

"Why don't you get your math folder now? I'll be done here in a second."

"I told you I wasn't going to work."

"It won't hurt, you know." But Robby sits there at Therese's desk. He begins to thumb through a hot rod magazine which he carries with him. He waits for her to finish, so they can talk some more.

# Just Keeping Up

Scott Tanner stands at the front door of Meadows Elementary. On each side, the wings of the one-story structure stretch out, forming a slight angle. Back across the street two churches, Methodist and Baptist, govern large plots of land. The air of middle America provides the breeze on this already warm morning in the first week of school. The early school bus arrives, and a small boy bounds off first, reminding Scott of "Cypher in the Snow," a film that deeply affected him.

> I mean, the kid died! He just stepped off the bus, fell into the snow, and died. And when the school people tried to find out more about him, they realized no one at school really knew him. He died of neglect . . . lonesomeness . . . I cried for him . . . I promised myself then that would not happen in my class.

Scott smiles at the youngster as he reaches the door, and he smiles back at the young, handsome fourth grade teacher.

Scott enters the building behind the first wave of children, checks in at the office, and heads off down the west wing toward his room. He passes the library, a third grade room, and two other fourth grades before he comes to his own. Each room bares its interior through plate glass walls to the corridor. In several of the rooms he notices colleagues making ready for the day's encounter. Once in his own room, Scott does the same. It's warm and he opens the low sash windows which line the outside wall. Above them plate glass rises to the ceiling. His room opens to the north revealing a grassy playground, a backdrop of thick woods. He sits at his desk and welcomes the first arrivers.

He is casual, at ease. He wants to get to know the students, and he wants them to feel free to come to him with their problems. He feels that's important and he works on establishing a good rapport. At 8:30 the class is nearly full and he takes attendance: "Anne" (bright red hair and bright intellectually). "James" (a tall, quiet, boy who needs encouragement). "Melissa. Danny. Katie. Donna. Steve." (More often it's Stephen, a slight, smiling child who quietly finds distraction from most activities.) "Margie . . . Margaret!" (a girl always about her own agenda). "Thom. Cristy. Joseph S. Jane. Daryl. Lucy. . . ." And so on, the list totaling thirty-two. "Will those absent please raise your hands." Everyone chuckles. Five absences again today—students who are on family vacations. They'll miss the first week or more and complicate Scott's planning. The real work cannot begin until the full class is present. Reading groups and math groups will be formed on test results, and testing must be delayed. Scott hopes that he can fudge his way through the remainder of this week, also giving himself time to wade into the massive curriculum guides he has been told to follow. Next week is testing and the first real lessons will take place. Things should get off the ground. This week means establishing rapport, getting to know individuals, setting routines, and handling paperwork.

Attendance completed, Scott begins the daily money collections. There are several, and it takes time. The students occupy themselves. "While I'm doing this, some of you should finish cutting and coloring your hands that we started yesterday. When I'm done we'll put them on the bulletin board." At the back of the room, a display titled, "Hand it to the Fourth Grade," is partially complete; traced and cut and colored paper hands with students' names dot the board; more than half have yet to be added. "Now I'll collect PTA dues. . . . Margie, please put your lunch away and start working. . . . Does anyone have PTA dues?" The students surround his desk. He is casual, smiling, accepting. In the class, the noise level builds as students move, and chatter, and wait. "Mr. Tanner, can I move from this desk to that one? I want to sit over there." He agrees, and the girl moves her belongings. Since the first day students have felt free to move to as yet unclaimed seats. Scott now notices the developing decibels: "Hey, what's all that noise out there?" Above the wall of youngsters he peers out. "If you've finished your hands, work on this English assignment." Packets and books are distributed; students settle into quiet work. One student whispers, "I hate English," and calls on the teacher to reexplain the instructions. "Oh, now I get it. Okay."

Money matters and paperwork have consumed enough time, and Scott finishes. He joins the class. "Bring your hands to the back of the class and we'll put them on the board." Students once again line up. Scott looks at each product, compliments the work, and asks where it should be positioned. While the boys and girls choose, Scott pats them on the back and smiles. "Margie, please put that comb away. This is not a beauty parlor." He tries to bring her back into the activity. "Do you have the English assignment done?"

For English, the students list the sounds various animals make. For most it is not difficult, but Margie has trouble. She comes to him, now, once again at his desk. She doesn't know the spelling of "meow." "Then spell 'ow,' if you can't spell 'meow.'" Margie masters this word, but cannot make the phonetic leap. Other students have now come to the teacher's desk. Eight witness her inability, and examine the various papers and objects on his desk. "Margaret, it's simple. Spell 'me,' then 'ow.'" She finally succeeds. He compliments her and thanks the other students for being patient. She returns to her desk, but immediately puts the paper aside; a bottle of glue captures her attention. She begins to cut and paste. Scott attends to the remaining youngsters. "Stephen, this is sloppy. Start again on a new paper." One by one the questions are fielded, and mistakes corrected. He makes the rounds of the class. Students are at work, but unpressured. They frequently take time to talk, to get drinks from the fountain in back, to sharpen pencils, to tease and taunt, to visit friends. If he notices these activities, they seem not to bother Scott. Students are, after all, getting work done. Only when the noise level rises, or a youngster oversteps the limits of behavior does Scott step in. So far, he hasn't had to do so often. But he is aware that to some youngsters he's already spoken several times. Stephen returns with a corrected paper. "That's much better. That's good."

With some time before recess Scott begins a review of the English assignment. He sits at an unoccupied student desk in the center of the room. The students eagerly volunteer to answer.

"Thom, what did you write for question 7?" Stephen unobtrusively moves to another seat, where he is away from Daryl, who has been bothering him. Bobby, James, and Danny are behind Scott in his present position, and they pay less attention. "Well, I never heard an animal make that sound before, but if you say so, I trust you." Outside, the first shift, the third graders are at recess. Their noise temporarily distracts the class, now cued that their own morning break is minutes away. The assignment review continues, less enthusiastically, until it is time to line up. Chaos momentarily breaks out, and Scott has the students return to their seats. "Now line up quietly and two-by-two. When everyone is lined up we'll go out." Mrs. Drew, another fourth grade teacher, enters to remind Scott that today is his turn to watch the recess. Her class has already exited, and Scott dismisses his own class.

The youngsters charge outdoors and their energies are dissipated over the vast playing area. Some students rush to the grass where stand swings and climbing bars; others stick to the asphalted surface bouncing basketballs and shooting for the nets. Off in the distance a group of youngsters nearly reach the permitted limits of the playground as they rush, tag and taunt one another. Stephen has incurred the wrath of another boy and comes charging, "Mr. Tanner, he's going to hit me!" Scott puts a stop to the chase and reprimands both boys. Alan has skinned a knee in falling from a swing. Tears and blood flow, and Scott sends him to the office. Katie and four other girls stick near Mr. Tanner through all this, filling his free moments with questions and comments. Suddenly, Scott grabs a wayward basketball and shoots. He misses, and misses twice more. The youngsters delight in his involvement, noticing that, "Mr. Tanner played ball with us." Quickly, the fifteen minutes are gone and he must usher them back to their classrooms. The whistle catches everyone's attention, but some are very slow to respond. The three lines of fourth graders are noisy and rocking. "We'll wait until everyone is here and quiet." They are yet boisterous. "I want it quiet before you can go in!" When the last stragglers reach the ends of the lines, he has Mrs. Drew's class start in, only half satisfied with their orderliness. And his thoughts jump back to the classroom, the English lesson, and ahead to the hours of school that remain this week.

* * *

The second week came, and with it came more students. Testing, grouping, and the real work of the fourth grade began and

Scott's planning could not keep up. Tests had revealed a wide range of abilities and Scott wondered how these differences could be met: "I can't give each student a different assignment each day in each subject. That would be impossible." The curriculum guides sat at home stacked on the dining room table, and each night they haunted; they were what should be done, what had to be done, but what Scott didn't know how to do. They were too much. He found himself sitting, staring blankly at reruns of Lucille Ball comedies, or sleeping until well into the evening. He was sapped of his energy, his motivation, and his patience.

The second week melted into the third, the fourth, and the fifth weeks. Planning remained the biggest problem, but it was joined by classroom management. Each day Scott brought in new assignments, usually dittoed worksheets and packets. Each day the Katies and the Annes and the Josephs finished early: "Mr. Tanner, I've finished this; now what should I do?"

"Don't come to me and ask me what's next! You have your math and English books you can study. But don't always come to me!" And Scott was hard pressed to see that the Stephens and the Margies and the Daryls finished at all. Students finished with the assignments, and students avoiding them moved about the room at will; some went to the library or restrooms while Scott worked intensively with reading groups or individuals. The drone and chatter were punctuated by frequent calls to order: Scott would raise his voice, and the students would settle. Momentarily, their activity resumed.

Scott grew frustrated. He did not seem to be able to plan so that the students would be engaged in the lessons for more than a fraction of the time. He did not seem to be able to monitor their actions and teach at the same time. Scott turned to the instructional coordinator for help. She offered to help him plan activities for the class, and to share materials he could use with individual students. But several days, then a week went by and she had not followed through on her offers. Scott was disappointed and was unsure whether he should approach her again. When several other teachers intimated, in conversation, that she was not to be trusted, Scott turned away.

Mrs. Drew and Mrs. Petaskey, the other two fourth grade teachers, had many years of experience between them. They were the kind of people to whom Scott would have readily turned for help. But they gave limited response. Mrs. Drew was cheerful and competent, but always seemed busy with matters involving her own class. Mrs. Petaskey was competent, but cold; the students did not like her even as much as they liked Scott. On Scott's birthday, the kids threw a surprise party for him at which Mrs. Drew administered an embarrassing series of birthday whacks. Yet two days before, Mrs. Petaskey's birthday went by, noticed but unheralded. With his two colleagues, Scott divided reading groups and shared the supervision of recess. But they did not help him with his class problems. And when they talked him into teaching science to all three classes—"Scott, didn't you teach science in your student teaching?" "Well, yes, but only for a short while, and I worked with sixth graders."—they actually added to his planning problems.

The first science classes were pain and pleasure. He pleaded with his own class to behave for the other teachers. "If you do nothing else for me today, go out and behave like little ladies and gentlemen." The other two fourth grades rotated into Scott's room for twenty minute periods. "They sat there, they discussed, they listened. I think they actually learned something. I wish I could teach like that all the time, all day long." But when his own class returned, they raved about how well they had behaved and praised the other teachers for such good lessons. "Mr. Tanner, it was so gooooood!" Scott did not react. But to himself he said, "Maybe it's me."

Recess was a reprieve. The hot days of early September had given way to mild and sometimes cool midmornings in November. For fifteen minutes Scott could be as he wanted with the kids. Girls would crowd around and hold his arms and jacket. Minor spats were resolved with a firm gaze and a directive. Disputes over balls and jump ropes and space were successfully negotiated. "Mr. Tanner, can I hold the door after recess?" A girl asks for a prized responsibility.

"Melissa and Cristy have already asked. You can do it tomorrow." The girl cries. He responds and negotiates for her to have the responsibility today. The problem is solved. Scott can play, roughhouse, and contest with the youngsters. They assure him of their affection on the playground.

In the classroom he felt the affection was betrayed. He planned as best he could. He rearranged the room and seating several times.

He altered the schedules. He increased the workload. The students frustrated his every effort. He called for their cooperation. He demanded their compliance. "Daryl, why are your papers not in the folder? You must stop roaming and settle to work. You've got a lot to get done." He set lower goals: "All right, give me ten minutes of quiet work. See if you can do that much," only to feel that these were not being met. Scott grew unsure of what kinds of academic performance he could expect from fourth graders. He grew impatient with their misbehavior. "I feel totally frustrated. I can't get these kids to be quiet and to do their work. They're not learning anything. We're wasting our time being here."

A parent questioned him during conferences about what went on in class: "Cristy comes home with no homework. She says that she's bored with school, that she gets everything done in just a short while and then has nothing to do." It was true. Cristy was one of the youngsters who consistently finished early. Scott could not keep up with her work pace. He suggested to the father that soon a learning center would be set up at the back of the room. It would keep the students more active and interested. The man pressed him for how soon it would be ready, and Scott committed himself to a one-week deadline.

His suspicion of his own inadequate performance seemed confirmed. Within a week a second confirmation came. Before a faculty meeting got underway, the teachers shared bits and pieces of their successes this year. Some spoke of the plans they were making for upcoming activities. Scott had none to share, and though no one probably noticed, he was shaken. "I can't go on any longer. The kids are frustrated and so am I. I've got to get things together." He turned to the principal for help. Mr. Kimball was well liked by the staff, though it was only his first year at Meadows Elementary. He was seen as a person who would take action. Scott was inclined to respect his judgment, and to trust him. He needed his help.

Mr. Kimball had observed Scott's class earlier, but everything went just as planned. The lesson was good and the students behaved well. None of Scott's rough points showed. Mr. Kimball was impressed with what he saw. Now Scott was faced with the difficult task of opening up, of revealing the problems unnoticed earlier. It had to be done. On the day after the faculty meeting, Scott went to the principal and talked. They talked for an hour and a half. Mr.

Kimball made a number of points that Scott found helpful. He arranged for Scott to observe a male elementary teacher in another school. He suggested that Scott adjust the morning schedule so he could meet with each of the four reading groups. Scott functioned exceptionally well in small groups, and this strength should be used. The meeting had been worthwhile, and several subsequent meetings reaffirmed the principal's support.

Changes were occurring in the class. Since the opening week of school, Scott had tried different desk arrangements, had created activity areas, and had adjusted schedules, searching for the right combination. These were surface changes. Deeper changes were occurring in Scott himself. The frustrations were wearing on him. The casualness with which he had handled the class dissolved and in its place a stiffness formed. After a cold and windy morning recess the students came in boisterously. "What is going on! You should come in and sit down. Get ready for the spelling test." Mutterings, excuses, and complaints were given no heed. A gruffness peppered Scott's manner.

The development of the learning center was a change that pleased Scott. Now functional, it relieved some of the pressures he felt earlier. New ideas and activities could be easily injected into the class, without having to engage every student. The Annes and Cristys could be kept busy while Scott worked with the reading groups. It was a tangible accomplishment. The learning center worked.

The work with the reading groups also provided a sense of satisfaction. With groups of four or five, more than with the whole class, Scott saw progress. The students, too, seemed to like their work in reading groups. Home-made flash cards provided the excitement one morning for the lowest reading group. "What does this word mean, Bobby?"

"It means pulling behind . . . like, on the ground." Scott pushed for a clearer definition, and an example of how the word could be used.

To the class, "All right, shhh!"

Two boys came to Scott in the group with papers: "Mr. Tanner, how is this?" He reviewed and praised their work.

He stopped to correct two students who had not been working as they should. "If you have nothing to do, you should have library books. If you don't bring books, you'll get a whack for each day you are without them." Scott didn't necessariy use the paddle, but the threat was now part of his manner. His attention went back to the reading group. For a while, the class was subdued. "What about this word? How do you pronounce it.?"

The lowest group responded enthusiastically. "I like doing this, Mr. Tanner."

"Good! We'll have more words tomorrow." He was pleased.

In the whole class setting, his warmth cooled. "Quiet! There's no reason for talking. You should be at work." The students, indeed, did more work. But not always were the demands met. "Daryl, I want you to do a better job than this. Take your time with the handwriting." The boy cried; the remark had unexpected impact. Scott's hard shell cracked. He returned to Daryl and comforted, consoled, and encouraged him. Daryl worked on, taking his time, refusing to be distracted by his friends.

The deep greens of the backdrop woods turned fall-colored, then brown. Leaves fell, and thoughts of Thanksgiving gave way to thoughts of Christmas. Scott waited for vacation. Even with its successes, teaching school had become taxing. The rewards were less than expected, the challenges more demanding. "Teaching requires so much work. There's something that's got to be done every night." Vacations were times to get away. They were times to put aside work and live a personal life. They were cherished.

As events would have it, the term from Thanksgiving to Christmas was the last long series of school days until nearly spring. For, shortly after school reopened in January, Scott became ill; strep throat kept him from school for a week. It provided an unexpected, but welcomed extension to the holiday break. Scott was reluctant to return to school. But January was bitterly cold, and natural gas supplies for Meadows Elementary and the whole region ran short, unable to keep up with demand. Stores, factories and businesses took emergency procedures to conserve. Schools too were affected. Early in the crisis school was open on a day-to-day basis. A telephone grapevine supplemented the local news broadcasts, and each evening brought word of tomorrow's status: open or closed. One morning Scott made his way through the frigid air and unmelting snow to the front doors of the school only to discover that news of the cancellation had not reached him. Somehow the grapevine had snapped.

Planning and teaching on a day-to-day basis was untenable. By February 1, many school days had been missed, and the long-range weather forecasts promised twenty-eight more days of the same calamitous weather. More decisive action was called for. The central administration decided to close those schools that relied on natural gas heating. Meadows Elementary was one. The few school buildings which had alternative souces of heating would remain open and would serve the entire system on a rotating basis. Students were to be provided assignments for work at home, and once each week they would meet the teachers at a designated school building to hand in completed work and receive new assignments. Additionally, teachers were expected to remain home to answer students' questions via phone, and to meet with small groups of students wherever and whenever that could be arranged.

Scott was not enthused about the arrangements that had been made. Few of the teachers were. Preparing work packets which had to stand independent of instruction seemed bound to produce limited results. Meeting with small groups of students was desirable, but difficult to arrange. Even in the first weeks it became obvious that the crisis would bring a halt to much of the work of his fourth grade class. Working at home some students did not complete the assignments, or permitted errors to go unchecked. Students did not come to the small group lessons which had been planned. "We waited for a while, but only Melissa showed up. So what I had planned was of no use. I worked with her, instead, on long division which she needed a lot of help with. We worked for about an hour and a half. In that regard I guess it was good." But overall, the effort seemed futile. For three weeks it continued, and then, as intended, spring vacation and a series of emergency days were placed back-to-back to provide a break which would stretch into March, when warmer weather was hoped for. The crisis, the vacations, the cancellations would be over. School would resume for the first time since December.

The days went by quickly, and because of the weather the break was hardly satisfying. Scott sat on Sunday, March 6th, the day before school resumed, with piles of ungraded papers and packets. He sketched out the classwork for the upcoming week. He wondered how much the students had forgotten, how much could realistically be learned in the remainder of the year, and how class routines and study habits had been affected by the prolonged closing. Even with these worries in mind he was ready to go back. The thought of getting back into a routine was appealing.

* * *

It's Thursday and the students have another new seating arrangement. They enter the classroom and wait until attendance, money matters, and paperwork are completed. Only fifteen minutes are needed for these preliminaries. Scott begins the day by assigning work. "All right, sit down. This sheet is what I want you to start on, and then do the assignment for your group written on the board." Several students complain that Greg has broken all of one girl's pencils. Greg denies the charge. "Did you do that, Greg?" A stern gaze at the boy brings no confession, and Scott drops the matter with no further comment. The youngsters now begin to blame Danny for the damage. The girl again appeals to Scott: "Mr. Tanner, Danny broke these pencils."

"It sounds like a personal problem that you two should settle." Again the matter is dropped.

"Mr. Tanner, you gave us the easiest worksheet."

"Good," and the matter is dropped. "Group 3, meet at the reading table. I want quiet in the class."

Scott sits with a small group. "Hi, gang!" he greets them warmly. "Bobby, you got a haircut, didn't you?" The reading begins, and with this group it goes slowly. Scott and the youngsters are patient as one boys reads. The class grows a bit louder, though the students are at work: "Shhh! Jana, sit down." The story is about a king and his kingdom. "Do you know the meaning of the word 'sire'?" Several definitions are offered and Scott accepts those that come close. A momentary gaze at two boys across the room attracts their attention and redirects their energies.

"How do you know so much about kings, Mr. Tanner?"

"I used to watch movies when I was a kid."

"Did they have TV's back then?"

"Of course, I'm not that old." Everyone laughs and Scott pats the youngster on the shoulder. They enjoy this reading group. The rest of the class continues, fairly quiet; no one seems to have finished yet.

* * *

Class that day went well. There were less hassles. Scott had not

. lost his touch with small groups. But problems with the whole class had not disappeared either. They were baffling. The problems came to a head later that month when a student's mother requested that her child be transferred to another class. Cristy's mom was a volunteer and had become familiar with the school. She made the request of Mr. Kimball but also spoke to Scott: "It's not that I think you're a bad teacher, Mr. Tanner. I just think Cristy learns better from a different style of instruction." Scott spoke with the principal and they decided that the request should be granted. Scott was left with many doubts: How could he explain the change to his own students? What would the other teachers think? Was he really that bad a teacher?

The matter was quickly handled, but Scott was stunned. "For three days I was really depressed. I was so disappointed in myself." The event was followed by a series of other events which helped to shift his focus. Mr. Kimball left Scott a note that he would be in to observe again. He had also arranged for Scott to observe another teacher. And the instructional coordinator, new since March 7th, announced that she too would observe his classes and offer help. The sudden interest in Scott's work was unexplained other than by the matter of the transfer. Yet the connection was never clearly drawn. Scott was caught up in a flurry of activity, and the transfer was all but forgotten.

Through April and May, the instructional coordinator came to Scott's fourth grade regularly. She made observations and shared those with Scott. She helped him plan activities that would interest the youngsters and occupy their time. "She told me that I have a natural ability for working with kids. I've always wanted to be really good at something. Some people have it in music, some in art, some in sports. She said mine was working with kids. And she said that I would be very easy to work with. I felt really good."

His appreciation of her help grew. They planned activities and coordinated the workload. Scott almost immediately felt the changes in his class. "I've kind of changed my whole personality. I'm still personable with the kids, but I'm also more critical and demanding. I'm giving them more work and putting deadlines on getting it done. Mrs. Jacks, that's the instructional coordinator, has given me a lot of ideas. She's bent over backwards to help, and she's really gotten me back on my feet. There's more preparation to be done, but I don't mind at all. It's really fun to teach now." Changes had developed quickly, almost before Scott realized them. He felt he was much more in control of the class than before, and that their activity had purpose. The changes were not total; many of the habits and attitudes formed earlier had remained. But things were looking better. There was promise. It was not all lost.

On the spring in-service day, Scott and Mr. Kimball rode together to a restaurant where they would join others on the staff for lunch. Mr. Kimball spoke of the past winter and the energy troubles they'd been through. He spoke about the next year: "You know, Scott, there's probably going to be an opening in the fifth grade next year. Do you think you'd like that position?" Scott had watched the fifth grade teachers work together all year long. He had longed for that kind of sharing of responsibilities. "Don't answer now, but think it over." For the first time, Scott knew that his contract would be renewed. But more importantly, Mr. Kimball had indirectly paid Scott a high compliment; he told Scott of the confidence he was placing in him. Scott was elated. This chance conversation had renewed Scott's faith in himself. He knew he would be back, better than ever.

*   *   *

Out on the playground the kids romp where, not much earlier, it was too cold to be. The grass has survived as it always does. In the woods, the trees which withstood the long freeze now promise spring. It's inordinately hot; 90° expected today. At 10:35, the recess whistle is blown and three columns of soon-to-be fifth graders line up at the doors, waiting to reenter.

Scott is in the classroom where he awaits the return of his students. Today is not his day to supervise recess. The students pile in from outdoors and settle quickly to work. Scott convenes a group at the reading table and they begin their review. A few moments go by and Scott interrupts. "Thom, if you don't get busy I'm going to warm your bottom." The boy, who is not in the group, makes some effort in that direction. The work continues. A note is sent from the office and Scott leaves. In the few moments he is gone, the kids begin to chatter; a few move around. As Scott comes back down the hall, "Teacher's coming," and the class settles. "I heard that!" Work resumes.

Three boys steal their new baseball cards from inside their desks to compare and count. "I've got this one."

"Yeah, but do you have one of the whole team like this?"

"How many do you have that aren't doubles?" They are quiet and seemingly out of Scott's line of sight. They follow this diversion as long as their intuitions dare allow them, then put the cards away and settle back to work.

Scott continues to work with the reading group. Lunch is nearing, and some students are finished with the morning's work. Joseph toys with a stick he found at recess. It becomes the focus of some attention. Several others want to hold it, swing it, bend it. Joseph takes it back, "I wonder how far it will bend." Suddenly a CRACK! as the stick breaks. Eyes dart from Joseph to Scott, and back again. Scott surveys the situation. "It's just about time for lunch. Those of you who are on safety patrol this week better go. The rest of you, make sure you've finished your work." Several youngsters leave. The reading group continues with Scott. The rest settle.

# Friend or Teacher?

Sandy Smith was born and raised in the affluent suburban community of Astoria. Her parents worked hard to provide a comfortable life for their two children. Theirs was a large and spacious home. The family was proud of the elegant living and dining rooms, but spent most of their time in the panelled TV den or the recreation room which occupied the basement. The closets contained downhill skis, water skis, golf clubs and tennis rackets. At the near end of the Smith's long back yard was a swimming pool, the center of family activity from June through August. The Smiths were an active family.

Sandy grew up loving sports. In junior high, physical education was her favorite subject; she lived for the three periods a week she could spend in the gym or on the field. She and several of her friends were always the leaders in PE; they would enthusiastically tackle all the skills and games taught by their beloved and admired Miss Caroll. By high school Sandy knew she wanted to be a PE teacher herself.

Sandy attended a small private college away from home. She found her college programs stimulating, enriching, and excellent preparation for teaching. Her college instructors provided her with the knowledge and experiences she needed to be a good teacher. They told her what it would be like; they prepared her for both the bad and good of classroom life. Sandy felt certain she would succeed as a teacher.

The summer following graduation Sandy moved into an apartment about a mile from her family's house. She had decided to try for a teaching position in Astoria. Many of her high school friends were also returning from college to settle down in the familiar surroundings of golf courses, tennis courts and racquet ball clubs, and Sandy looked forward to spending her free time with her old friends. She liked being close to her family. Of course she had access to their house and, more importantly, their swimming pool. In early July she submitted her application to the Astoria school system, took a summer job as a recreation leader for the municipal parks, and stopped by her parents' pool every evening for a swim.

Sandy looked forward to teaching. The core of her existence was a multitude of individual and group sports, and Sandy wanted her students to enjoy athletics as much as she did. She wanted students to hit tennis balls, strike volleyballs and kick soccer balls with zeal; she wanted them to relish the excitement of competition.

No PE positions became available in the system that summer. Sandy signed up for substitute teaching, and for the next two years she subbed and tutored in the Astoria schools. Substitute teaching was a valuable experience. It gave her a chance to get used to the teacher role, learn the basics of teaching, and to become adept at controlling student behavior. Sandy gradually learned that students had to be watched. Constant supervision was a necessity. The aphorism "give 'em an inch and they'll take a mile" was realistic. Students would always want more: more free time, more rights, more privileges.

By the end of two years, Sandy had built up her confidence. When she was finally hired to fill a PE vacancy at Astoria Junior High School, she had no doubts about her ability to discipline students. She thought, "I won't have to worry about these kids getting out of control. I know I can deal with them. If you can handle kids as a substitute, you won't have any problems as a regular teacher." She approached her first full-time year feeling enthusiastic, committed and self-assured.

Sandy was assigned to teach all of the seventh and most of the ninth grade girls' PE. During the week before school she spent some time talking with other teachers in the PE Department. Ella Grimes was a middle-aged woman who was adored by the junior high schoolers. She was warm and personal with her students. Ella gave hours of her time after school, and was always willing to sponsor a club or chaperone a social occasion. Sandy admired her ability to get along with students so well. Despite her own self-confidence, Sandy knew that she was an amateur; Ella Grimes was a pro.

Sandy's other colleague was Dan Wilson, the head of the PE Department. His loud voice reinforced his authoritarian manner. His hair was straight and, depending on how he combed it, usually covered most of his ears and fell down across his forehead. The boys in his class today were tomorrow's Astoria High School athletes, and he must prepare them well. Mr. Wilson spent an hour showing Sandy how to keep the attendance records and take inventory on the equipment. He further informed her that at the beginning of the year his and her seventh grade classes would be combined.

The months of September proved warm and sunny. Sandy often had her classes outside playing kickball.

*   *   *

The ninth grade girls amble out of the locker room door and find their seats on the bleachers at the side of the gym. Sandy converses with the students casually. There is some joking around, some discussion of class activities, and some ruminating about last night's television shows as the students wait for everyone to find her place. Most of the conversation is about the "in" fashions. In a lively way Sandy participates in the conversation with her style-conscious students until they are abruptly interrupted by the ringing tardy bell.

"Shhh!" Sandy repeats this a number of times before the girls respond. The students are dressed for physical education. Many have new outfits: sweatsuits, shorts, and shirts matching in color and design. There is some talking while Sandy takes the roll. "Shhh!" Sandy repeats the signal for quiet. The students continue to talk softly.

Sandy finishes taking the roll, puts down the attendance chart and describes the class activities for the third period class. The students become restless and some even complain. Sandy ignores the comments and asks the students to go out to the football fields. The students run ahead of her.

Once at the field Sandy stands on the side as she gives directions: "Roll the ball in so it can be kicked." Judy, the pitcher in the game, rolls the ball but it bounces on the ground rather than rolls smoothly.

"I said roll it, don't bounce it." Sandy's verbal demand is accompanied by a demonstration. She walks over to the catcher, picks up the ball, and rolls it back to the pitcher. The ball hugs the ground as it moves toward Judy and nearly stops at her feet. Judy picks up the ball and rolls in the next pitch just as she has been instructed.

A few girls actively participate in the game and stand ready to catch the ball when it comes their way, others appear disinterested and lethargic. One girl combs her hair, another glances at the adjoining field to see if she is noticed by the boys who are playing soccer. Sandy encourages the girls to play hard; some girls respond to the verbal encouragement with nonverbal signs of exasperation. Sandy wants the ninth graders to learn how to play kickball correctly, to get involved in the game and see how exciting the sport can be.

Play stops when Sandy yells, "The winning team will not have to run a lap after class. Not let's really play hard." Some girls react to the statement by playing harder; they play the game as Sandy wants it played—with vigor and vitality. A few students still refuse to participate. Playing harder means working up a sweat and sweat is the last thing the girls want—they have hair and boyfriends to consider. One girl yells to a friend, "This sucks!" The friend smiles and nods in agreement. Similar comments are made by other students. Sandy does not hear the comments; she is wrapped up in the game.

When the game ends, the losers are told to run around the track; some run as instructed, others walk. The winners walk with Sandy back into the school to change for their next class.

A few minutes later Ella Grimes joins Sandy near the bleachers as the girls wait for the bell to ring. She looks at the girls and rhetorically asks how they are. The students do not respond verbally, most simply smile, affirming Ella's presence. Suddenly a question from a student cuts through the silence. "Mrs. Grimes, is there any way I can transfer to your class? I'd like to be in your physical education class." The girls and Ella laugh at the query; Sandy is sobered. The remark reminds her of a fear, a fear of not being liked and not doing a good job.

\* \* \*

A few weeks of teaching brought Sandy face to face with a problem she hadn't experienced before. As a substitute she knew she had to set limits and be consistently strict; there was no opportunity to get to know the students well. But as a regular teacher she was getting to know the students and wanted them to like her. It was important to her that she and her students have a congenial relationship. She wanted to show that she shared the girls' interests; she hoped they would share her love of sports. The problem was: How does a teacher stand firm, enforce rules and act tough without alienating students?

Sandy liked students; she enjoyed being around them and playing sports with them. She reflected, "I guess I am like a good friend to these girls. I like that. But being a friend makes it hard to get tough with them." When the roles of teacher and friend became confused, the students, particularly the ninth graders, were difficult to control.

The seventh graders were easier to discipline. When they stepped out of bounds they could be controlled by intimidation. The ninth graders were more defiant and could not be coerced. Sandy often tried to bribe them to get them to participate. She used such inducing statements as, "I'll give a ten-minute break to anyone who plays hard," or, "The winners do not have to run a lap around the track." These, however, proved ineffective. The students developed an immunity, a "so what?" attitude toward rewards. They appeared to know what Sandy was trying to do and they refused to cooperate.

The combining of Sandy's and Mr. Wilson's classes lasted for several weeks. Mr. Wilson put Sandy in charge of the beginning of each class period and made her responsible for the mundane preliminaries: exercises, drills, laps. He remained in the office. As soon as he emerged, however, the power was transferred. He automatically assumed control, establishing rules for the games and boundaries for the activities while Sandy stood to one side. The inequity in their relationship stood out sharply the day Sandy asked whether the girls and boys could trade soccer fields. The boys had always played on the large field while the girls stayed in the smaller area. One October day as the students ran out to the field and Sandy and Mr. Wilson followed, Sandy asked if her class could switch places with his. There was silence after the question and then the silence was broken with an abrupt, but polite "No!" The unilaterial decision was followed with a short perfunctory explanation. "Your girls already have enough room, they don't need any more space." Sandy accepted his answer and carried on.

As the year progressed Sandy kept looking for ways to create more enthusiasm and active participation, especially with the older students. She continued to use rewards, such as fewer exercises or no laps, as part of her contingency management system. Sandy also used competition; teams were established and competed against each other. Sandy, however, was often more involved and enthused than the girls. Although there was cheering by the winners, many girls seemed bored and unconcerned with either winning or losing.

One terrible day the use of competition as a stimulus backfired. The students decided it was more fun to lose than to win. It occurred in a small ninth grade class with only ten girls. None of them liked sports—particularly volleyball. The students from the "winning team" served the ball while the students from the "losing" team let the ball drop, untouched, in their court. The losers took pleasure in letting the points mount up against them. Sandy was both frustrated and frightened by the experience. She just kept recording the points, but in her mind she was thinking, "What am I going to do if they continue to refuse to play? What will the principal think if he sees this happening?" Sandy realized the limits of rewards and competition. Students could choose not to respond to any stimulus. They could decide not to participate, regardless of what the teacher said or did. What did a teacher do then? Fortunately, the students never repeated the losing behavior. During their next class they played properly.

Despite the pitfalls of establishing simultaneously both the discipline and the cooperation Sandy hoped for in her classes, she continued her friendliness toward the students. She involved herself in the extracurricular life of the school, initiating a gymnastics club, advising the ninth grade Social Committee, accompanying students on ski weekends, and sponsoring evening volleyball games. Like Ella Grimes, Sandy became part of the mainstream of school activities.

The level of student participation in Sandy's classes improved as the year progressed; the students worked harder and cooperated more. The change was slight but noticeable. Sandy was never certain why the students started to work harder. Had they changed or had she? Was it because of the extracurricular activities she initiated? The friendship and closeness which evolved appeared to be an outgrowth of the extra effort and concern Sandy demonstrated. Since Sandy was willing to sacrifice her time for the students, the students seemed to reciprocate by becoming involved during classes.

Sandy's relationship with Mr. Wilson also underwent changes

when a revision in the schedule forced him to be in another part of the building. The teacher who took his place was, like Sandy, new and relatively inexperienced. He was unfamiliar with the procedures and had difficulty controlling the boys' classes. Soon after his arrival he asked Sandy for help, and Sandy became the leader rather than the follower. Mr. Wilson's absences helped her realize her strengths as a teacher. She found that she did not have to rely directly on Mr. Wilson for a decision; she herself was fully capable of developing her own activities and giving her own directions.

* * *

It is warm outside. The ground is just beginning to thaw from the harsh winter. Sandy walks into the gym and announces that the students will be inside working on gymnastics since it is still soggy outside. She takes the students to a small room adjacent to the gymnasium. Mats cover the floor as the ninth graders bend and stretch their way through opening exercises. The room is hot and musty from the heat and sweat generated by previous classes. Sandy has carefully planned the activities and exercises, and she demonstrates each skill to be accomplished. The girls seem excited. They practice, and as they do they challenge one another to do as well. Sandy focuses more on their learning the skills than their enjoyment of the activities.

There is a lot of joking among the girls, but Sandy is intent on helping them and avoids casual conversations as she walks around the room. "Judy, lift your leg higher for this skill. Sally, bend that knee more." Judy and Sally respond to the comments promptly and adjust their bodies as instructed. When the preliminary exercises are over the students get in four groups of eight girls each. Sandy demonstrates what the girls will be expected to accomplish at the stations she has set up for them. The girls are instructed to move from station to station until all skills are practiced. Sandy blows her whistle and the students begin twisting, turning and flipping through the drills. Sandy circulates, continuing to give direction and encouragement.

The most excitement centers around a dive-roll maneuver. Sandy has two mats rolled up and placed side by side. The students run up, dive head first over the mats, complete a somersault and end up back on their feet. Sandy watches the students and finally tries one herself. "Okay, let's put another mat next to these two and see who can do it." The students at the other stations stop to watch while another mat is moved into place. Sandy gives additional directions on how to do the dive-roll and then demonstrates again. As she returns to her feet following the dive-roll she turns to the girls and says, "Now, do it just like that." The girls appear ready and begin duplicating Sandy's feat. As each girl completes the jump the rest of the class cheers. All but one girl successfully completes the jump and she has decided not to attempt it.

There are only a few minutes left in the class when Sandy blows her whistle again, "Okay, let's do one more tumbling exercise and call it quits." The students line up behind Sandy as she demonstrates the final tumbling exercise. Every student participates. Only a few appear bored and even they try the exercise when it is their turn. Each student gets two turns. Sandy watches and offers suggestions. "Okay, I guess that's it. You can all get changed now."

Sandy follows the girls out the door and thinks about today's activity; she is satisfied. "It was a good class—particularly for the ninth graders. They worked hard."

* * *

As the year drew to a close Sandy felt more self-assured in her interactions with students. She understood that teachers and student roles are different and that those differences must be respected by both herself and the girls. Being just a disciplinarian or just a friend produced problems. Sandy began to learn how to be both. She found that a healthy relationship with students was the result of personal concern and involvement, not jokes and discussions on clothes. She learned that gaining the respect of students meant understanding and being open to students without destroying necessary teacher-student differences. She became a teacher who was also a friend.

# Making the Team

Calvin Carlson began his first year of teaching calm and confident. He had good reason for confidence. In a year when teaching jobs were difficult to obtain, Cal had had six offers.

Cal was older than most first year teachers. He was twenty-eight. He had had a broadening set of experiences since graduating from a small liberal arts college. During college days he worked at youth camps, as lab assistant at college, and as trainee at two government national laboratories doing research in physics. He was drafted and spent two years in the U.S. Army, much of which time was spent in Viet Nam in the sensitive position of military policeman. Cal saw a good deal of life patrolling the bars and back alleys of Saigon and escorting supply convoys throughout southern Viet Nam. After his discharge he returned to the Midwest and went to work for a major oil company handling custom application of fertilizers. That did not satisfy Cal, so in the fall he enrolled at the state university in a program leading to a Ph.D. in physics, the program he was starting when he was drafted. For three years he did advanced graduate study, working in physics lab as a research assistant and teaching undergraduate physics courses. It was during this period that he married Linda, a childhood friend who was now teaching elementary school.

During those three years of graduate study, Cal became uncertain about the career line he had chosen. Jobs in physics were very hard to get and besides, he wasn't sure he wanted the cloistered life of the physicist. He had been urged and pushed by teachers and counselors to become a research scientist, but he was not convinced that such a career would match his talents and interests. He wanted a life more involved with people than with weights and masses. While not obviously outgoing or gregarious, he still felt that he would be more satisfied in a people-oriented profession. Teaching became the obvious alternative. For one thing, his new wife was a dedicated and enthusiastic elementary school teacher. His mother, a brother, a sister, and a number of relatives were also teachers. He had been surrounded by teachers all his life. The more he thought about it, the more attracted he became to the idea of becoming a teacher.

Cal broke with physics and enrolled in a teacher education program at a college not far from his home. He would become a secondary school mathematics or physics teacher. Although he felt a little strange sitting among college sophomores and juniors in the basic education courses, Cal became very involved in his teacher preparation program. He found that he and his wife had much more to talk about once he had decided to become a teacher. His year of training went extremely fast. He enjoyed all but a few courses. Like many other teachers, he found student teaching immensely satisfying and reassuring. He felt fortunate that he was able to have skillful, cooperative teachers in both physics and math. They established a strong relationship and Cal felt that he received valuable feedback and advice during his student teaching. He felt he was ready. Apparently, a number of school personnel directors and chairmen of mathematics departments where Cal applied thought so too.

Carlson is very large. Not huge, just large. He seems bigger than his 6 feet, 4 inches. He seems heavier than his 230 pounds. While not particularly muscular or athletic-looking, he has a stolid, heavy presence. His body is thick and round and, one suspects, capable of exerting a good deal of strength. His eyes are quiet and steady behind heavy, dark-rimmed glasses. Normally, his face is calm and without expression. He wears a full mustache, but hardly a modish or frivolous one. It is substantial, covering his entire lip. His straight brown hair is carefully parted and slants across his forehead. By current standards, Cal's hair is short. His hands and face look well-scrubbed.

Cal gives careful but not obsessive attention to clothing. In general, his dress is modest, inexpensive and modish only in fabric and color. Often, his tie and shirt and pants look like they have been carefully coordinated. His shoes are always shined. His concern is for neatness, rather than cut or fashion. His clothes and appearance give the impression of a small-town bank vice-president, one who is not attracted to the far-out or the deviant. Altogether, his size, his calm expression and his clothing give him the air of being a serious, no-nonsense person.

Cal was assigned to Hayes Junior High School in Easton, an old and comfortable suburb. He was to teach eighth grade math. Much to Cal's surprise, the principal asked him to serve as department chairman of the eight-person mathematics department at Hayes Junior High School. Although somewhat apprehensive about these responsibilities, particularly in his first year of teaching, Cal took on the task with quiet pride at having been asked. He saw it as a sign of the administration's confidence in him and this, in turn, gave him a sense of personal confidence. His teaching assignment, then, was to teach four periods of eighth grade mathematics, to serve as department chairman, and to be on the district-wide math curriculum committee.

Hayes Junior High School is organized on the "house plan" at the seventh and eighth grade levels. Students are not merely divided into grade level, but also into units of approximately 100 within each grade level. Four teachers are assigned primary responsibility for the academic instruction of their 100 house members. Although each teaches his/her own individual subject—mathematics, English, history or science—four teachers are expected to plan and share as a team. They are scheduled so that they have at least one common planning period each day. One of the advantages of this plan is that it helps each subject matter specialist get the perspective of other teachers on the individual student and together, to bring what they believe is a more holistic perspective to the student's year of study. Also, it provides the potential for the teachers to bring several disciplines to bear on common themes, whether it be the metric system or Greek mythology. As Cal saw it, it provided an immediate support group to which he, as a beginning teacher, could relate.

As Cal sat in what was to be his classroom a few days before the opening of school, he had a subdued, but clear sense of excitement that what he had been preparing for was about to begin. Although his path to room 128 in Hayes Junior High School had been somewhat round-about, he was sure he had found the right place. As he spoke about his plans and expectations, his characteristic deliberateness was evident. "Teaching is really important to me. I have been pressured to do other kinds of work. I have worked in business. I have been in the service. I have worked in research in physics. People tried to encourage me to do other things because I could make money in them, but I decided I really want to teach and teaching is really important to me. I guess I've wanted to be a teacher for as long as I can remember, even back in elementary school. My whole family, with the exception of my father, is in teaching."

Unlike many male teachers, Cal wasn't thinking about a short-term career of being a teacher and then moving into administration. In response to questions about his career plans for five years, he said, "I still plan to be in teaching. I don't know whether I'll stay here forever. Maybe I'll try elementary teaching somewhere, but I do plan to be teaching. I don't think that I would ever want to be an administrator. I don't know if I will always be in this school system or not."

Cal felt that he had many reasons to be relatively confident. There was not only his successful student teaching and his ease in getting a job, but also his sense of self. He knew that his greatest strength as a teacher would be organization. "I'm organized in my personal life and in my professional life and I think that that will be a strength. I'm also big. I think being a man and being a little older could be a strength, too."

Like most beginning teachers, Cal had some apprehension about keeping control of his classroom. Basically, however, he saw himself as "a strong disciplinarian." When asked if he thought the students might give him a rough time, being a new teacher, he replied, "Sure, I think they will try, but I think they won't succeed. They're going to know that I am new to the building, but they won't necessarily know that I am a first year teacher. If they ask, I will tell them. I think that they will try to give me a rougher time, but they aren't going to get very far. They will know that they have to behave themselves when they come into my room."

On the other hand, Cal anticipated that he would achieve good relationships with the students. "I think that is very important—not to be their friend or buddy, but to be friendly and have a good relationship with them."

Nor was there any lack of clarity about what he was aiming for.

When asked to describe his view of the ideal teacher, he said, "I think the ideal teacher is someone who would be enthusiastic, would have a good knowledge of the subject matter, would be interested in kids, and would help them learn and pay a lot of attention to them."

The only real apprehension that Cal had was with the added role of department chairman. He wondered whether the other teachers would accept such a neophyte as their department leader. But, if they thought he could do it, he thought that he'd do it and do it well.

Easton was not an average American community. Nor did its citizens think of themselves or their community as average. It was an upper middle-class community consisting primarily of single-family homes. Easton had undergone immense growth in the previous fifteen years but the part of town in which Hayes Junior High existed was the older and wealthier part. The school was nestled in an area of shaded and curved streets with very English names such as Greenwich, Lennox and Brighton. While not all the children came from comfortable homes, the majority who attended Hayes Junior High School were the sons and daughters of the managerial and professional class. These parents were very concerned with their children's academic performance and therefore, they were very concerned with what happens in school.

Hayes Junior High School had a special meaning to the Easton community. Before Easton went through its growth spurt, the Hayes building was Easton High School, a school well-known for its superior academic program and outstanding athletic teams. So, although the current building was old, rather worn and somewhat ill-suited to being a junior high school, it was, for many of the leading citizens, something of a shrine. After all, they had gone there. It served them well. It was a place of tradition and stability in a changing Easton world.

Indeed, Hayes Junior High School gave the impression of being a shrine to the achievement of many members of the community. Along the main hall, mounted high above the oversized lockers, hung huge portraits of the distinguished graduates of Easton—the giants that had stridden these halls, the symbols of what the community wanted the school to perpetuate. Under each picture was a list of accomplishments. The faces stared down at the latest crop of Eastonians, measuring their promise. The district's long-time congressman peered down along with corporation presidents, distinguished writers, a World War II hero and pilot ace, a distinguished professor or two, and the most well-known graduate of Easton High School, "The Silver Server," tennis player Jay Prince. Hayes Junior High School exuded both tradition and high expectations. For a new teacher, the stakes were high.

*   *   *

It's after lunch on Friday, the second day of classes. Cal sits quietly at his desk in the front corner of the room reviewing his notes. Between bells the students filter in and move to their desks. One pipes up, "I don't understand this math!" referring possibly to the homework Cal had assigned.

"Come in after last period, then," says Cal as the bell rings.

The students appear relaxed, sitting or standing around their desks. One automatically removes gum and throws it in the basket. Cal rises and immediately asks the whereabouts of two students who are missing. Several people answer at once. Cal begins filling out a tardy slip as two boys noisily enter. In a flat voice, Cal says, "Vance and Chris, come in for twenty minutes at 3:30. We went over the rules yesterday." The boys grimace and take their seats.

Cal goes on. "We talked about the rules yesterday, but I want you to add another, rule 13. When you come to your homeroom in the morning, come in to stay. I will post these rules tomorrow." (It is Friday and two or three students look at one another.) Cal then goes over the grading procedures to be used in the course and describes the rules covering homework. It's all very matter-of-fact. Then, he stresses the influence of homework on grades and how he will award the four homework grades: "plus," "check," "minus," and "zero." "Also, your attitude of participation in class will influence your grade." He then asks them to take out their homework papers and tells them that, although normally the papers will be graded first, today they will go over them in class. "How about number 7 on page 14? Okay," and then in response to a waving hand, "Judy."

"Twenty-seven."

"Okay, number 9." Pause. Hands, this time half the class. "Greg."

"Thirteen."

"Okay, number 14, next page." Pause. Hands. "Tiffany."

"Nine." Wild waving of hands. "No! wrong!" five or six voices report.

"Okay." Cal stares at hands. "Rick."

"Minus nine."

"Okay." Cal turns to the board and writes out the problem in a clear hand, talking the students through the steps as he goes. When he comes to the final step, he says, "Minus thirteen. Next, number 18. Okay." Hands. "Ken."

"Minus eleven."

"Okay." And so it goes for twenty-five minutes. The teacher rarely varies from the pattern: question number, name, receiving an answer, and confirming the answer with an "Okay." When an answer is wrong, Cal doesn't declare the answer wrong. The fellow students do that. Also, his request for a further answer is indication enough. Cal is calm and businesslike, a show of contrast to the bubbling energy of the class. After twenty-five minutes, he says, "Okay, hand in the papers." Without a pause, the papers roll in from the back seats to the front. Cal takes out a folder and collects a stack from each student in a front seat.

"Now, turn to page 22. You have problems 1 through 20 for homework. I'll do problems 1 and 2 to get you started." Cal writes the problems on the board and walks them through the various steps. "Okay, you can begin working on your homework. Work alone. If you have a problem, raise your hand and I'll come down." Cal seems like a giant in this small room with these skinny, pre-pubescent students. When he sees a hand raised, he leaves his desk and purposefully moves to the student's desk. He often kneels on one knee, making him eye-level with the student while he quietly answers his question or explains a problem. Then on to another puzzled youngster.

Cal moves from student to student, quietly answering their questions and explaining how to work the new problems. The two boys that came in late, Vance and Chris, are more engaged in conversation than working on their problems. One raises his hand. "May I sharpen my pencil?"

"Yes." Vance saunters slowly to the pencil sharpener. Once there, he grins back in triumph at Chris. Having taken enough time to acquire an exceedingly sharp point on his pencil, he saunters back. Cal appears not to have noticed any of the by-play between the two boys. He turns to his desk in the corner and begins to go over the homework papers. A hand is raised. "May I go to the bathroom?"

"No."

"But I have a bloody nose."

"Do you have a handkerchief?"

"No."

"Okay." Cal quickly writes out a note and the boy, with head back and nose in the air, stiffly walks out. By and large, the class is undisturbed by this. Most are busy with their problems, although some stare vacantly in space and others talk quietly together. Vance and Chris, in the first seats directly in front of Cal's desk, sporadically work and talk. With five minutes to go in the period, the noise level starts to rise. Four students have come to Cal's desk with problems, thus unintentionally providing a shield for the two boys. They begin to take advantage of it. The boys, with one eye on Cal and one eye on each other, trade punches on the arm. Other students begin to talk and laugh.

In a strong but not harsh voice, Cal says, "Let's keep it down!" There is a momentary hush, but then a constant murmur. The two boys, Vance and Chris, begin to talk and fool. The boy with the bloody nose jauntily comes into the room with a broad smile on his face and goes to his seat. Anticipating release by the bell, the noise level rises. Cal is about to say something, when the bell rings. As soon as the bell is over, Cal says, "Okay," and the students move toward the door. Cal stands and says, "See you tomorrow."

Several turn to him and one girl, fixing Cal with a condescending grin, says, "Tomorrow! You won't see *me* here tomorrow."

With his first smile for today, and a slightly embarrassed one at that, Cal says, "Okay, right." The students smile back and rush out. As the room empties, Cal goes to the board and erases it and returns to his desk to review his notes during the three minutes between periods.

New students file in. Just as the bell rings, a boy rushes in and says, "Can I get a drink?"

Cal says, "Yes, but bring back a detention slip." The boy's face falls and he moves from the door to his desk and plops down. As soon as the bell rings, Cal gets up from his desk and goes through a pattern very similar to the one in the period before. This class is a more advanced eighth grade class and their mathematics this year is algebra. The class is more serious and there is less window-gazing and talking. All the students seem eager to answer the homework questions, but not quite with the fervor of the previous class. One girl, however, Wendy, is intent on getting the teacher's attention whenever possible. Wendy looks, by face and figure, to be two or three years older than her classmates. She has the clear mark of a future Easton cheerleader. But in the meanwhile, she seems to be practicing how to be noticed. Wendy leans forward with arm waving and coos, "Oh, Mr. Carlson! Mr. Carlson!" Cal's response to students is typically dry, unemotional and businesslike. There is little expression on his face, whether the student is enthusiastic or distracted, correct or incorrect. His reaction to Wendy is consistent with his pattern. However, her energetic participation results in her getting called upon much more often than other students.

When problems are being worked on during the latter portion of the periods, Wendy finds many opportunities to come up to Cal's desk or to invite him to help her at her seat. Cal complies, staying for a few moments and then going on to help another student.

\* \* \*

Cal's day starts rather early. He and his wife rise around 6:30. Cal is out of the house by 7:00 and drives a half hour from his home in a suburb on the other side of the city. He is typically one of the early arrivers at the building, getting to school forty-five minutes before homeroom begins at 8:23. Cal is careful and orderly. He likes to be well-prepared and have things worked out in advance. He uses that time to put final touches on plans for the day. Homeroom period lasts eleven minutes. There are announcements to be made or administrative chores to be taken care of. Cal enjoys this early morning start with his eighth grade homeroom. The students are fresh and eager. He is relaxed and available to the students. Sometimes they talk to him about the mathematics homework; sometimes, about sports. Although Cal enjoys these talks, he doesn't initiate them. He tends to be a conversational counterpuncher in his contacts with students.

After homeroom, Cal has a forty-eight-minute team planning period. These meetings are the heart of the Hayes house plan. Cal feels fortunate to be part of a house plan. He feels that his team really has helped to orient him to the school procedures and peculiarities. It's something of a built-in support team for him. While the team plans various activities for the students, there is also a good deal of discussion of individual students. Cal can check to see how students who are having trouble in math perform in other classes and thus, he has a better picture of how to help them. To Cal, team planning period is an important part of the day in his first year of teaching.

Cal begins the first of his four eighth grade math classes at 9:30. Each period is approximately forty-eight minutes. Cal is pretty much the same from class to class. The same text is used in three of his four classes. The stress is on core mathematics concepts, concepts which will aid greatly once the class gets to algebra in the next year.

After two math periods, Cal has either study hall or a student conference period. He and another teacher rotate the responsibility for the study hall. The study hall is no problem. The students all seem to have work to do and a firm reminder that they shouldn't be talking gets them back in line. Shortly after noon, Cal has three-quarters of an hour for lunch. Cal makes a point about eating in the teachers' lounge. At the beginning of school, the principal urged that the teachers get to know one another better this year and Cal feels that he should comply. He also wants to get to know his fellow teachers. Although he is somewhat quiet and reticent at lunch, again the counterpuncher, early in the fall he feels very much at ease with his fellow teachers. He generally eats with the men and an easy camaraderie begins to develop.

At 1:00, Cal returns to his classroom and teaches the third section of math eight. Particularly early in the year, he is able to use the same lesson plan for his first three periods. After this, Cal has his last class of the day, the algebra class, the advanced group. There is a good deal of variation of ability in this class. One of the boys is a math whiz and later on in the year will go on to enter state mathematics contests. Cal thinks this is good, but his real interest is in the kids having trouble. When he worries, he worries about them. At 2:38, Cal's teaching day is over. He has a conference period when students can come in to do makeup work or to get special aid, but nothing that calls for special plans. Cal likes this individual work with students. He looks upon it as a problem-solving activity. They have a learning problem and he needs to talk it out and find a solution. The number of students varies in these conference periods. However, the pace is normally leisurely and he feels that he can give adequate attention to those with difficulties.

The official school day ends at 3:30 and the building quickly thins out. Cal stays around for another half hour, straightening his room, sorting out the day, occasionally talking to a janitor or a fellow teacher or possibly a student until 4:00. At 4:00, he heads home with his briefcase full of work, passes the gym where the stuff of Easton's athletic aspirations are training themselves for their hoped-for rendezvous with destiny. He passes, too, the gallery of selected alumni and goes out the front door. Directly in front of the school is a small town square, fifty yards by twenty yards. It has the war memorials, a flagstand and some benches and decorative shrubbery. Although it is right in front of the school, it is not considered "school turf." Over the years, it has become a free zone, a refuge for Hayes Junior High's rebels, an alienated and fast crowd. This lovely little town square is strewn with soda and beer cans, cigarette butts and papers, candy wrappers and the rest of the youth culture's litter. On a normal day, fifteen or twenty students stand around in sullen groups, getting, it seems, the only sense of community they can in this high-pressured, achievement-oriented school. If they can't feel effective or wanted in school, they can perhaps feel effective and wanted in the park. Cal walks by, preoccupied by the day. Occasionally, he is distracted by a burst of laughter or a shout. He is sure it is not aimed at him.

He gets in his car and heads home; as usual, enjoying the ride. He has a lot to think about this year. It's not just the teaching. It's being a department chairman. He believes that the teaching is going well, but he is not sure what's expected of him as a department chairman. He is taking care of the paperwork, but he is not sure that he is providing the kind of leadership that he should.

When Cal arrives home, he knows he has some projects ahead of him. He and his wife, Linda, are redecorating the house they bought and moved into three days before the start of school. Cal still has carpentry to do. The work with his hands provides him with two hours of diversion from his new all-consuming occupation. At 6:30, his wife and he sit down to eat. They don't have children yet, so they have time to talk about common concerns, to compare notes, to plan and talk about their work. They always talked about teaching, but now that Cal is "one of the guild," he feels that the conversations are much richer. At 7:30, Cal gathers up his briefcase and goes down to his small office in the cellar. During the first half of the year, he is normally there until 11:00, until his wife tells him "enough is enough" and he puts away his work for the evening. She kids him about trying to be "Superteacher" and he enjoys this. He feels that things are really clicking, that he has found his niche and is making steady progress. So, in the early months when she calls him "Super-teacher," Cal has a sense of quiet satisfaction.

Although Cal is not an extrovert or particularly socially outgo-ing, he thinks it is important to get to know people. He realizes that there is a little more to keeping one's job than simply being a good teacher. In true Easton spirit, he want to be "part of the team." And there is a sense of team in his school. But then, not everybody is really on the team.

Cal's principal is a handsome, athletic man in his late thirties. Although he is generally interested in all aspects of school, one senses a particular interest in the sports program. The principal gets on well with all of the teachers, but he gets on particularly well with men who share his interest in sports. There is a good deal of talking in the teachers' lounge about sports and there is also a faculty bas-ketball team. The principal participates regularly. Cal, while not an avid fan, has some interest in sports and becomes part of these conversations and decides to join the men's faculty basketball team. It means he has to come back one night a week, but he enjoys it, and after all, he is becoming part of the team.

Cal feels that right from the beginning, he established a good relationship with the principal. After all, the principal hired him and a place like Hayes Junior High probably had many applicants. Dur-ing the early weeks of the school year, the principal stopped in and observed. In the conference that followed, Cal received feedback which was quite positive. The negative comments were very few and really in the nature of things to work on. Cal also sees a good deal of the principal in weekly departmental chairmen meetings where policy is discussed. Cal is relatively quiet in these sessions, but he gradually feels more at ease during these meetings of the school's inner circle. In effect, Cal feels early on that the principal made a positive judgment about him and believes that he is the one teacher about whom the principal does not have to worry. While this is no reason to relax his efforts, Cal does find it reassuring.

*   *   *

It's been a rainy, cold fall. This early November day seems more like a December day. After lunch Cal goes back to his room to get ready for his 1:00 period. As usual, he goes over his notes and records. As usual, too, the small room is very orderly. The desks are in neat rows. The board has been cleaned after the last class. There are no papers on the floor. Cal's desk is the picture of order—folders neatly stacked, his briefcase on top of his desk, but also, neat and tidy. Cal is in a colored, short-sleeved shirt with a tie that matches his pants and shirt. Many teachers don't wear ties and occasionally Cal will not, but on the whole, he feels more comfortable in a tie. As the bell rings, the students come pouring in. Their voices are loud. A few yell questions at him at his desk. He answers calmly. As the beginning bell starts, Cal remains at his desk, going over his notes. There is noise in the room.

Cal begins to take roll. Everyone is here and almost all are talking. Five minutes go by before the class begins. Then Cal calls them to order. There is a momentary quiet and then, when Cal asks for homework, the noise begins again. Cal is talking with individual students. The students seem unmindful of his request for quiet. Two girls are combing their hair with huge combs. Three boys are throwing wads of paper into the wastebasket in the corner of the room. There is much joshing and hoopla about this. Daryl, who is quite big for his age and who has been in and out of trouble most of his time at Hayes, arrives late, but with a pass. He also has a cap on and keeps it on as he noisily sits down.

Eight minutes into the period, Cal begins to go over homework. The students quickly settle down. They have had problems with the homework, so Cal goes over the general rule of signs in mathematics. They seem to want to know this and quickly become goal-directed and responsive to Cal. When he feels they have mastered the rule, Cal says, "Another thing before you start doing individual work. I would like to give you an idea of tomorrow's quiz." The students straighten up for this. However, once their individual work starts, many seem to drift off. It begins snowing, the first time for the year. Five or six students just gaze out the window at the snow and then gradually more begin to talk about it. Ten of the students are doing some work and twelve are clearly fooling around; Cal seems not to notice. However, he moves from one student to the next in response to their requests for help. When Chris' behavior is especially distracting, Cal quietly reprimands him. Shortly after, Chris gets out of his seat and showily shoots a paper wad at the corner waste basket.

Cal says flatly, "Sit down, Chris," and after grimacing, Chris takes his seat and gets to work.

It begins to snow harder. Now four are working and eighteen seem to be talking, passing notes or gazing out the window. Cal asks for their attention. He mentions that apparently a number of them are having a similar problem with the homework problem. In the ten minutes before the end of the period, he goes over the problems in a familiar pattern, this time trying to explain the individual steps. Then the two boys, Vance and Chris yell out, "Mr. Carlson, Mr. Carlson," or simply yell out the answer. They seem to be doing this more for the benefit of the rest of the class. When Cal has his back to the class, there is a good deal of preening and playing to the crowd. It seems Cal is being tested by these boys. They are trying to find out how far they can go with him. Although Cal calls on them more frequently than others in response to their requests for attention, he deals with their answers, not their behavior.

Cal is not particularly concerned about how Vance and Chris have been behaving. Cal says matter-of-factly that Chris has a behavior problem and that Vance is hyperactive. He says they're a little "off the wall," but he is aware of it. He thinks that he could be "on top of them all the time," but says they need to behave that way to stay interested in the material. Cal seems unconcerned with the potential of a severe discipline problem developing.

* * *

Hayes Junior High has a monthly school newspaper. It is eight pages and typed, but contains photography and illustrations. It is called *The Cub Reporter*, (since the totem of the high school is the Bengal Tigers). In an autumn issue, three of the eight pages are devoted to stories and photographs of the football team and cheerleaders. Cal is pictured with the school's three other first year teachers. The issue also contains a story on him.

Teacher Feature: Mr. Cal Carlson<br>by M. K. Barnes

Mr. Carlson is a native of Maple Grove. He went to college at Warner College, where he majored in physics and worked on his Ph.D. in physics. During his last year he went to Confar College to get his certificate to teach. Mr. and Mrs. Carlson have been married for three years and have a fearsome mutt named "Zeus." They live in Northtown where Mrs. Carlson teaches fourth grade. Mr. Carlson likes fishing, water skiing, outdoor activities, and sports. His hobbies are gardening, listening to piano and organ music, and woodcutting. He also has a collection of 350 straight razors. He thinks students and teachers are enthusiastic, and he's very excited about being an eighth grade math and algebra teacher at Hayes.

As Cal moves from the fall to the winter, the testing behavior of Chris and Vance and a few other students gradually disappears. Thirteen-year-old boys who had been showboating in Cal's class begin to quiet down. The erratic work patterns of some of the students begin to fall in line, although not completely. The noise level often gets high, but students quiet down as soon as Cal begins to talk.

In his own low-key way, Cal has a consistently positive attitude toward students. In class, he appears neither particularly friendly nor unfriendly to them. He maintains a somewhat somber, poker-face throughout his instruction. But when he talks about them one at a time, he talks about them with care and concern. When asked to describe a good teaching day for him or a particularly satisfying experience, he always refers to the individual success of the students: a slow learner who is beginning to respond; a student who had a block on one math concept whom he was able to help; a learning-disabled student mainstreamed in his class for whom he was able to develop some special exercises.

As Cal gains confidence in his instructional skill and gets a stronger sense of the students, he begins to experiment with individualizing instruction. Then he moves on to the contract plan, a variation of individualized instruction. He attended a math conference in Cincinnati and came back with several new ideas. There is still large group instruction in his class and it is still part of the basic pattern. "Okay, how about question 19? Daryl." The student answers. "How about question 24? Julie." And on and on. This pattern, which is repeated over and over again, does not seem to annoy the students. He uses "okay" on the average of once every eleven seconds during drills, but neither does this repetition get on students' nerves. It seems he just keeps moving forward, undeterred by student peccadilloes and other distractions. The classes are predictable. Although there is no glamour or excitement, clearly, the students are moving forward with him. They can think in mathematical terminology. They can solve his relentless mathematical problems.

*　*　*

It is the twentieth of January. As soon as the bell rings, Cal brings the class to order. He has a lot of work to get done today. He is louder, slightly more forceful. Cal spends the first five minutes going over a new concept. Then he tries some problems on the students and the pattern of questions and answers begins.

Normally, Cal's room is orderly, but plain. This month the room is heavily decorated along the metric theme. Everything in the room has a metric measurement alongside of it: the flag, the door, the speakers, the window, ceiling tiles, boxes, desks. All of this is designed to raise "metric consciousness" and to develop a sense of metric lengths.

Toward the end of the lesson Cal makes a speech fluff, mispronouncing a word. In a flat voice and the slightest smile he says, "I'm having trouble spitting out the words today." The class seems to enjoy it. He blows another word, saying, "right-reading" instead of "sight-reading." They laugh and this large man blushes. There is a little groan, but he makes a quick announcement about a test. They file out in cheery fashion.

Cal has the next period free, and a young janitor knocks and comes in.

"Hi, Art."

"Hi, Cal. Do you mind if I clean up in here now?"

"Be my guest."

As Art cleans up the baskets and Cal straightens up his desk and cleans the board, they talk about sports. Art is out of the room in six or seven minutes. Cal remembers from one education course that there is a great deal to be learned about schools from the custodial staff and secretaries, and he enjoys talking with Art. They are about the same age and they have had some common experiences, like military service.

As the spring comes and the cruel, cold winter gives up its grip on Easton, Cal has a sense of accomplishment. The principal has been in again, and the feedback was very good. Not only has Cal been playing on the faculty basketball team, but he has been regularly taking part in a Friday afternoon "culture club." On Friday afternoon, many of the faculty go to a cocktail lounge two or three miles north of the school. A good portion of the teachers go on a semi-regular basis. The principal tries to get to all of them, but if he's not there his assistant is. They talk about school, the district, sports, television, politics. It's a week's end of relaxed unwinding. Cal has come to enjoy these Friday afternoons. It's part of being on the team, part of the school community.

When Cal was in graduate school before he taught, he noticed his wife had what he called "a spring slump." It got harder for her to get through the teaching week and she was easily irritated. Most of all, teaching became more exhausting. Although his wife said that other teachers had that experience, Cal thought that perhaps she had it more than others. This spring, Cal's first spring at full-time teaching, he had the "spring slump." He felt the students did, too. There were no major problems in the class, but things just became much harder. He didn't think the classes had much bounce, and everybody, including himself, seemed dead on their feet. In late May, however, he got his energy back and so did the class.

On April 29, in the midst of his "spring slump," Cal has his major conference with the principal. In Easton schools, first year teachers are visited at least three times, and each visit is followed up with a conference. This particular conference was to discuss Cal's overall performance. Cal was not at all concerned about this meeting, but nevertheless, he was quite pleased when he was given a superior rating by the principal and told that he was being recommended for reemployment. The overall performance continuum follows: outstanding; superior; excellent; above average; satisfactory performance. The fact that he didn't get an outstanding rating did not bother Cal. He did not believe that he was outstanding yet. The principal wrote on Cal's performance evaluation. "Cal is a very positive influence on the staff and students." Further, he remarked, "Cal's classes are well-planned and he presents the material well." Finally, he wrote, "Mr. Carlson has achieved his growth goal in excellent fashion. He has worked well with his house team and has done an exceptionally fine job as department chairman, especially considering that he is a first year teacher in this school."

In conversation with the principal about his reactions to Cal's first year, the principal echoed these same sentiments. He was clearly pleased with Cal and with his own judgment in selecting him. He felt that a major factor in Cal's success was maturity, the fact that he was twenty-eight and not a "regular rookie." Cal had clearly made the team.

Cal had made it in his own eyes, too. At the end of the year, he acknowledged that he had some mild apprehension before the year began, but there was no real doubts about the profession he had finally joined. After all, he reflected, he had had a lot going for him. He was older. He had been able to choose his job from several possibilities. He was in a good school with a good, supportive group of colleagues and administrators. He had no trouble with the subject matter he was teaching. He also had some guiding understandings. For instance, he said, "Students look for two things from their teacher: that he be good at discipline and that he be a fair grader." Cal stayed close to such essentials while keeping in mind the individual needs of students. At the end of the school year, with only one or two student failures and with a contract for the next year, he had a clear sense of accomplishment.

Cal had found his groove and he was moving slowly, steadily forward.

# Everyone is Watching Me

Julie Carson fits well the scale of her kindergarten classroom and its miniature appointments. She is barely 5 feet, 3 inches tall. At 110 pounds she seems scarcely heavier than some of her students. Her brown-framed reading glasses call attention to her large blue eyes. Her quiet voice reinforces the visual impression of frailty and shyness.

As is frequently the case, first impressions are deceiving. Though quiet and soft spoken, Julie's voice sparkles with enthusiasm, particularly as she talks about her teaching. She speaks in a thoughtful manner, choosing her words carefully. Her calm and deliberate manner dispels any hint of frailty and instead suggests inner strength and steadiness.

Julie dresses carefully and without pretense. Her clothing is always appropriate to the active role of a kindergarten teacher. Her soft brown hair is cut above her shoulders and is unpretentious in style. She wears little jewelry or makeup and presents a fresh, natural appearance.

The decision to become a teacher did not come early in Julie's life. In high school she thought it stupid when some of her friends joined Future Teachers of America. Who would want to be a teacher? She wanted to be away from school. She knew she would never be a teacher. However, as a high school junior she volunteered to help with a local Head Start preschool program. Julie found that experience enjoyable but did not think about teaching young children as a career.

Like many other freshmen entering college in the fall of 1972, Julie was uncertain about career plans. She was good in math and chose that field as her major area of study. During her freshman year, she found that she could handle the math courses, but they left her vaguely unsatisfied. Julie decided she didn't want to work with numbers the rest of her life, and began to examine other options. She knew that she wanted to work closely with people, and the positive experience with young children in the Head Start program stuck in her mind. Perhaps a career in teaching could provide the satisfying interaction with people which she was seeking.

Julie had no single model for teaching as a career choice. None of her close friends or immediate family had been teachers. She did have a sister-in-law who was a teacher, but Julie had no real idea of what teaching was like. Her involvement in the university's early career experience program was discouraging and did little to provide her with a teacher's perspective. Julie found herself spending ten weeks grading fifth grade math papers with almost no interaction with children. She found that this view of teaching differed little from that she had known as a student. Teaching was simply passing out work, collecting it, grading it, and doing what the principal said.

This limited view remained unchallenged until her junior year, when Julie enrolled in a special teacher education program for teachers of young children. Instead of the usual one quarter of student teaching experience during the middle or end of the senior year, Julie's student teaching began in the fall of her junior year and lasted until June. She was placed with a first grade class in an open school setting, and remained with that class for the year. Instead of abstract courses in the theory and practice of teaching, Julie's courses in methods were closely connected with the actual experience she was having in her classroom. Julie found that she could use her student teaching experiences to test the knowledge and practice the skills she was learning in her courses. She now began to acquire a teacher's perspective on teaching, from the first day of school to the last. For Julie, teaching became living with children for an entire year: having good days and bad days, having disagreements with children and having satisfying times as well. Student teaching allowed Julie to become well acquainted with all of the children during the first quarter of the year, when classroom observations were stressed. During the winter quarter she took on more responsibility for planning and teaching. By the spring, her cooperating teacher was rarely in the classroom, and the class was hers for the quarter. At the end of the year, Julie knew she was ready. She knew that teaching a class of young children was possible and exciting. Julie felt she had a complete view of the school year and was now ready to be out on her own.

Julie's senior year went quickly. Her husband Rob was accepted to law school, and Julie knew her job would provide their only income. She graduated in March and began substitute teaching in the city's public schools. Julie found that substitute teaching lacked the rewards she had known in her student teaching. She found that the temporary status of a substitute teacher made it difficult to work with the students or establish the kinds of relationships she had developed during her student teaching. She encountered the all-American pastime of "bait the sub." Often Julie found herself eating breakfast at 6:30 waiting for the phone call with her assignment for the day. As she waited, she could feel her stomach tighten and turn over at the thought of what she would be doing that day, where she would be. Substitute teaching became so aversive that at the close of schools in June, Julie took a job as an office clerk. She decided that she would rather clerk than substitute teach if she could not find a teaching position in the fall. Julie applied to many school districts in the city and surrounding area. The summer was practically over before she was contacted by Cleburne Public Schools, a nearby district seeking a replacement for a teacher taking a year off for graduate school. With a great sense of relief, Julie accepted the offer and was assigned to teach kindergarten at Annandale Elementary School. Even though it was a terminal one-year contract, and would mean a long drive from her new apartment in the city, Julie was very happy to have gotten the job.

Julie planned to teach until her husband's graduation from law school and then for a couple of years thereafter. She expected that teaching would be put aside while she started a family, and then she intended to return to her career. She mused, "Teaching is very important to me. You are working with people, not numbers, papers, or machinery. In teaching there is the potential for continual growth, learning something new every day, changing each year. I worked this summer as a clerk, made good money, and when I came home I didn't even have to think about my job until I arrived at the office the next day. But there was no opportunity to work with people. There were no rewards. In teaching I can do things on my own, I can work hard in the evening and weekends, and I can say I have succeeded. Teaching is a profession, not a job."

On the evening before the first day of school, Julie expressed concern about her own sense of perfection getting in the way of her teaching. "I have always done well in college—I may be sort of a perfectionist—and I get a really good feeling when somebody praises me and tells me that what I have done is really good, or the best. But as a first year teacher I am not going to be the best. There are so many things to know, I can't be on top of everything. The other teachers are already familiar with the curriculum and the parents and the students."

She was particularly apprehensive about relations with parents. "When anybody yells at me," she confided, "I cry. I think I have good reasons for the things I do in my class, and I am afraid that if I get upset I won't be able to talk about and explain my reasons. I didn't have very much experience in dealing with parents when I was student teaching. So many parents with their first child in kindergarten are concerned that everything is right and that their child is progressing. Frequently when parents come into kindergarten classrooms and see the children playing, they may not appreciate the educational aspects of play. So it is terribly important that I be able to explain the things that are happening in my classroom.

"You know," she continued, "I am replacing a beloved teacher who had taught at this school for several years. She was expected back this year, so as a new teacher I am a complete surprise to these parents. They don't know me, and they don't know what to expect from me and I understand that. I met some parents who were at school while I was setting up my classroom and one remarked how young I looked. Parents know I'm a new staff member, but I try to let them know that I have other experience. I try not to publicize the fact that this is my first year."

Being the only new teacher in her building and a first year teacher, Julie expressed concern that other teachers would be watching for her mistakes. She felt that she would "stick out like a sore thumb." Feeling that she would be highly visible, Julie knew she would have to work extra hard. Hard work, however, was highly consistent with Julie's notion of the ideal teacher, "Teaching is work; you are not there to spend time and go home when school is over. It takes a lot of work to do the job well."

Annandale Elementary School was located at the edge of a large cornfield. Across the road lay a new, moderately expensive housing development. Recent construction of homes and apartments in the school attendance area had strained the school's capacity. In a rural-suburban section of the county, the school served an almost completely white neighborhood of farmers and blue-collar workers.

Julie made her classroom warm and inviting even though it was too small for the thirty active five-year-olds it contained. It was carefully cluttered with piano, easel, shelves, houskeeping furniture, and tables and chairs enough for all children to sit at once. There was little open space on the floor, and children were cramped into small areas between tables. Movement was impeded by these clusters of children. There was no one space large enough to seat all of the children on the floor without considerable crowding.

It was the third day of school. The uneven hum of children's activity was broken by the soft tinkling of a bell Julie held in her hand. A hush settled evenly throughout the classroom as the children stopped what they were doing and looked to their teacher.

"It is twenty-five minutes past nine, and almost time for us to begin to clean up." Julie spoke in a straightforward, conversational tone. "If you are at a stopping place you can begin to put your things away. If you are not finished, you can take about two or three more minutes and finish up." As she turned to set the bell on her desk, the room lurched into activity as the children began to pick up and put things away.

"Nathan," Julie spoke in a relaxed voice, "Nathan, if you are finished, look around for someone else to help." As she spoke she pointed to a group of children cleaning up blocks in the corner. Children scurried about in a knowing, businesslike fashion, putting away blocks, straightening books on the shelf, putting math materials in their boxes and then on the shelf. While the children worked, Julie was in constant motion, going calmly among the children, giving assistance where needed. Julie called her children by name as they finished their tasks and the room was arranged. "Lisa, Todd, Clinton, will you sit down at the table, please." Singly and in clusters the children completed their clean-up tasks and sat at one of the six tables in the room, talking excitedly. Julie continued her measured movement about the room, helping the last few children with their jobs. The children sitting at the empty tables became louder and louder. Turning from the group she was helping, Julie looked toward the noisiest table, "Charles, will you and Mark sit in the chairs, please." Though soft, her voice carried an "I mean it" edge, and the two boys slid down into their chairs, exchanging grins.

The last child found a chair at a table. It had taken just five minutes to move from an ongoing, full-dress, free play period to relative quiet for the next activity. The clean-up process carried with it an aura of order, calm, and serenity. The children and teacher seemed to know what they were about. It was as if it were the third month of school instead of the third day.

"I need four helpers. Nicole. . . ." Julie's voice was lost in the din of chair legs shrieking against the tile floors and mingled cries of "Teacher!" and "Me!"

"Class." There was a slight strain in Julie's voice. Then again, more calmly, "I will choose helpers who are sitting quietly at their table."

"Renee," she called out, looking at a quietly seated girl. Most of the children dropped in their chairs, frozen, with beseeching eyes aimed at their teacher. "Jimmy, and Charlene," she concluded. Julie quietly gave instructions to the four proud helpers, who with painful precision began distributing sheets of paper and crayons to each child. The class grew restless as little fingers carefully separated each sheet of paper and placed it on the table. The teacher's aide, sensing that things were moving slowly, helped distribute the crayons.

"Class." A note of frustration sounded in Julie's voice. "Please leave the crayons and paper on the table until I have given you directions." Noting the growing air of unruliness in the thirty five-year-olds seated at the tables, Julie helped complete the task of passing out paper.

Julie started explaining the activity. She would read a story about a mouse who moved up, down, to the right, and to the left, and the children were to draw lines to show the direction the mouse had moved in the story. It had taken five minutes to distribute paper and crayons, and many of the children had lost interest in the activity. Charles slid down in his chair until his chin rested on the table top. With a big breath he sent papers flying and giggled softly to himself. "Charles," Julie spoke, walking quietly to his table, "will you sit in your chair." She continued her directions, her voice more strained though not louder. Over half the class had already begun to use their crayons. The directions completed, Julie began to read the story. Although the story was short, she had to stop several times to explain the directions. Many of the children were plainly confused, but most attempted to follow their teacher's instructions.

At the end of the story, Julie announced that the children might color whatever they wanted on their papers. Many of the children had already been coloring what they wanted, and were not interested in more of the same. They jumped up from their tables to turn in their papers and crayons to the teacher. The children crowded around her, each trying to show his or her own paper. The noise level rose dramatically. Julie vainly tried to comment on each paper shoved at her as the children jostled to be near her. Charles and two other boys began running and sliding between the tables.

Another five minutes passed. In an eager and surprisingly loud voice, Julie called from the midst of the children still vying for her attention, "Class, everyone sit down. We are going on a lion hunt!" For the next four minutes, the entire class was held spellbound as Julie created the fun and excitement of this traditional imaginary excursion. Though using a quiet voice, Julie was capable of a wide range of effects as she spoke. The children were delighted and clamored to do it again.

Shaking her head with a big smile, Julie softly asked the class to line up to go outside. With astounding calmness the class easily formed into a single line, snaking among the tables and chairs that crowded the room. In a loud whisper, Julie reminded her charges about moving quietly through the halls. Almost automatically Julie moved up and down the line of children, touching those who were not listening, separating Charles and another boy. Returning to the head of the line, she opened the door and led the class out.

Julie's days were full. She would leave home early in the morning to drive to school. During the half hour drive she would leave the car radio off and mentally review her plans for the day. She liked to arrive at school by 7:45, which gave her time to make sure the room was completely set up and ready. The children began arriving at 8:15 and Julie liked to greet each one of them individually. She considered this just one way that she could help each child feel as if he or she were a special person. The children chose certain activities to work with until everyone arrived. It was during this informal time that Julie collected money, took care of notes from home, or observed children. This period lasted about fifteen minutes, and was followed by a fifteen-minute group time on the small rug area. Children would help with attendance, the calendar was updated, and any business relating to the day was dealt with. Then the children selected their work/play activity, or rules might be reviewed, or new materials introduced to the class. A half-hour work/play period followed. During this time Julie moved from child to child, interacting with children as they went about their activities. Clean-up came after the work/play period, and an active game or song or outside play usually followed clean-up. When the children returned from the playground they got a drink, used the toilet, and then rested at the tables while music was played on the phonograph. Then Julie read a story to the group, and gave them about twenty minutes of whole-group instruction. The class ended at 11:00 with a clean-up period and an evaluative discussion of the day's activities.

Because the kindergarten children were dismissed thirty minutes before the rest of the students at Annandale went to lunch, it was convenient for Julie to eat with the teacher aides rather than the other teachers. Annandale remodeling required that the faculty use part of the school's office for their meal. Julie felt that it would be adding to the crowd for her to eat with the other teachers in the office. After a quick lunch, Julie would begin preparations in her room, getting ready for the afternoon class which arrived at 12:00. The schedule for the afternoon was much like the morning, though she found the afternoon class more mature and easier to work with. The afternoon class was dismissed at 2:40, and then Julie would begin preparations for the next day. Julie usually stayed in the building until 3:30 or later. On the drive home, she tried not to think about school, but turned the radio on and relaxed.

Julie's husband was spending a great deal of time studying in the law library, thus placing most of the housekeeping and cooking responsibilities on Julie. At the start of the school year, when Julie was particularly busy, Rob would pitch in with the chores, and they would frequently go out to eat in the evening. After supper Rob would return to the law library, and Julie would begin work on her plans for the next week and final preparations for the next day. "Teaching is more than an eight-hour day," she explained. "I think that one of my greatest strengths as a teacher is having things well planned. I really enjoy what I am doing, and I want to do my best. This is always the way I have been." Julie spent two and one-half hours each evening and six or eight hours each weekend preparing for her teaching. Rob also studied until late in the evening, and he gave her strong support in her teaching efforts.

Julie's principal, Mr. Grove, turned out to be another source of support. Even before school began, Julie expected that the principal would provide assistance if problems arose. Julie found Mr. Grove both understanding and encouraging of the innovations she was trying in her class. Julie felt him to be fair and talked to him without fear of recrimination. Mr. Grove approved of the way Julie was teaching, and she saw his suggestions as positive and useful. In mid-November Julie was formally evaluated by the system's elementary school supervisor. In a conference after the observation, Julie was pleased to find the evaluation positive and the feedback helpful.

October was followed by an unseasonable, cold November, a prelude to the coming winter. Julie began taking a more direct approach with those few students who were not attending in group activities. She was not angry or forceful with those children, but instead of her earlier strategy of ignoring them, Julie became calmly consistent in her demands that they behave as she requested. When children did not comply with her verbal requests, Julie took the time to guide them to their places; this represented an intentional change in Julie's classroom management strategy. Julie was thoughtful and explicit in her standards of behavior for the children in her class. She consciously worked to be consistent in her enforcement of these standards. She used praise liberally in a natural, sincere manner, but not lavishly. When she found it necessary to speak to a child about his or her behavior, she did so politely with a minimum of fuss and bother. She called the name of the misbehaving child, and precisely stated the name of the behavior to be changed and how it should be changed. For example, she would say, "Charles, the puzzles are to be used on the table. Please sit at the table to work the puzzle." In the instances when she did not know how to deal with difficult or unusual behavior problems, Julie sought advice from Mr. Grove, and then dealt with matters on her own.

As October and November passed, Julie became increasingly confident of her teaching. She began to make "fine-tuning" adjustments in her teaching. Julie felt that perhaps her daily schedule was causing behavior problems and wasting valuable learning time because of the many changes from one activity to another. To reduce the number of transitions during the day, Julie eliminated some activities and lengthened others. She found this action effective; reducing the number of occasions when it was necessary to have absolute attention and quiet resulted in fewer management problems. With longer instructional and activity periods, children became more involved and were able to accomplish more.

Julie's own approach to teaching included much less whole-group instruction than used by the other teachers in the school. Building on her student teaching experience, she had planned a program where many materials grouped in activity centers and small-group activities took the place of whole-group instruction. Julie recognized that the time individual children spent in activities at the sand table, art center, library corner, science and math center, and at working puzzles or imaginative, dramatic play would be as effective for each child as would her instruction to all thirty children at once. As with the adjustments in the daily schedule, Julie's skill and confidence in her individualized approach grew as she made changes.

The first parent conferences came quickly in November. Though anxious about these conferences, Julie understood the great importance of close parent-teacher relations. She had been keeping parents informed of classroom activities through a newsletter, and when necessary made contacts with parents regarding their child's progress. Julie was aware that good public relations were vital to her style of teaching: "It is going to be tough to please all of the parents. Every parent wants something different for his or her child. Most parents of Annandale's students are conservative with their children and fundamental in their approach to education. Some parents want kindergarten to be strict preparation for the first grade. Others—the middle-income families—don't necessarily want it that way."

The first round of parent conferences went well. The parents were interested and asked questions which Julie could answer. She made sure that parents understood the reasons for what was happening in their child's classroom. She fostered feelings that their children were in a good place. Julie was pleased that she was able to listen to parents and respond without defensiveness. With the uncertainty of parent conferences behind her, Julie brought her full attention back to her teaching.

In and out of class, Julie continued to maintain honest and fair relationships with her students. She knew that five-year-olds were very sensitive and could be upset or hurt by seemingly little things which she, as an adult, might not be aware of. She listened carefully when children disagreed with her point of view and she carefully explained her own action. As in the beginning of the year, Julie continued to maintain a calm and rational approach to her students. In her communications with the children, she continued to stress her reasons for acting in a certain manner. Julie felt that her students saw her as a friendly person who let them work and helped them, and, if she got upset with their behavior, let them know why she was upset.

It was obvious that Julie enjoyed the children in her class. She liked watching them and being with them. Frequently she accompanied her class to art, music or gym even though she didn't have to be with them. Julie found her students loyal and resilient, and they expressed their satisfaction in their smiles: "The times that I've been mean, or felt that I've been mean, they still smile and say, 'See you tomorrow!'"

An important part of Julie's notion of the ideal teacher was being able to get along with the other teachers. She found that being both a kindergarten teacher and a first year teacher made that difficult. As a rookie, Julie felt that in the morning before school started she needed to be in her room making last minute preparations for the day; not chatting with other teachers. As a kindergarten teacher she was on a different schedule from that of the other teachers. When her lunch was over, other teachers were just beginning theirs, but that was Julie's time to prepare for the afternoon class.

As the Christmas vacation neared, Julie adjusted her schedule so that she could spend more time with other teachers before school started in the morning. Julie helped other teachers with after-school and evening Parent-Teacher Association activities. As a newcomer to Annandale school, she was ignorant of some of the folkways of the school staff. Julie missed out when a notice was posted in the teacher's lounge about a meeting of the faculty "Culture Committee." She later discovered that this was a euphemism for a faculty gathering at the local pub! Julie got along well with the other teachers, interacting positively when they were together. She found it easy to talk to the older librarian next door to her classroom, and with a young male teacher whose sixth graders frequently worked with the kindergarteners in one-to-one situations. On the whole, Julie found the faculty friendly to her and generally supportive.

A severe winter and a natural gas shortage closed the Cleburne schools for a month. Julie met with small groups of pupils in their homes and prepared materials for parents to use with their children. Julie found that the makeshift teaching during the break had several positive effects. Working with small groups in homes greatly increased her knowledge of individual children. More important was what parents had learned about their own children and the tasks of teaching. Many parents working with the packets found that their children were unable to function at grade level. Julie found that parents were now more interested in what their children were doing in school, and that home-school cooperation was maximal. And parents were telling her that teaching was not as easy as they had once thought!

By the end of March, Julie noticed changes in her teaching and her life at Annandale. The long school closure during the energy crisis forged a new feeling of closeness among the faculty. First year and experienced teachers alike were faced with the uniqueness of planning for school activities outside the traditional classroom. Julie felt this experience formed a stronger bond with other teachers than would have occurred in the normal school setting. She became more connected to the social life of the school faculty.

Returning to the normal school attendance patterns brought all of Annandale's teachers face to face with the realization that much remained to be completed in the remaining weeks of school. Julie was aware that many of the school district's established objectives for kindergarten remained to be met. Julie was also aware that her one year contract would soon expire. Surprisingly Julie felt closer to the principal, in spite of the increased observation as the final evaluation neared. She felt more secure, in spite of the fact that the kindergarten teacher she replaced would probably return in the fall.

As the tentative April skies surrendered to May's strong sunshine, Julie thought about her year. At the beginning she had written everything down in her plans for teaching. She wanted every minute accounted for. After almost a year she still planned for every day, and for the big blocks of time, but she understood better what she was going to do, and didn't have to write in such detail. Julie had increased her ability to judge how long activities would take, so she no longer put down scheduled times. She continued to make adjustments which improved her already highly effective teaching. She added a quiet work time to her daily schedule in order to provide a better setting for her prereading groups. Julie kept adding to her notes of things she would do differently next year: pacing groups and children at various levels, and beginning the year with a more strict approach to behavior in whole-group activities. Julie realized that she was learning a lot about children and about teaching, and was eager to use her new-found knowledge to improve her teaching next year.

Unexpected good news came for Julie with the closing of the school in June. The regular kindergarten teacher on leave from Annandale had decided not to return to teaching. Julie was elated when she was given a regular contract for the following year. But as important to Julie as the contract was the sense of accomplishment and a new sense of identity: "At the beginning of the year I was very excited and scared, and nervous about how I would do at teaching. I felt all the other teachers would be doing so much better because they were all experienced. I was always comparing myself to them. I also thought that everyone would be watching for my mistakes. I was worried about how I would do, but because I felt everyone was watching me, I was determined to do well. Throughout the year I fluctuated between thinking I was doing a good job and thinking I wasn't. I would do something well, someone would comment on it and I would feel a little better, but then I would snag on something else and fall back to feelings of insecurity. I think by the end of the year I realized that I was going to make some mistakes and I took them in stride. I didn't get as low as I ever did at the beginning of the year. I stopped down-grading myself for being in my first year of teaching. Experience isn't everything."

Julie Carson was highly motivated to teach. She began the year with feelings of insecurity common to many first year teachers. She also began at a high level of competence and intense drive to succeed. She met problems thoughtfully, relying on her thorough preparation and advice from her principal. Her expectations of the job and of children were realistic; misperceptions were minor and quickly corrected. By the end of the year Julie Carson knew that teaching was as she had anticipated: challenging and rewarding. She knew that she could teach, and teach well.

# The Best of Both Worlds 12

The room is large, well lit, and carpeted. There is a minimum of furniture; display cases, clothes racks, and cash registers have not yet arrived. Toward the far end students lockers cover one wall, and in front of them are clustered tables and chairs for twenty students. This is the class area, occupying less than a third of the room space. This is where Donald Cross will teach his first year.

\* \* \*

It's the beginning of the second day, a Friday. Don is there early to arrange chairs, to organize papers, to review once more what will take place today. He's anxious. Yesterday did not go as planned. The students were unresponsive, and though he covered the material he had intended to cover, he felt much was missing. Students wander in and go to their lockers. Don greets each one, handles leftover paperwork, and converses casually with some of the students.

Don knows the students by name. He's already had extended conferences with each student and parents. The nature of the merchandising program was explained, and some expectations for student performance were defined. Don got to know a bit of background about each student and was confident that they were prepared for the work ahead. He was confident of their maturity and their commitment to his career program. "These students are different. They know where they're headed."

Eighteen students were assembled. Don collects his thoughts

and returns to the table that serves as his desk. It's 8:30, time to begin class. For the next hour and a half these students will be his charges. These high school seniors will expect him to teach them the fundamentals of merchandising. For the next nine months they will hold these expectations. The anxiety returns. Attendance: everyone is here.

"I got so wrapped up yesterday, I forgot to say I'm glad to be a part of the new ideas that are going to take shape in this place. This is going to be a different kind of school, requiring extra efforts of all of us. I hope you realize that, and that success at your jobs will depend on how much effort you're willing to make." The class is quiet.

Don distributes a list of expectations, some from school policy and some from policy set by merchandising firms in the area. Policy is important. Just as employee expectations must be understood in every firm, so too here, that would be the case. The class reads the sheets silently. He asks for questions. There are none. The expectations apparently are clear. Don distributes cards to be signed by parents and returned. A student ventures a question as Don passes by. He responds quietly to the student. Another student asks a question aloud; Don responds aloud. Don distributes a personal phone book supplied by the telephone company to each student: "Now that you are entering the business world, you must get used to keeping telephone numbers handy. It will save you a lot of time in the long run. I expect you to keep these booklets handy at all times." The students receive the phone books with no comment. Don collects papers distributed yesterday; they were to be signed by parents and returned. Several students do not have the sheets. He speaks to them individually.

"I'd like you to take a moment to fill out this information form. It will help me in placing you in jobs. Then print your name on one of these file folders. That's where your work records will be kept." The students begin the tasks. One students stops, confused. He asks for further explanation. Don responds. Moments pass and another student asks the same question. Don tenses. He bites his lip and places his fingertips firmly on the tabletop. "Okay, I did say it twice, so now listen. . ." He smiles at the students but wonders if they're listening. He wonders if his instructions are clear. Papers are collected.

"On this small piece of paper make five circles, like a bull's eye. Place in the center-most circle the person you feel is most important to your success in this program. In each circle out from the center, place the next most important people." The room is quiet as the students work. Don urges them to finish quickly, the third time today he has done so. "Okay, now everyone should have placed themselves in the center of the bull's eye. Because success here will depend mostly on you. What did you put down for second most important? Miss Cauley?" She responds that the employer is second. "No, I think that the teacher is second most important. I'll work with you in training for your job. Maybe later on the employer will be more important." Several students erase their answers. The discussion ends.

The class continues: another brief exercise, another questionnaire. One student queries, "Mr. Cross, did you have to use such big words on this questionnaire?" Don excuses the vocabulary: "Oh, you'll see that you'll learn many new words this year." A few student questions and he again says, "Please listen. I've repeated this three times. Am I clear?" Don finishes the class by explaining, once again, how this program will be different than the students' prior school experiences. This is to be a performance-based approach to learning, not the "traditional" approach. The students listen quietly. Momentarily he pulls an example from his business-world experience. "Examine the Pierre Cardin sweater in this picture. Look at the color combinations and the style. How can these traits be turned into selling points? Suppose I were . . ." The example brings him to life. He knows the business. The students catch on. It is short-lived. Don returns the discussion to the program until the class ends at 10:00. "I'm a new teacher. This is a new program in a new school. We're talking about new, new, new. We're putting it together, together."

A few students linger. One wants to know what the merchandising laboratory will look like when it's completed. Don shows him the blueprints. Another inquires about a conflict in scheduling. This too is handled. Soon all the students are gone, and Don is left to his thoughts, the stacks of paper in front of him, and his worries about next week.

Mr. Phillips, his supervisor, has asked him for an outline of the year for the merchandising program. Don does not feel he can yet project that far ahead. He isn't sure what he'll do next week. Yet neither does he want to disappoint Mr. Phillips. "After all, he's my boss." So, before Mr. Phillips asks for the outline again, Don wants to have something to present. But how can he?

His thoughts carry him back to last night. He had felt bad about yesterday's class and had called a friend, a woman teacher, to talk. It was good to talk to her. He felt like crying, but didn't. And when he'd hung up the phone, he felt empty again. The anxiety returned. In the middle of the night he awoke and could not fall back asleep. "There are five whole days next week! What'll I do?"

* * *

Donald Cross was new to teaching. He had had no teacher preparation; his undergraduate degree was in business management. For five years he worked in the merchandising world and found it unsatisfying. The get-ahead ethic ran counter to his manner and character. Yet he understood that the business world would always function on that principle. During those years he derived satisfaction from his contacts with youth. He was a Big Brother; he volunteered for work in church youth organizations; he was a youth leader at an institution for juvenile offenders. He liked working with youngsters. When the opportunity arose to combine his business knowhow with his commitment to youth, he jumped at it. As a teacher of merchandising he would combine the best of both worlds. He was enthused. The decision to go ahead represented a big change in his life, a new career. He wanted it. Temporary certification was granted, and he was hired to mastermind the new program at Rutherford County Vocational School.

The school itself was new. The diversified curriculum drew students from everywhere in the county to study in such programs as auto repair and maintenance, data processing, commercial food preparation, and Don's own merchandising program. His program would be like the others in its intent to incorporate laboratory experience into the classes. But, unlike the others, Don's program would include on-the-job training. Students would spend part of their school week actually working in local merchandising firms. Don himself was responsible for both the classroom/laboratory and the field components of the program. For all practical purposes, he would have to develop the program from the start.

In the weeks before school began, he busily planned and organized. He met with students and parents and teachers. He set up his contacts in regional merchandising firms, the place where, within the month, he hoped to have his students employed. He ordered texts, materials and furniture to outfit the lab. At times he would flashback to his years at the M. J. Bell Company, the firm he had left to take this position. It was frightening in that all the work, all the responsibility, all the pressures were there again. He found himself getting caught up in the race. But this had purpose that the other did not have. There was a higher goal here. That would make a difference, he felt.

In many ways he would organize and run the program as if it were the M. J. Bell Company. He would be the supervisor, and the students would be the employees. He would relate to them in this manner because it would be their best preparation for on-the-job success. He would conduct himself as a businessman and would expect a similar response from the students. The expectations would necessarily be high. There would be no problems: the students knew to what they had committed themselves, and he had learned to deal with youngsters whose behavior could be far worse. The "company" would function smoothly.

*   *   *

A week of classes has gone by. Furniture has been added to the lab space, though it is yet not complete. Routines have been established. Mounds of papers have been processed. At 8:30 only thirteen of the students are present. Attendance is taken and, just as in his business experience, the day starts with its complement of procedural matters. "One of the most important forms you'll fill out all year. . . ." introduces the accident procedure form. It must be completed and returned "by Monday. No excuses." Fire drill procedures. Absentee and tardiness procedures. Five more students have, in the meantime, arrived. They must be apprised of what is going on. The new textbooks are assigned. "Please take care of them. You'll have to pay for damages." In this and all the procedures, the consequences of breaking policy are made clear. Don asks to see the appointment calendar each student is to have gotten. Six of the eighteen have them. The others excuse their failure in various ways. Don is concerned about the poor response; he is upset. This would not have happened in the business world. "Those of you who don't have them must do so by Monday. This is considered an incomplete assignment." The class is quiet. There have been no questions so far, no voiced concerns.

Don distributes blank job applications. The students will practice completing them. He reviews the form and tells the students how he wants them filled out. He quizzes them for possible answers. "Mr. Collins, what do you have to say?" Collins has been talking to another student and does not know how to respond. "You're not listening, Mr. Collins." The students work on quietly. Don encourages them to make the most of their past experiences. "Be honest, but put yourself in the best light. Don't act like you've got nothing to offer."

For several minutes now a girl has had her head on the desk. "Miss Walsh, are you okay?" There is some movement, but no response. A different kind of quiet touches the class. They watch Mr. Cross and Miss Walsh. "Miss Walsh, will you please sit up." There is a challenge in his voice. She meets it with a moan. She is half asleep. "Miss Walsh, if you cannot sit up and attend to class, then leave and report to Mr. Phillips." She props her head up.

Business continues. Mr. Cross, at the front, directs activity. His suit, his posture, his demeanor bespeak the value of that world. He addresses the students as Mister and Miss. Boardroom etiquette is practiced. He does not lean on furniture, he does not sit on tables, he does not use slang. These would not be appropriate in a merchandising firm; they are not appropriate here. These are standards he holds for himself and for his students. They are learning.

Don distributes an assignment sheet to the students just before the class ends. Explanations are hurried, just as they are at the start of a busy workday. The students rush off to the next class. Don faces the next six hours of planning and worry. He looks at all that must be done for next week. He worries that at 4:00 he'll hardly have begun to get things done, and then his weekend will be filled. "It's difficult to separate personal life from professional life. It's hard to put the briefcase down at the end of the day."

* * *

The weekend has come and gone. Monday flew by, filled with procedural matters and continued work on job applications. Tuesday's class begins much as has every class since the first. At 8:30 only a portion of the students have arrived; some students seemingly ignore the school's policies about promptness. Attendance is followed with checking for overdue assignments and completing paperwork. Several students have not yet turned in accident procedure forms. School work permits must also be completed and returned; several students have not done this. The indicators Don would like to have of a smooth-running merchardising operation are not yet in evidence. Appointment calendars are not in hand. "Mr. Fulton, is this the way you'll respond on a complicated assignment too? All you had to do was get a calendar book." Don is puzzled and bothered by the continuing lack of student response; many do not complete even simple assignments, and in class they remain distant.

"Let's continue now working on the applications for the Steiner Merchandising Mart company. I'll be around to check your work. I don't want any mistakes, and it must be neat. Remember these applications could represent you to a prospective employer." Students continue the task begun several days ago. "Mr. Cross, what should we put down for Expected Salary?"

"Put the minimum wage. It's $2.30 per hour." Another student challenges this fact. He believes the minimum wage is less. Don listens to him, but brings the discussion to an abrupt end: "Put down $2.30, please."

As the students complete the forms, Don starts a dialogue with one student about the information he has supplied on the forms. The exchange serves to highlight the best responses and suggest how other responses could be put more positively. Momentarily the boardroom gives way to the classroom, the supervisor to the teacher. The class attends to the dialogue and learns from it. Another students raises her hand: "Mr. Cross, I need to have a textbook assigned to me." He is distracted from the dialogue. Don gets a book and hands it to the student. "You would not do this in a business meeting. I don't mean to be personal, but you've got to be better prepared than this. I would prefer that these matters be handled before or after class." The dialogue is lost. Questions posed to other students generate less response. Mr. Cross, the supervisor, again emerges and addresses the meeting.

At 10:00 the students exit. Don breathes a relieved sigh. He wonders if the students feel they are learning. Job applications and interviews are of immediate importance if the students are to secure positions in local firms. Yet somehow this all did not seem like real "content." He's worried too that even with this preparation, some students will not do well. They might miss job possibilities because of simple mistakes. Don thinks to himself how different the administration of a school program is from the administration of a merchandising operation. The difference was unexpected.

Mr. Brighton, an enthused student, returns to class. "Mr. Cross, you don't have to worry about the students not answering questions. They don't know each other yet, and aren't comfortable speaking up. And I don't answer because I always answer. They'll get better at it." Don appreciates the concern but is not consoled. "I can understand when they try to answer and cannot, but I can't accept it when they don't even try." Don is open with this student as he would be with a business associate. He shares his goals, his disappointment, his fears.

*     *     *

By the end of the third week, the confidence and hopes with which Don had approached the teaching task were all but shattered. The initial feeling of having many things to do gave way to being overwhelmed. Students' reluctance to respond now seemed to be refusal. The measures of a good business operation were missing. Don's confidence in his ability to plan and teach was shaken. "I don't know how to do this; I've never done it, you know." On Friday of that week, he reflected back over the events that were making his life hell.

"I feel like I'm running scared. There's too much to do and I don't know where to begin. Students should all be placed in jobs by next week if they're going to get the required number of hours of on-the-job experience, and I haven't even contacted all the firms yet. Most of the firms are in a seasonal slump now; they can't hire anyway. I should have known that. Everything takes so much time! What does it matter? These kids are hardly ready for interviews anyway. Last night I couldn't sleep for worrying about placements. I don't know how to do things. I can't type and all my dittoes have to be hand written. I don't know how to run a ditto machine. Yesterday, before school, I got a master stuck in the ditto machine—no, it was the thermofax, and it started to burn. Five teachers were standing there waiting to use it! I'm feeling inadequate.

"Guilty. I want to put the briefcase down when I go home, but I can't. If I go out, I feel like I should be working. Even when I'm with friends I can't stop talking about school. They get turned off.

When I see friends who are teachers, I'm always asking their advice, their help. I'm a leech. I'm a charity case, always asking for a dole.

"I don't know how things run around here. I've been keeping the students right up till 10:00. I didn't realize they were supposed to have time to switch classes. Finally, their English teacher asked me whether the students were at fault for always coming late to her class. I apologized and said it was my fault. It won't happen again.

"Being a teacher is just different from being a merchandising trainee. When I did that, I had daily visits from my supervisor. I had a training manual that I could follow; it spelled out these things. There were periodic reviews to tell me how I was doing. And there were fellow trainees whom I could talk to; we went through it together. In teaching there are none of these things. I didn't know that.

"I've been sick. Partially it's the flu, but it's also the worry. My stomach is in knots. Last night I cried. I actually cried. The lady next door came over. She knocked, and I thought, 'What the hell does she want!' I opened the door, and there she stood with a piece of cake and a big bowl of soup. And I cried. I just cried. I hadn't been with anyone to let something out, and I felt so bad because I was feeling so negative and here she was bringing me food. She says, 'You haven't eaten in days, I bet.' I'm losing weight and I look pale . . . I'm wiped out . . . I must get away. . . . Things will be okay.

"Today was the worst. I spilled the beans to my supervisor. Before school, Mr. Phillips came into the room, and I'm so paranoid, I could have sworn he was holding a flag saying, 'When are your students going to be placed?' Well, I just came out and was candid with him, and told him how bad it looked. And he was very calm, but very direct and factual. He said exactly what I knew he'd say, and though I have reasons for everything, he made it clear that placement was one of my major responsibilities. 'You know, Mr. Cross, I was very free with you about how you spent your time and made your decisions before school started. Well, now we may have a real, real problem.' I had done everything I thought could be done before school started. I had all the parent conferences and had formed an advisory committee of people from each firm, and we met. But none of that helped. None of that counted. I didn't know . . . He's my boss. He knows what's going on. He made his point. I felt so stupid; I felt like crawling into a hole. The whole program could be in jeopardy! Just like in my nightmares. I felt like a worm.

"Then the students started coming in and class had to start. By the time I got all the paperwork out of the way, and had given some students info about the interviews I had set up for them, I was way behind. I could see them getting impatient, and some didn't like the times I had arranged for them. Some were very patient and accepting. But others started getting up and asking, 'Can I go at 2:00 instead of 1:00?' 'Is this for Huffman & Company or for M. J. Bell Company?' It was chaos! I was becoming impatient and yelling. I felt no one was listening. And in comes Mr. Phillips again. And he could see what was going on. Well, it wasn't all that bad, I know, except in my own mind. Many students were just sitting there quietly, waiting. Mr. Phillips came in to ask me about some invoices. It dawned on me that that's why he came in earlier. But I didn't give him a chance! Instead, I spilled the beans. Well, I had to tell him eventually anyway."

The three weeks had been hell, but there had also been good days. On several occasions he had good responses from students. On one day in particular everything went well. All the students participated; some even volunteered for extra work. He had the feeling that he fielded questions well, and felt that the group work was very productive. On days like this, Don realized his hopes for teaching, and he knew that things could go well for him. The company ran smoothly. On these days he'd say, "I feel like I've accomplished a lot. I'm proud to be in this position, proud to be a teacher." And in consideration of the worst days, "I just need time."

Time, of course, was what Donald Cross had plenty of. From October to June he would have the opportunities to come to grips with the tasks of teaching, with the students and staff of the new school, and with himself. The next several months were to be a rollercoaster ride: incredible highs and abysmal plunges. Don was not ready for it, but he survived. And he grew. Out of the year emerged a different teacher, a different person, than had entered the class that September.

Donald Cross had begun the year hoping for and expecting the best of his students. He was confident that they were able and willing to meet the high expectations set for the program. But quickly he had reason to doubt this assumption. The sleepy Miss Walsh incident was but the first of many. The students' lack of response on assignments and in class led him to query one day,

"Why do you want to fail?" The students did not respond. In spite of poor results, he continued to hold high expectations for their performances. In job interviews and eventually in on-the-job situations he expected a mature, adult, and well-trained response from each of the students. To accept less than good work was to condone poor work; that would not prepare students well for the business world. Don felt he had an obligation to both the students and employers to maintain high standards. He also had obligations to the new school. Those standards placed him in a bind: the students had to be given opportunities to display responsibility on their own, yet he himself felt ultimately responsible for their performances. Left on their own, many students would not meet the standards; they would fail. Constant pressure, continual reminders, and pleading encouragement would help them now, but not in the long run. It would also make him the teacher he did not want to be.

Don wanted to be the businessman. In the business world, the boss sets the pace, and the employees eagerly follow. Their commitments are in harmony. Acceptance of responsibility is not in question. He felt if he could establish the routines and atmosphere of the merchandising firm, he would be performing, for such a program as this, the essential teaching acts. The role of teacher would follow. He knew he would have to make presentations, develop skill-building exercises, design tests, and fulfill other such tasks, but these would flow from the content and the climate of the merchandising program. So he set out to be the model businessman—supervisor in this case. He recreated his own work-world experience for the students—the employees. He was Mr. Cross, the businessman; he was not Don Cross, the church volunteer, the youth leader, or the Big Brother.

The segmenting of his business manner from his personal manner was a conscious act. It was something he had done as an employee of the M. J. Bell Company. In the boardroom it was demanded. Entering the classroom, Don realized that it was his knowledge and experience in merchandising, not teaching, that qualified him for the position. And so his business manner again became his dominant style. Don Cross, the person, was also alive, but hidden, and not allowed to enter the classroom. He once expressed, "I don't have time to get wrapped up in feelings." The person he knew himself to be was not part of his intended teaching style. This conflict between his outward and inward selves had once before been a problem. It had left him unhappy with his business career. As the year went on, it seemed headed that way again.

Miss Walsh's attitude continued to plague Don. She was belligerent. He talked with the counselor and Mr. Phillips about her. He wanted her out of the program. "She'll do great in an interview, because she can be very nice when she wants to. She'll charm her way in. Then when she gets the job, she'll be hell to train. I can just see her now, refusing to do class assignments." They listened to him, but did nothing. After several weeks of discussion, the matter was settled at another level. A visiting administrator overheard Miss Walsh lampooning Mr. Phillips to her friends. She was called to the office, but did not report. The administrator was infuriated. She was expelled. Don felt relieved, but sad that it had to happen that way. And just as he had predicted, Miss Walsh had, in the meantime, secured a job—one of the precious few Don had found. It was disturbing.

More disturbing, however, was the reprimand from that administrator that Don should not have let the student "mess up." He was told that such students could not be allowed to represent the school. Don explained that he had wanted Miss Walsh out of the program weeks earlier, but was not supported. His explanation fell on deaf ears. He still was held responsible, and he felt his job was in jeopardy.

The incident struck a deep chord within Don, one which had uncomfortably sounded, off and on, for all the years of his adult life. He was in search of a place for himself, and had not found it. Success, achievement, and the work ethic were part of him. In the past he had been successful in his work, but remained unsatisfied. This venture into teaching was a gamble. He was not sure of success, but it held a promise for satisfaction the business world could never offer him. In order to find his place, he took the risk. Failure had seemed remote.

With the reprimand, however, his growing doubts were confirmed. It began to look more and more like he was losing the gamble. At the beginning of the year, Don had instituted weekly meetings with Mr. Phillips to seek his advice and to keep him informed. Those meetings continued, and though they were helpful in many ways, they did not alleviate the feeling of loneliness in the face of this venture: "I can talk with him all I want, and he listens. But when it comes right down to it, it's my responsibility. The pressure's on me.

Everyone else can just walk away from it." When a counselor re-
signed because of pressure from the administration, and several
teachers threatened to do the same, Don realized that careers were
being made and broken at Rutherford County Vocational School.
He did not want his new career to end in failure.

The pressure on the students had to be maintained. The businessman remained dominant. As furniture for the lab area was installed, Don called on the students to bring items to fill out the
displays. The lab had to look complete; it had to be usable. "Bring
used items from home, and ask at the places you work if they can
spare some inventory. You can give me all the excuses you want, but
it's not results." As he pressured and challenged the students, Don
told them not to take it personally: "Take it as a business thing."

But many students did take it personally. His demands were
met with hostility and sometimes personal affronts. Don pondered
his reputation in the school: "Most of the students like me; some girls
who are not in my class are always stopping in to talk. Some students fear me, I think. A few don't respect me." In one classroom
exchange a student blurted out, "We're not learning anything here.
We haven't all year." Don was hurt, and the students could tell. The
student retracted his statement, and the others spoke in Don's de-
fense, but Don was not consoled. Another of his fears were confirmed: the students were not learning.

Don was frustrated. He felt he was just putting in time, getting
nothing accomplished. Planning was becoming more difficult.
Translating his own business knowledge into classroom lessons to
which the students would respond was increasingly demanding.
There were too many other things to do as well. Planning became
the avoided chore. "It's like I'm setting myself up to fail. I know I
need to sit down and write out what has to be done in class. If I did
that, I could feel like I know where I'm going. But I just can't bring
myself to do it. I go home at night and think of all the things that
need to be done, and I feel like throwing in the towel. Look, this is
Friday. With all the work I've got to do this weekend, it might as
well be Sunday night."

His frustrations in school created problems in his personal life,
too. The demands of energy and time left him with little of himself
to offer his friends. "To them this is an alien career. They don't want
to hear about my problems with Mr. Williams, or my ideas about

guest speakers. My personal life is falling apart: my mother wants to know why I haven't been home for so long; my friends want to know why I'm never around. I feel a trapped-in frustration. It's getting to be just like M. J. Bell Company, pressure and all. I get so depressed."

Don dealt with his depression in a variety of ways. He'd shift activities, do something completely different, and try to work it out of his mind. At other times he'd try to think it out, reason it through, deal with it in his head. Increasingly, he found other people helpful at these times: "I used to be a soloist. I'd never go to anyone for help. Now I find that others who listen are very helpful. I was told when I started teaching to find someone to talk to. That's been excellent advice. As I talk things out, they seem to get better, even if only for a while." And when nothing else worked, Don prayed. "Sometimes that's all there is left to do."

In November, for the first time, he voiced his doubts about whether teaching was for him. In December, he doubted that teaching could be worth it: "I can hardly wait until June. It's not just being depressed. The job's just not worth it. I was told it's all part of the first year, the growing pains. I was told it's a bitch. They were right."

It happened that Miss Walsh's expulsion was reversed when the matter reached the central offices of the school system. Several weeks after her abrupt departure, she was brought back, escorted by Mr. Phillips. In the middle of the class they entered, and amidst the stares and quiet acknowledgments of the students, she took her seat. Don smiled and welcomed her back sincerely. He knew she had been through a lot. "I'm sure we'll be able to work things out."

Problems with student performances continued. One student missed the only job Don had any hope of her securing. "She has a C average in math; how was I supposed to know she wouldn't be able to pass a simple math test!" Another student, Mr. Arturo, was caught stealing at the place he worked. The company fired him and he was expelled. Again Don was held accountable for something over which he felt he had no control. "Mr. Phillips asked me if I had ever reviewed company policy with the kid. Since when do you have to read company policy to know that stealing is wrong!" Another student was suspended from her job for violating company policy.

Don was encouraged by Mr. Phillips to talk with each of the job supervisors. It sounded like a good idea in light of all the problems that were arising. It would serve to "cover" him too. It backfired. The students were irate. Miss Walsh demanded to know why he told her boss to "watch out for stealing." Mr. Collins wanted to know why the supervisors were told to be strict. Don had not given these instructions to the supervisors, but the intimation was there. The students sensed they were not trusted. Don could not explain fully: he could not tell the class that Miss Powell was found in the stockroom when she wasn't supposed to be on the job. He could not reveal that Mr. Arturo was caught stealing a twenty-dollar bill. The student assault was strong; they had taken his move personally. He was not prepared for this challenge; it would not have happened in a merchandising firm. His self-defense was ineffective.

Mr. Williams complained, "Mr. Cross, you've done nothing to help me get a job." It was well into the school year, well past the deadlines, and Mr. Williams was still unemployed. He forgot interviews. He hadn't even secured a work permit. His class attendance was sporadic and consistently tardy. Students commented one day when Mr. Williams arrived early: "Look who's here! Why are you here so early? Are you sick?" Mr. Williams was popular; he had been elected class president at the start of the year, beating Mr. Brighton. From this post he challenged Don's authority. His blatant irresponsibility would have been serious enough. But he also was quick to rebuff. He provided a regular stream of commentary to Don's instructions. Don corrected and reprimanded him, but would not contest with him for the students' favor. On a cold January day, Don tried to get the students working on setting up displays. They were sluggish. They protested that they did not understand his instructions. Mr. Williams stood and explained the same point, and the students responded. Mr. Williams turned to Don and said, "Why didn't you explain it that way?"

Don was slowly becoming paralyzed. "The students really feel that I'm working against them, not with them. I'm afraid to ask what they think of the program. I'm afraid to look at them for fear they'll not be listening. I'm afraid when they come up to me that they are going to ask to get out of the program. We're supposed to take a breakfast field trip next week, and I'm afraid to bring it up to them. What if no one shows up?" The good days and the responsive students did not offset Don's growing fears and doubts. His earlier indecision about what to do was now accentuated by the worry that action would lead to further problems, or be met with disdain.

Don continued to meet with Mr. Phillips, though not as regularly. He did not want to be "discovered" in his inadequacies. He did not want to be reproached. "I've seen Mr. Phillips talk to the other teachers. He can really be unreasonable, asking them to do things over which they have no control. I still talk with him about my concerns, but I don't reveal my fears." A friend told Don he was paranoid. "He's probably right. I've got too many fears and insecurities which keep me from doing what I know needs to be done. What I need is a good kick in the pants. Someone to tell me to stop feeling bad and start getting things done."

Don also kept himself open to the students, but he did not disclose as much as he had earlier. Mr. Brighton was the exception. He became, through the year, a trusted sounding board. He was enthused about the program and the possibilities it opened for him in the business world. His participation was full. Don trusted his judgment. After class, Mr. Brighton would linger, finishing his work or explaining a new idea. Sometimes he interpreted: "When you overemphasize things too much, you give students a reason to not listen," and, "When you make simple things look complicated, you confuse us." Don listened and took to heart such advice.

The breakfast trip Don had hesitated to arrange was poorly attended; only six students arrived at the meeting place. Don bought them breakfast before the tour of the facilities began. He felt good about the response of the students who were there, but was disappointed that others did not come. The next day in class, talk focused on "Mr. Cross bought us breakfast!" Don overheard the comments and thought, "Gee, it was such a simple thing for me, but it made such an impact on them. I never realized how much impact a teacher can have."

By March there was a marked difference in Don's classroom manner. With only a few months remaining, he could see the end. "It is a revelation of survival. I know I will make it to June, and I want to make the most of what time is left." He became less formal. He allowed more of himself to come through. He began to use humor, some sarcasm. "Oh, I don't crack jokes for *them*. They're for me. I'm saying what I think and feel. I used to formulate my ideas all the time. Now, I'm more spontaneous. If I'm sarcastic, I'm feeling that way. That's the way I am." Don also felt more direct. "When there's something to be done, I tell them to do it. With some it works and with some it doesn't, but at least I've done what I could. I used to be more uptight about things; now I'm relaxed. I'm doing what I can."

Don was developing a sense of confidence. He began to understand that he was, indeed doing an acceptable job. His students were learning, albeit not as much or as fast as he'd hoped. In most cases, the on-the-job evaluations from their supervisors were laudatory, even if classwork was poor. "It boggles my mind when they ignore assignments, and they know it's going to affect their grades. I don't understand it. If they'd just try in class, they'd be getting really good grades." Don came to feel less responsible for the students' performances. He'd do everything he could and then the responsibility was theirs. "I'm low-key. I state the facts. I tell them, 'I'm on your side, and I'll help you get things done, but you've got to make the move.' But I don't allow them to affect me the way I used to. Like, if they got angry, I'd worry about what I did to make them angry. Now the checkpoint base is in me. I do what I think is best."

Through the year, Don came to see his students in a different light. He realized that some of the students would not succeed in the business world: "They just don't have the skills or the personalities that are going to make them attractive people to employ. And they're unwilling to learn. I'm hopeful, but it really lies in them to do it." He realized that some of the students didn't care about the program, and were not particularly convinced of its value for them. He laughed, one Friday, about the difference between himself and the students: "Look at me! Here I am concerned and wanting them to be concerned about what will occur on Monday. But they're high school kids: they've got the weekend on their minds. If I were a kid, I would too." He realized that his own bearing may have been evoking negative reactions in some of the students. "Students' acting out is often a sign of confusion, not a challenge. When I come on strong some of them get very defensive. They don't hear what I'm saying. That's why I've tried to change this. I'm factual. I lay the situation on the line. And I take on my 'Can I help you get this done?' attitude. They respond a lot better."

His relationship with Mr. Phillips changed as well. He met with Mr. Phillips to keep him informed, but now he made decisions on his own. "Why should I ask him to decide matters that will affect only me? I've got to make these decisions for myself. I used to go to people with that urgent 'help me' need. I was inexperienced, and I was afraid of trying things. Now if I want advice, I ask. But I make the decisions.

"I've also gotten over the need for solace from others. You know, that 'I've made a mistake, help me get over my terrible feelings about myself.' Oh, it's still there, and I'm fighting it. It's a terrible time to be a teacher when you're still trying to deal with your confidence and your ability to see yourself as having something to offer. But I'm getting over it. And teaching is helping, because it's such an onstage thing. I can't afford to have moods."

In spring, another set of tasks presented itself to Don: preparations for next year. There were students to interview, contacts to be set, materials to be ordered, problems to be anticipated. The thoughts of quitting which haunted his work through the winter months faded. "I owe it to myself to stick it out. My credentials need it if nothing else. Even the worst of times, I realized I couldn't be happy with myself if I didn't return."

\* \* \*

It's May, a Thursday morning. Students are assembling. Less now, than before. Mr. Williams is gone. Mr. Arturo is gone. Two others as well. Don readies a movie screen and projector. Students talk to one another and occasionally to Don about school matters. At 8:30, when it's time to begin, five students get up and move to the lab area. "We're going to destroy this place and the merchandise." Don looks up at them and senses they are buffooning. He smiles.

"This movie we are going to see today is the last of a four-part series. It fits in well with what we've been studying about American commerce." The students return to their seats and the film is begun. Don thinks, "Good, I didn't overreact. A teacher must learn so much from the students, more than they learn from him." The film continues. The students seem interested.

When the film ends, Don directs them to take five minutes to write a brief summary of the major points of the film. Some of the students get started immediately. Others delay. Don says it would be acceptable to work together. He sits at a table looking over assignments and papers. A boy and a girl begin fussing with each other about desk space. Don calls to them, "Sheila. Tom. All right, cool your burners. Let's be a bit more mature about this." The two quit their fussing.

Ten minutes pass before Don calls for the summaries. As the

papers are collected, Miss Walsh raises her hand. "Mr. Cross, I've been offered a full-time job at the store after I graduate." The announcement is a bit of a surprise, but not completely unexpected. Donna's work had improved steadily, and Don had told the students that some of them would be offered jobs if they were good trainees. Don is pleased and proud: "Did you all hear that? Donna has been offered a full-time position at Steiner's. That's really commendable. That's a good firm to work for."

The activity changes. The class is planning a quiz game. Students seem to be involved in the idea and somewhat concerned that it go well. Don sits at a table as the students come to him for advice. He stands and moves to the chalkboard. He calls on the students to write on the board when they know an answer. He gives the first answer, and writes it. A few minutes pass and no students have responded with answers of their own. Don seems at ease. Finally, Mike Freyer goes to the board and places an answer correctly. Other students page through the books for the answers. Some coax Joan Cauley to write all the answers on the board. They badger her, but she refuses. Now a sense of cooperation develops, and the class decides that Charles Brighton and Bill Collier should write the answers as the class gives them. Don does not tell the class what to do. He occupies himself with other matters. In a few minutes the board is covered, complete, correct. Don steps in and conducts an oral review. When, after some time, he begins to draw the review to a close, a student asks him to clarify several points. He does so.

At 9:30, just enough time for a planned quiz remains. Don distributes papers on which answers will be written. The questions will be given orally and in conjunction with a series of slides. "Look at the slide, listen to the question, write your answer. Think in there somewhere." The quiz begins. If it is to be finished before the end of class, there must be a time limit on each slide. It moves quickly. A student mocks Don by asking a question too quickly to be understood. Don says nothing but looks at the student. Another student snickers at the mockery. After a minute or so of silence, the student asks the question again, now slowly, almost apologetically. Don responds politely to his inquiry. The quiz continues. Don moves from table to table helping the students. They complain loudly about the time limit. The students argue among themselves about going on to the next slide.

At 9:45, the quiz continues. Some complaints, some challenges, some questions. Mostly quiet and work.

\* \* \*

As the school year drew to a close, Don reflected on the relationship that had developed between himself and his students: "They hate the school, the program, and maybe me. I suppose I understand that, although I regret it came out that way." Don felt he had the ability to relate to kids, but had not used it. He had been so sure that his work with youth had prepared him for any problems that might arise. He trusted that in the long run, "next year, when they're working, or maybe five years from now when they see what it's like, they'll understand why it was important to do these things. They'll understand why I taught the way I did." He was also proud of what they had accomplished. As he looked at the students, he thought about how far they had come since September: "They really have learned a lot. When I compare them to some of the new students who are here to be interviewed for next year, I can see how much they've grown. Some of my students are ready for full-time positions." Don had vacillated in his understanding of his students. He had assumed them interested and capable; he had thought them bored and ignorant. He had been encouraged by their signs of learning and destroyed by their disdain. He had treated them as adults and had pampered them as children. He had loved them and hated them. They were his pride and his embarrassment.

In the classroom, the businessman gave way to the teacher. "I tried being the businessman; that's where I was comfortable. A teacher needs structure, but not the businessworld structure. To most of the students that was such a foreign world that it had no chance of succeeding. They turned it off. Besides, it's a facade. It separated me from them. I was more concerned about getting things done than about the students. When I related to them as a teacher-advisor rather than a businessman, I saw changes. Sometimes for just a few days. And I see how other teachers make the best use of their rapport with the students. That's where I'm going to begin next year."

Don listed the causes for the changes he'd gone through. First, there were the growing pains—mistakes which once made, would forever be avoided. "Trial and error teaches." Secondly, the school year moved on with an inevitability of its own. "There are cycles to the school year: predictable ups and downs; vacations that renew energy; months that promise to never end; there are beginnings and endings. When I realized that, it made my year seem more sane." Then there was a reassurance when other people's predictions about teaching came true. "I was told that some students would quit their jobs without thinking, and it happened. I was told that I would become a better planner, and that happened." There was comfort in knowing that his experience paralleled others' experiences.

Don realized he had become more bold in his use of resource people, and at the same time more self-reliant. He called on people to do what they could, and he himself did what only he could do. He had also become more patient. He realized that time alone would solve some problems, if he would just wait. Finally, he came to understand that teaching offers very little direct gratification. "In business the rewards are all up front. In teaching the rewards are few, small, and often indirect. A teacher must settle for that or be frustrated."

Personally he had gone through a year of grave doubts and misgivings, but also one of promise and hope. He had learned much about himself. "I like being called 'teacher.' I never realized how much people look up to teachers. When I'm introduced to someone as a teacher, I almost feel as if I must straighten my tie. It's a really good feeling."

# I Think
# I Can...I Think I Can

"She's kind, considerate, and loving."

"She talks too loud."

"She helps you when you need help."

"She sometimes has her bad days and gets mad."

"She tries to like everybody in the class the same."

"She yells."

"She reads us stories."

"She doesn't make things clear."

"She's fun."

"She's not strict enough and we can't get very much done."

She is Ellen Gilder, new fourth grade teacher.

Ellen Gilder came to teaching with high hopes and big ideas. Employment at Rosecrest Academy meant so much to her—small classes, all the best facilities, intelligent well-mannered students, plentiful materials, no lesson plans to turn in, and an opportunity to work side-by-side with the most respected members of the elementary division. She was looking forward to a very special kind of first teaching experience. And, indeed, her first year was special, only not quite the way she expected it to be.

The first days were busy with faculty meetings. Learning what it meant to be part of a faculty of an exclusive private school was no easy task. The teachers seemed aloof, so cold. Ellen wondered if she would find someone she could relate to, someone to share ideas with or swim with or play tennis with, but the teachers seemed so unapproachable. She felt like an outsider, like someone being watched and judged by her clothes, her style, her demeanor. She hoped that would change.

Even her teammate, Mr. Hetherington was distant. Ellen couldn't understand how the person assigned to be her helper and the person with whom she would share a classroom and thirty-four ten-year-olds could be so indifferent to her. He gave no smiles, no words of encouragement. Only the stiff aura of politeness pervaded. The headmaster, a robust, white-bearded administrator had admonished her early to sit back and observe the life of the school before making decisions or acting on impulse. Ellen learned quickly that in a private school "image" is important. She was told that when parents pay $3,000 tuition for a specially structured kind of education, then they expect the traditions of the school to be preserved and observed. She knew the parents must believe their children were getting an excellent education and she felt it her responsibility to provide it.

Forewarned, Ellen plunged ahead; eager to begin, enthusiastic about the opportunities that awaited her. A bright, responsive, energetic young woman, Ellen had grown up with education in the best sense. Her interests ranged from anthropology to dance, from film-making to sewing and each activity was pursued with a great deal of enthusiasm. The fullness of living seemed to radiate from everything she did. Her parents, both respected members of the academic community, made a wide variety of opportunities available to her at an early age. They prized her individual development and change. Travel, the arts, and interesting people from all walks of life were a part of her early life experience. She attended a progressive private laboratory school and a small but rigorous liberal arts college where she achieved honors. As far back as she could remember she had wanted to be a teacher. Though several of her college friends chided her for wanting to do something "anyone could do" as they went off to graduate school in business, medicine, and the law, Ellen stuck with her love of children and her love of learning. Following her undergraduate education she entered a large state university for a year of teacher preparation to attain an elementary teaching certificate.

While in high school Ellen had met Bill. They went to college together and after college spent time together. They were planning

marriage the summer before Ellen was to begin teaching. She had
applied for and accepted a teaching position in the city where Bill
was employed. Then early in the summer trouble began. Bill decided to call the relationship to an end. Ellen was broken-hearted.
She moved back home with her parents and began looking for other
jobs. Through an old friend she learned of the position at Rosecrest.
She needed something to fill the void in her life and she thought
work would keep her busy. She had too much time on her hands, too
many regrets, too many feelings of rejection and frustration. She
needed a success, something to boost her morale, something to help
her believe in herself once again. A teaching situation like Rosecrest
seemed heaven-sent. She knew she would be challenged by the position. Her only fear was running out of good ideas to keep the children actively involved. With the support from her family, her desire
to become a good teacher, and her need to forget, Ellen welcomed
the beginning of the school year.

The first week meant meeting and becoming acquainted with
thirty-four children who for the purposes of most instruction were
divided alphabetically into two groups. Mr. Hetherington divided
the curriculum so that each of them taught the same lessons twice
during the day. Ellen was surprised and a little disappointed with
her responsibilities. While she had expressed an interest in teaching
language arts and reading, she was given instead social studies, science, handwriting, and spelling. In addition she was assigned to be
part of the preschool program one morning a week. Her lunch was
also considered to be part of her teaching duties. In the lunchroom
she was in charge of a table of elementary children where she and
they practiced proper table etiquette. This schedule gave Ellen little
time to prepare for classes or relax during the day. But that was all
right. At this point in her life Ellen felt that she could and would
devote all her time to teaching. The emotional part of her life needed
time to heal, so the hours she devoted each evening to preparation
for the next day's work were fine with her.

Ellen was very encouraged by her students. "Each day I enjoy
my fourth graders more. After the first day I began to identify them
as individuals. I am utterly amazed at their diversity despite their
similar backgrounds. There is an amazing gap between the most
mature and least mature children. There are some to whom I can
talk as if they were my dearest friends, and others who see school as

a joke and look for silly ways in which to get attention. In terms of their school work there is also a great deal of variety—both in how well they do and how much they do. How difficult it is to plan a lesson when one-fourth of the class won't understand even after I teach it, and the rest of the class may or may not catch on! I'm not sure what I'm going to do about the children at the bottom of the barrel who cannot even grasp the *instructions* for a test. Socially they do all right with the others, but they are in constant need of special, extra attention which would bore the others. Yet I cannot ignore the fact that these kids have not understood what was taught. I don't know if I should fail them or what I should do. Having only seventeen students at a time is a luxury. All sorts of discussion, joking and informality are possible. I've noticed distinct differences in the two halves of the group. One group seems more reliable, more self-confident, more independent than the other. It amazes me how much I've learned in just one week. Things are going just too smoothly."

As a part of introducing new teachers to the school and the school traditions, each new teacher was asked to share something special about themselves to the students in an assembly. Ellen chose to read aloud a favorite childhood story, *The Little Engine that Could*. She was surprised at her ability to get in front of the whole school and read. As she read "I think I can. I think I can. I think I can." she found herself gaining in confidence and actually enjoying reading. A week after the assembly a little second grader came into her room and told her that she had made her mom buy the book for her. Ellen was touched by the enthusiasm and thoughtfulness of the child and this gesture was the first tangible evidence she had to show her that indeed she would influence the children she taught. What a thrill!

The classroom for the fourth graders was a large, brightly lit room with movable desks in straight lines facing the board. In the front of the room were two teachers' desks—one large, well defined, and orderly; the other small, set to the side of the room, and piled with books and papers—Ellen's desk. A side of the room had built-in lockers for the children. One-third of the room could be separated from the rest by an accordion partition. It was in that space during a science lesson in the second week of school that Ellen's bright bubble burst.

Thursday afternoon Group B came to science unsettled. The children were all chatting, unable to sit down and get to work. Ellen, ignoring their rowdiness, began the lesson about measuring water temperatures. The students were up and running—filling beakers and picking up thermometers; threatening to sprinkle, spray, and pour water on one another. Ellen, believing that if she'd ignore the bad behavior the children would settle down and attend to the lesson, continued the demonstration. Three children started pounding rhythmically and loudly on the table tops and moving chairs squeakily. Still, Ellen continued to talk about the lesson, but she was becoming unnerved. This had never happened to her before. She wondered why the children were behaving this way. Didn't they want to learn? Didn't they like her? Didn't they think she could teach them or make them want to behave and listen? What was going wrong? The lesson had gone well with the other group; they hadn't acted this way, but now what was she going to do? Stop. (But then what?) Yell. (That would show them that she had lost control.) Send students out of the room. (Was that even allowed in this school?) Call for Mr. Hetherington. (But she wanted to be able to stand on her own two feet.) Ellen turned around quickly hoping some answer would come to her and as she did she dropped the thermometer she was holding. It shattered across the floor. Silence spread across the room like a wave of cold air. The pounding and squeaking stopped. One of the children who had been beating rapidly on the table top looked up at Ellen as if to say, "What's the matter with you? Can't you take it?" and shouted, "You BROKE it!"

"Well, I guess I did."

"What do you mean, you *guess* you did. You *know* you did it. You BROKE it. Admit it." The student taunted her. Before Ellen could respond the bell sounded and the students stampeded out of the room leaving their teacher frustrated and distraught. "When this happened to me I felt lost. I thought they were trying to hurt me. I took this kind of behavior as a direct assault on me. I don't know what I'm going to do. When I was student teaching and something like this would happen I would say to myself, 'Only a few more weeks and I'll be out of here,' but now I can't do that. I have to face this and handle it or I'm going to be in big trouble."

It was during that second week of school Ellen awakened to the permanance of her situation and the responsibility it entailed. As a

student teacher when disruptions occurred she had her cooperating
teacher to lean on and she knew she would be leaving. Now she had no
one. She felt she must prove to herself, to her students, and to Mr.
Hetherington, that she could handle any situation. But what was she
to do about the outburst that had occurred in science? Should she
ignore the behavior and begin again as if nothing had happened?
Should she explain to the whole class her feelings and encourage
group discussion about the incident? Should she talk to the three
principle troublemakers individually and let them know that their
parents would be called if this happened again? Should she talk over
the problem with Mr. Hetherington and follow his suggestions? She
would not have the group the next day because of a special school
program and, as Monday was a Jewish holiday, many of the children
would not be in class. Ellen adopted a wait-and-see attitude. The
next week all seemed forgotten.

Then came the initiation of parent conferences. The parents of
each child were called for twenty-minute interviews. They were
arranged at a time when both teachers were free. After the conference Ellen would write up what was said and these notes would be
filed with the child's permanent record. Ellen felt a bit awkward at
first through these meetings. She found herself becoming more attentive to the children whose parents she would be meeting that day.
She was surprised at the parents' responses to her. Parents would tell
her, "Joey really likes you. He thinks you are so pretty." Then they
would turn to Mr. Hetherington and praise his teaching abilities and
tell him how much they felt their child was learning. "The parents
are *incredibly* concerned over their children's achievements and 'place
in the class.' They all want to be called if anything goes wrong and
they want to help with everything the teacher thinks needs work. I
feel badly because I see the needs of the children as being partly
academic and partly emotional. I feel that a good portion of my day
is spent conferring with the children in one-to-one discussions of
their problems or feelings. Many of these pushy parents are causing
their kids more harm than good by emphasizing academic achievements and neglecting their social development." Ellen felt her subject matter was not valued highly by the parents and that too many
remarked about her youthfulness. The parents didn't seem pleased
about having their children encounter a new, inexperienced teacher.
It was during these conferences that she began to question her own
values in teaching. What was more important—helping the children

learn or making school enjoyable? What kind of teacher did she want
to be? A nice one or one that earned parents' respect?

Ellen was seeing herself as being too kind, too concerned about
the children's feelings. She wanted to be respected, too. She wondered if she could inspire learning *and* be loving or if these were
mutually exclusive qualities for teachers.

Ellen began constantly comparing what she did and how students responded to her with reactions given Mr. Hetherington, and
she felt she was always coming up short. She was beginning to see
herself as not quite good enough. Because of the time-consuming
nature of the conferences, as these doubts grew within her she was
not able to think them through. "My desk is chaotic, my brain is
chaotic, and my nerves are frazzled. For the first time, I yelled at a
child in front of the class. I couldn't take Judy's talking and disrupt-
ing any more. Everyone was shocked into subdued silence until the
bell rang to go home. I felt *awful*! Then crazy Judy stayed after
school to keep me company! Some of the rest of the class, perceptive
as they are, have spoken to me about her. They say all the teachers
have problems with Judy. They say things like, 'I like you Miss
Gilder. The only time you're mean is to Judy.' or, 'I still love you
Miss Gilder. Everyone has to yell at Judy.' I get lots and lots of love
from the children and that's great. But what about respect?"

The sixth week of teaching Ellen described as the worst week of
her entire life. The vivacious, strong-willed teacher of the first week
was replaced by a wide-eyed, soft-voiced, despondent woman full of
self-doubt, anxiety, and fear of failure. During this week she was
reminded of her times with Bill; he had called her just to see how
things were going and to tell her about his new girlfriend. On top of
that, Mr. Hetherington had been sick for two days and Ellen had
been required to teach all thirty-four students all subjects. She also
had playground duty which left her no time for herself. The students dealt some crushing blows when, during Mr. Hetherington's
absence, they kept asking Ellen when he would be back so they
could "have some peace and quiet in here." She had tried to organize
an "International Foods Festival" as part of her social studies unit on
tracing your own personal family history. The festival had been
chaotic largely due to Judy's loud and unruly behavior which
habitually disrupted many of Ellen's creative lessons. She wanted to
see herself as in control, but she couldn't—not with Judy. She found
herself being constantly tormented by doubts of what to do. She had

trouble sleeping. She questioned her own values and abilities. "If I can't be accepted for the kind of person I am as a teacher, then maybe I'm not cut out to be a teacher."

In the mornings as the alarm would awaken her, she would find herself saying, "Oh, my God, I have to go to school and teach. What am I doing? Why am I doing this? Will I be able to handle the kids? Will I ever be able to get Bill off my mind?"

Thanksgiving vacation came just at the right time. Ellen's high school class had decided to have a five year reunion over the break. It would be a good rest for her away from school and Judy and a chance to see Bill. Ellen had begun reaching out to other faculty members at Rosecrest. She became friendly with the dance teacher and learned that they both shared an interest in Ellen's old home town. The vacation allowed them an opportunity to become better friends as they drove there together. Ellen also began going swimming after school with the new second grade teacher, in the school's natatorium. The exercise and the conversation were welcomed. Gradually Ellen was getting to feel a part of the staff. The single women included her in their frequent "dinner meetings." She invited them to her new apartment near the school and they to theirs. Though Ellen longed for male companionship and a real social life, she welcomed the company of her colleagues.

Ellen returned from the holiday renewed, at least determined that she could keep herself together until Christmas. Only three weeks of Judy's behavior to be endured. Things had not gone well with Bill. His half-hearted promises of "we'll get together" left her feeling uncertain and frustrated. Did they still have feelings for one another or not? She didn't know but she *did* care.

Then it was time for the headmaster's first official review of her teaching performance. Awesome. "He was ten minutes late for the conference; he seems to be very busy at all times and obviously other things took precedence over our conference. He was kindly, solicitous when asking how things were going for me this year. He asked me about my summer plans and I mentioned perhaps going back to school for a Master's degree in reading. He replied, 'That would be a good thing to have,' and I wondered, 'Why—is he already planning to get rid of me?' He told me he thought that this year's new teachers at Rosecrest were the best they could be. He was pleased yet offered no praise other than to say he liked my vivacious personality. He asked if I had any problems and I replied that I had a problem controlling the class because of one child's disruptive behavior. He became quite paternal, assuring me that it was not my fault that she was this way and promising to set wheels in motion to get her medicated or sent elsewhere. (Oh, dear! Because of me?) At Wednesday's faculty meeting he mentioned problem children in the school and how they would no longer be tolerated. I guess I shouldn't feel any more responsible for bringing her case up than anyone of the other teachers—*all* of whom agree on her lack of self-control. I left the conference twenty minutes late for my next class and in a mixed emotional state. I wish he had said specific things about my teaching performance. He could have commented either positively or negatively. He's never been in my room though. Oh, well, I guess I feel empty as a result of that conference. I'll have to keep plugging along."

Problems with Group B persisted though Ellen always was ready with creative, inspiring activities to involve students in the learning process. In social studies each child was given a country to be "his own." Investigations of customs, traditions, geographical highlights, historical significance to world development, language, and religion were encouraged. Each child had a special contribution to make through his own studies and the class explored the world together. In science the children learned about the metric system by exploring their environments in metric measures. Looking at the ordinary became special. Handwriting lessons were made into opportunities for creative expression. Not only did Ellen encourage expressive language but she allowed the students to illustrate their writing. At one point in the year she had children make books for the preschool and together they visited the preschool where the fourth graders shared their stories with the young children. Because Ellen was interested in the reading process—so much so, in fact, that she applied for and was accepted into a Master's program in reading at a nearby university where she took evening classes—she made reading a part of every class. Reading aloud to the students was her forte. She always held a book in reserve. When a lesson was not going well or children finished early on work that was assigned, Ellen would pull out the book of the moment and the class would become silent, eagerly anticipating the sequence of the story. Reading aloud soon became Ellen's ace-in-the-hole. When all else would fail, the book would pull things together. As Ellen read she seemed to become a part of each character. Her vocal and visual interpretations inspired the children to want her to read more and more, and she did. Her reading time, though not a part of the formal curriculum, became the focus of much of the children's attention.

Before Christmas was a hectic time. Rooms had to be decorated and attentions were drawn to holiday festivities. Ellen anticipated an opportunity for rest and travel. Bill was still on her mind. She wanted to go visit him, to try to work things out. Instead, largely because her parents wanted her to, she decided to visit her grand-mother in California. Even Ellen's reading was not working the magic it had on Group B and Judy. The children were really taking advantage of her kindness and she knew it but felt powerless to do anything. Though appearing to be calm and patient while all around her was chaos, inside she felt trapped in failure. Each day as she observed how calm and quiet Judy was in Mr. Hetherington's class, she was reminded of her shortcomings. "Some days when it seems like every minute with Group B is a trial by fire. I can't even face Mr. Hetherington. I know how easily he handles them and it's like being slapped in the face to try to explain to him my problems. 'Don't let them get away with that rude behavior,' he says. So what do I do about it? There's the problem; if they don't cooperate be-cause *they want to* there really is no 'or else.' And don't think they don't know it. When they start working me over—talking loudly or rudely on purpose—I get angry inside but also embarrassed and upset at their ability to behave so poorly in my classroom. I see it as a reflection on me and my poor teaching or lack of motivation." When the children would come to her and ask her to "*please* do something about Judy," she was reminded of her shortcomings. Ellen believed that she had to reach every child, that she had to be loved and respected by each one to be a successful teacher. To top things off, two parents called Mr. Hetherington about Ellen's inability to con-trol the group. According to Mr. Hetherington the parents said that Ellen's classes were chaotic and that something needed to be done. Ellen was most upset about this. She wondered why the parents hadn't come to her directly about the problem. "Don't they consider me a teacher?"

Vacation was good but coming back to school was not. There was nothing she wanted more to do than walk out, leave the job and

the badness behind her. But she knew she couldn't. She had to try
again. Before vacation the two groups of children were reorganized.
When school began Mr. Hetherington announced to the class that
Miss Gilder would now be teaching math and language arts. Ellen
was dumbfounded. Not only was she unprepared for class but she
was completely unfamiliar with the children's math skills. What a
blow. Judy's behavior was going from bad to worse. The first week
back she made three children cry in class. She threw one girl's books
on the floor, pulled a chair out from under another, and kicked the
third girl in the face and made her lip bleed. She had generally taken
to picking on girls in the class who just couldn't take it. The boys sat
with idle curiosity, watching. Ellen, with a surge of determination,
talked with the elementary school principal about the problem.
(Though she struggled with a case of guilt feelings.) At her prompt-
ing, the Judy issue got off the ground—a parent conference for
disciplinary reasons would be held the next week. The frustration
and anger that had been building for five months must be faced.

Ellen could never have anticipated the events of the next week.
Tuesday at 3:00 A.M. while she was sleeping, a man broke into her
apartment. When she heard the breaking glass and footsteps she
screamed loudly. Luckily her neighbor heard the noise and called
the police. As the intruder rummaged through the apartment shouting, "Shut up or I'll kill you," Ellen was terrified. The police came
just as the man was fleeing and they took him into custody. Ellen
was distraught. Her life had been threatened. She felt incapable of
coping with added stress. She felt she could no longer stay in that
apartment and how could she possibly face school, Judy, and the
rest of the children? Early in the morning she phoned the school and
explained to the headmaster what had happened. She spent the day
at her parent's home trying to pull her thoughts together. As if all
this weren't enough, she had to go back to school facing Judy's
parents in a conference. It would have been easy to quit. She felt like
she had had enough. But what choices did she have? None, she
thought. She had to keep going.

The students and staff were very supportive of her. When she
returned to school on Wednesday, they were curious about the incident but they were all very kind. The children were well behaved,
so concerned, so helpful. That afternoon was the conference.
Thoughts of the confrontation with Judy's parents consumed Ellen

the entire day. She wondered if she had done the right thing in sharing her problems with the headmaster and the principal. What would the other teachers say? How would the parents react? What changes could she expect as a result of the conference? Would she always feel that she was the cause of the problem?

The meeting was very formal. Each person present described his or her assessment of Judy's behavior. Ellen was surprised. "Although privately supporting me and my feelings about Judy's behavior, during the formal meeting I was the only teacher willing to admit that this child was a severe problem in a classroom situation. The other teachers agreed that she was verbally cruel and antisocial, but *only* when unsupervised. Perhaps this is true but at the meeting this point of view made *me* look like the reason for the meeting, the weak link in the chain, which once removed would solve the problem. Luckily the principal stood up for my point of view and prodded the other teachers to rethink and restate their points of view until it became somewhat clearer that this was not merely a personality conflict between myself and the child. Nonetheless I left the meeting feeling extremely incompetent and incapable since it was only my classroom where she misbehaved. It was not a pleasant event."

To complete the events of the week-to-end-all-weeks, a temperamental child, Tony, decided that Thursday was his day to act up. In the middle of a spelling test he stood up and slammed a friend of his on the back with his fist and stormed out of the room screaming obscenities. Judy leapt out of her seat to chase Tony. Ellen felt panicked. What should she do? She handed the spelling list to one of the students and told her to finish giving the test. She got the victim who was sobbing loudly and took him to the hallway where she confronted Tony. She showed Judy back into the room telling her to sit down and be quiet. She told Tony that physical violence was not permitted in the classroom, that he would have to learn to control his anger while he was in school. With that Tony stormed down the hallway threatening to walk home. Ellen let him go and returned to the classroom. The children, a bit taken back by the incident and by Ellen's direct control of it, were progressing on their spelling test. While she felt that her nerves were shot, she was pleased that she had exercised her authority and taken direct action in dealing with the students.

Throughout the year despite frustrations afforded her through Judy, Ellen generally had held high regard for the students' feelings. She was never too busy to listen to a child's story; never too distraught to give a quick smile or a wink to a child in need of affection. Throughout the year she treated each child as someone special. And, in turn, loving adoration from most of the children flowed back to Ellen. "We love you, Miss Gilder." "We voted you the prettiest teacher in the school, Miss Gilder." Ellen began to realize that the affection she had shown for the children was coming back to her, and being nice did have its rewards. Oh, nothing that a standardized test score would measure, but the rewards in the kindness the children were developing in their treatment of one another were valued highly by her. In the next two weeks Ellen's attitude toward herself and her teaching changed. She gained more confidence in herself; she became more accepting of herself and less tolerant of student misconduct.

Following Spring vacation the headmaster asked Ellen to house-sit. Ellen looked upon this request as an act of trust. She felt that the headmaster must believe in her competence or he wouldn't have given her the responsibility of caring for his property while he was away. Then she received in the mail a contract for the next school year with a note describing her raise in salary. She was elated and looked at this as another act of confidence. She was beginning to believe that she was going to make it through the year and even want to return to teaching in the fall.

She was asked at the end of the year to prepare an assembly for the school which would be attended by students from all grades and any interested parents. This was quite a responsibility. Relying on her past successes in teaching synchronized swimming, she organized a special interest group of girls from grades 3-6 and began putting together a swimming circus complete with clowns, seals, dancers, horses, lions and other circus characters. She took complete charge. With the aid of Miss Evans, her after-school swimming partner, Ellen's show went like clockwork. Through this she was able to show the entire school that she had made it; not only had she survived through the first year but she had actually succeeded in teaching. She received many compliments on her ability to work carefully with the young swimmers.

"I could see myself as a teacher now. Before I was somebody

pretending to be a teacher. I just couldn't believe that I was responsible for these children. I now realize that we can spend a whole period talking and things don't have to be so organized all the time. I now realize that I have the power to call a parent or send a note home or tell a child to stay in from recess. Now I know I should do what's best for me and not be afraid or fearful. I've liked giving of myself—it's something I've needed to do. I've learned to be more mature. I think I'm becoming grown up. The kids have helped me. At first I was trying to be what everyone at the school wanted me to be. Now I know that to make it as a teacher I need to be myself and accept myself for what I am. It took a whole year but now I am confident and relaxed. I am strong and tough when I need to be. I think I've made it."

# Epilogue

We are grateful to the teachers who participated in this study for their cooperation and assistance. The stories in this book are a glance at their initial exposure to the professional world of teaching. Two years have passed since the information for the stories was gathered. The following brief descriptions provide an update of what the twelve teachers are currently doing and how each views teaching as a career option.

*Linda Fuller*—Linda continues to teach French at Clear Creek High School. She does not want to teach much longer because she intends to marry and wants to be able to travel with her husband. She is more relaxed and confident, but less enthusiastic than she was when she first started her career as a teacher.

*Dave Hardy*—Dave is teaching at the school described in the story. He is undecided about how much longer he will teach; he enjoys the students but finds the managerial aspects of teaching frustrating.

*Donna Hastings*—Donna is in her second year as a primary teacher in a rural school district. Although she is undecided about her career, she believes that she will move to a warmer climate and possibly leave teaching.

*Joyce Bond*—Joyce became a mother toward the end of her second year. She continues in her original teaching position, although she had given up coaching in order to spend more time with her family.

*Bill Moore*—Bill plans to continue teaching and finds his interactions with both students and fellow professionals to be enriching. He is presently teaching at the same school and grade level described in the story.

*Therese Gorman Stevens*—Therese is no longer teaching. She was married one year ago and has chosen, temporarily at least, to pursue personal interests more actively than professional ones. She is substituting and hopes to find a regular teaching assignment soon.

*Scott Tanner*—Scott is no longer teaching. At the present time he is working in the finance and credit division of a large corporation.

*Sandy Smith*—Sandy is teaching physical education at Astoria Junior High School. She plans to continue her career as a teacher and is pursuing some graduate work in education.

*Calvin Carlson*—Calvin wants to continue to teach and, at the same time, pursue some graduate work in education, particularly administration. He is teaching at the same school and grade level described in the story.

*Julie Carson*—Julie wants to continue to teach, at least until she starts a family. She has completed some graduate work in education and continues to teach kindergarten at Annandale Elementary School.

*Donald Cross*—Donald is teaching merchandising at Rutherford County Vocational School. He does not plan to continue teaching as a career, however, and cites student irresponsibility and disinterest as the primary reasons for pursuing other career options.

*Ellen Gilder*—Ellen will finish her master's degree in reading this year. She expects to stay at Rosecrest Academy another year; eventually she would like to pursue a Ph.D. in education.

# Something to Consider: Study Guide

In reading each of the stories you may have gained some insights about the first year of teaching which you did not have before. Hopefully, the accounts have prompted you to think about yourself in regard to this important stage in professional development. And, hopefully, you have had the opportunity to discuss these matters with others who are concerned and interested.

In order to help you focus your reading and reflection, the authors have organized the following study guide and activities. First are a series of questions which concentrate on important aspects of individual accounts. You may want to respond to them as you finish each account. Second are a series of questions which call you to compare the experiences of the different new teachers. You will want to have read most of the accounts before you respond to these. Finally, a number of activities are suggested which will point to ways you can go beyond this book in learning more about the first year of teaching, and more about yourself as a new professional.

# Story Study Questions

Linda Fuller                                           *I've Done It On My Own*

1.  What effects did the rural school environment seem to have on Linda's teaching?

2.  What do you think Linda expected from teaching? What did she get?

3.  If you were Linda, how would you have dealt with the poetry she received? Do you think this is a common problem for new teachers?

4.  How would you work with an auditorium study hall? What did Linda do that seemed appropriate? What would you do differently?

5.  Linda's teaching did not seem to change much during the year. What influences teachers to change or not to change their teaching behavior? Why do you think Linda's behavior did not change?

6.  The locker inspection incident posed a dilemma for Linda. Should she have gone along with the administration or should she have supported the students' right to privacy? What would you have done?

7.  Based upon what you have read, do you think Linda Fuller was an effective teacher?

Dave Hardy                                    *Mr. Hardy, Mr. Hardy!*

1.  The religious and education background that Dave brought to
    his first year of teaching was different than that of most new
    teachers. How did this background seem to influence his teach-
    ing experience? What is it about your background that may
    make your first year of teaching unique?

2.  Describe the conflicts Dave confronted between his own values
    and the community's expectations. Do you judge that Dave
    handled these conflicts well? How much should a teacher attend
    to the community's expectations?

3.  How would you describe Dave's teaching methods? In what
    ways are these methods similar to those of your present and
    former teachers? Do you learn when a teacher employs these
    instructional methods?

4.  Dave's personality seemed to play an important part of his first
    year experience. In what ways might his personality have
    played a part in his teaching?

5.  What factors seemed to contribute to Dave's professional de-
    velopment over the year?


Donna Hastings        *I Should Definitely Have It by Thanksgiving*

1.  Donna looked forward to a good year. She based her anticipa-
    tions on a number of beliefs about the school and community,
    prospective students, teaching and learning, and herself. What
    were these assumptions and beliefs? How might these have af-
    fected her performance? How might these have affected her
    experience as a teacher at St. Ambrose?

2.  For a group to be effective, clear, decisive leadership may be
    necessary. Assuming that a classroom of students is a group and
    the teacher is a leader, what characteristics would an effective
    teacher-as-group-leader have? Compare these characteristics to
    what you know about Donna.

3.  In August, Donna felt proud that Sister Theresa had high ex-
    pectations for her teaching ability. But Donna was also intimi-

dated by these expectations. Imagine a time when you felt like Donna did in August. What were your feelings? What did you do? What was the result? If you were to find yourself with similar feelings when you begin your first teaching position, what might you do to put your anxiety to work for you rather than against you?

4.  A change of role can be attended by anxiety and identity crisis. Donna experienced both. She reported a considerable degree of anxiety; she reported that she was both the person she had always known and the new Miss Hastings, teacher at St. Ambrose. Do you think that an identity crisis and anxiety necessarily accompany a change in role? How does a person blend old roles with new roles?

5.  Donna felt her living situation affected her teaching experience and that her teaching experience, in turn, affected her after-school life. Was this influence inevitable? What might your experience be when you begin your first teaching position?

6.  Donna's response to Sister Theresa's outburst and the follow-up conference was dramatic; her classroom behavior changed greatly. Describe and evaluate the changes. Consider whether the changes Donna made improved her experience in the classroom or improved student learning.

7.  Evaluate Donna's decision to resign. Was it the best decision for Donna? for students? for Sister Theresa? Were there alternatives from which Donna could have chosen a course of action? What would you have done given similar circumstances?

Joyce Bond                                                    *Math Teacher*

1.  What messages did Joyce send to her class on the first day of school about the kind of teacher she was?

2.  What are some possible explanations for the difference between Joyce's reactions to the class as a whole and her reactions to individuals?

3.  Over the course of the year, Joyce's teaching seemed to change. How would you describe these changes? To what influences would you attribute these changes?

4. From the first week of school and for some time thereafter, Joyce had problems maintaining classroom discipline. What would you have advised Joyce to do to help alleviate the problems? Can the suggestions you would have made be used by any teacher?

5. Though teaching can be frustrating, it can also be very rewarding. Did it seem that Joyce's frustrations and satisfactions balanced one another? What would you find frustrating in teaching? What will be the sources of your satisfactions?

Bill Moore                                               *Just So They Have Fun*

1. Bill thought teaching was an art. Do you think teaching is an art or a science?

2. How effective were Bill's classroom management techniques? What classroom management practices were evident in Bill's teaching? Is there a difference between classroom management and classroom discipline?

3. Would you describe Bill's classroom as traditional? What does the term "traditional" mean?

4. What problems in instructional planning did Bill seem to confront? How did Bill's planning change as the year progressed?

5. Bill seemed to think he needed to be "tough" on students. Did he come to think that way as the result of his own beliefs, or was it because of the environment in which he taught?

6. How did the supervisor define effective teaching? How did Bill define effective teaching? What behaviors do you feel effective teachers exhibit?

Therese Gorman Stevens                                  *When There Is No Way*

1. Therese lived through some very difficult personal developments at the same time she went through her first year of teaching. Yet these changes seemed not to affect her work as a teacher. How is your personal life likely to affect your professional life? How do those who are close to you feel about your becoming a teacher?

2.  Therese was one member of a teaching team. In what ways did the three teachers seem to work well together? In what ways were they not really a team? What do you feel to be the advantages and disadvantages of team teaching?

3.  The youngsters whom Therese taught were growing up in an urban environment. They were poor, most were black, and all were classified as Educably Mentally Retarded. None of those background characteristics were part of Therese's own experience. How important would you say it is for a teacher to understand the backgrounds of the youngsters he/she teaches? How can a teacher learn what is important about the youngsters he/she teaches?

4.  Through most of the year, Davey presented Therese with some of her most difficult challenges. How did Therese attempt to deal with Davey and his behavior? How would you have approached this youngster in the situations described?

5.  Therese reported that as a teacher she felt "vulnerable" in a way she had never felt before. What do you think she meant by that? Are people who have just begun their teaching careers likely to feel vulnerable?

6.  When Therese received her first formal observation by Mr. Roberts, she was disappointed and disturbed by not receiving any comment from him regarding her performance. What kinds of feedback would you expect from an observing principal? What would you do if you were given no feedback after an observation? What would you do if the feedback were negative?

Scott Tanner                                                        *Just Keeping Up*

1.  Scott had a difficult time planning to accommodate the needs of the wide range of students in his class. He found it difficult to understand and use the large curriculum guides that he was given by the school district. Name three steps that you might take faced with such a problem?

2.  In what way did Scott's growing frustrations seem to affect the classroom climate?

3. Describe the differences among Scott's teaching behavior when he was on the playground, when he was in a reading group, and when he worked with the class as a group. In what kinds of teaching situations do you feel you will do best? In what kinds of situations do you anticipate problems?

4. Scott could have felt that he was pressured into developing the learning center by Cristy's father. How should teachers respond to parents when the parents seem to put pressure on them? Was Cristy's father reasonable to raise such a question with Scott?

5. Several times during the year Scott reported that his confidence in himself was shaken. What incidents led Scott to feel bad about his work as a teacher? Would you have interpreted these incidents in the same way? What events seemed to restore Scott's confidence?

Sandy Smith                                         *Friend or Teacher*

1. What expectations did Sandy have about the behavior of junior high school students? Were those expectations realistic?

2. How did Sandy think substituting would benefit her teaching? Do you think substituting was a positive or negative influence on her teaching?

3. Describe Sandy's relationship with Mr. Wilson at the beginning of the school year. How did the relationship change as the year progressed? Why do you think it changed?

4. How did Sandy attempt to create enthusiasm toward physical education activities? In what ways were Sandy's efforts counterproductive?

5. How did Sandy's relationship with students change during the school year? Where do you think the change took place? Did the change have a positive or negative impact on Sandy's effectiveness?

6. What does it mean to be both a teacher and a friend of the students? How does the teacher role conflict with the friend role?

Calvin Carlson                                                    *Making the Team*

1.  Cal was part of a "house plan." What is a "house plan" and how does it function? While this plan seems to have been beneficial to Cal's getting started as a teacher, how might it have been otherwise?

2.  In Cal's mind, being twenty-eight and having been through military service and other work experience were helpful in his teaching. What effect do you think his age and his experience had on his first year of teaching?

3.  How would you describe the social system of Hayes Junior High School? What were the values of the parents, and what were the values of the principal and teachers?

4.  Calvin tended to overuse one particular questioning pattern. What was it? State three or four alternative ways Cal could have reviewed the homework and checked to see if the students understood it.

5.  How did Cal react to being tested by some of the boys in his class? Do you believe that such an approach is effective in all cases?

Julie Carson                                                      *Everyone Is Watching Me*

1.  Teaching was important to Julie Carson. How would you respond in an interview for a teaching job, to the questions: How important is teaching to you? Why is teaching important to you?

2.  It was important to Julie to be able to explain to parents and to give reasons for the things that she did in the classroom. Can you give clear explanations and thoughtful reasons for the teaching materials and methods you plan to use in the classroom?

3.  Julie was concerned about parents knowing it was her first year of teaching. How do you think parents react to first year teachers? How will you respond when parents ask about your previous experiences? How will you feel if they ask?

4.  Julie was a motivated and self-disciplined teacher. Much of her

success in her first year of teaching might be attributed to her thorough planning, in the evenings and on weekends. What are your feelings about spending time away from school on planning or preparation? Would it change your view of teaching if you knew that teaching, particularly for the first year, was a fifty-hour-a-week commitment?

5. Julie's husband Rob was understanding of the demands of the first year of teaching, and was cooperative with respect to housekeeping responsibilities. What potential stress points can you identify in a marriage relationship which might be caused or contributed to by demands of the first year of teaching? In what specific ways might these potential conflicts be avoided?

6. Julie was concerned about her visibility as a first year teacher, and about making mistakes. How do you feel about being new, about being watched, and about not always succeeding in your teaching? How might these feelings affect your teaching or your relations with those with whom you work?

Don Cross                                              *The Best of Both Worlds*

1. Don would say that he changed from a supervisor into a teacher as the year progressed. Why did he seem to think that was an important change to make?

2. Don recalled the year when he was a supervisor-trainer at a merchandising mart. He compared that year to his first year of teaching. What differences did he note? How important might these differences be to you?

3. Through the year, Don shared some of his thoughts and feelings with a trusted student. What conditions probably existed to allow that practice to develop?

4. How did Don deal with depression? What methods would you be most likely to use if you were feeling low?

5. Many times, Don felt that the students he taught were un-motivated toward school work. Considering the students and their situation, what might have made that true? What about

Don's way of working with the students might have made that true? What would you have done to motivate the students if they were in your class?

6. At several points in the year, Don realized that he wasn't really as much a part of the school as he wanted to be. How important do you feel it is for a new teacher to become and feel like part of the school?

7. Don reported a considerable conflict between his professional and his personal life. What kinds of conflicts did he note? How would you have resolved such conflicts in your own life?

Ellen Gilder                                          *I Think I Can . . . I Think I Can*

1. What did Ellen expect the year would be like?

2. Ellen had many adjustments to make during her first year of teaching. Which ones were most troublesome to her?

3. Suppose the bell had not saved Ellen in the thermometer incident. If you were she, how would you have handled the situation?

4. Parent conferences were a big part of school life for Ellen. What questions would you ask a parent during a conference to help you gain insights into a child's behavior? How frequently should a teacher contact the parents of his/her students? For what reasons?

5. New teachers sometimes feel they should be loved, admired, and respected by ALL students. Ellen felt she had not been successful with Judy. What did she do to try to correct Judy's misconduct? What more could she have done?

6. Ellen believed that love for children and respect from children are nearly antithetical. Are they? Why do you think she believed this?

7. Ellen was always comparing herself with her teammate, Mr. Hetherington. Why might she have done this? What differences did she see? What advantages did team teaching have for Ellen? What disadvantages?

# Comparative Experience Questions

The questions and activities below should help you explore your own feelings about the first year of teaching. They were written with all of the stories in mind.

1.  First year teachers have many problems both major and minor. Which ones do you recall most vividly from the stories? Why was each situation a problem for that teacher? Would this situation have been a problem for you? If so, what possible solutions would you consider?

2.  Each first year teacher wanted to get along well with students, but also knew that a teacher must maintain discipline and impart knowledge successfully. Which teachers found this a dilemma and how did they attempt to resolve it? Why do you think the other teachers felt no conflict between the role of friend and the role of teacher?

3.  The teachers had many views about what good discipline was and how they would go about maintaining it. Which teacher's approach was closest to your own?

4.  All but one of the first year teachers found enough joy or satisfaction in teaching to carry them through till the end of the year. Where did the joys and satisfactions come from? Speculate about how much each teacher's personality, professional goals and teaching situation influence his or her willingness to continue teaching.

5.  Entering a new role in life involves changes which may be stressful, and beginning a career as a teacher is no exception. Can you identify the changes which caused stress for the first year teachers? In what ways did they try to ease the stress?

6.  Sometimes new teachers are surprised when situations occur in teaching that they did not expect. What surprises did these first year teachers have? What might they have done to avoid the surprises?

7.  As the year progressed, changes occured for the new teachers. What kinds of changes did you notice? What changes would you want to make during your first year of teaching?

8.  The community in which you teach may have some impact upon the attitudes you have toward your school and your students. How did these first year teachers get to know their schools' communities? What else might they have done to help them understand more about community life? In which stories do you think knowledge of the community made a difference in what the teachers did? What happened?

9.  Sometimes new teachers feel alone in the school. They would like someone to give them advice and be helpful. To whom did these new teachers turn for support? Were they helpful? Why or why not? What other sources of help can you identify?

10. School faculties can seem cliquish to new teachers. What did the first year teachers do to become included in the faculty? Was it important for these teachers to have friends in the school? What do you think affects a teacher's need to become part of school life?

11. Prospective teachers have often heard the horrors of becoming a first year teacher. But many say, "I'm going to be different." What insights have you gained from reading these stories which will help you "be different?" What concerns do you still have?

12. Do you still have some questions about what it will be like to be a first year teacher? Make a list about what it will be like to be a first year teacher? Mak a list of those questions and interview someone currently in his/her first year of teaching.

# Index